ROUTLEDGE LIBRARY EDITIONS:
HUMAN RESOURCE MANAGEMENT

Volume 26

THE THIRD WAY

THE THIRD WAY

The Promise of Industrial Democracy

DENNIS LAWRENCE

LONDON AND NEW YORK

First published in 1988 by Routledge

This edition first published in 2017
by Routledge
2 Park Square, Milton Park, Abingdon, Oxon OX14 4RN

and by Routledge
711 Third Avenue, New York, NY 10017

Routledge is an imprint of the Taylor & Francis Group, an informa business

British Library Cataloguing in Publication Data
A catalogue record for this book is available from the British Library

ISBN: 978-1-138-80870-6 (Set)
ISBN: 978-1-315-18006-9 (Set) (ebk)
ISBN: 978-1-138-28837-9 (Volume 26) (hbk)
ISBN: 978-1-138-28838-6 (Volume 26) (pbk)
ISBN: 978-1-315-26794-4 (Volume 26) (ebk)

Publisher's Note
The publisher has gone to great lengths to ensure the quality of this reprint but points out that some imperfections in the original copies may be apparent.

Disclaimer
The publisher has made every effort to trace copyright holders and would welcome correspondence from those they have been unable to trace.

The Third Way

*The Promise of
Industrial Democracy*

Dennis Lawrence

Routledge
London

First published in 1988 by
Routledge
11 New Fetter Lane, London EC4P 4EE

Set in Palatino, 10 on 12 pt
by Witwell Ltd, Southport
and printed in Great Britain
by T. J. Press (Padstow) Ltd.
Padstow, Cornwall

British Library Cataloguing in Publication Data
Lawrence, Dennis
The third way: the promise of industrial democracy
1. Management — Great Britain —
Employee participation — History
I. Title
331'.01'120941   HD5660.G7

ISBN 0–415–00252–4

Contents

Acknowledgments

I am grateful to each of the organisations or institutions listed below for permission to quote from the works ascribed to them as publishers:

Allen & Unwin, C.D. Darlington's *Evolution of Man and Society*, Bertrand Russell's *History of Western Philosophy*, Joan Robinson's *Economics: An Awkward Corner* and Thomas and Logan's *Monodragon*;

Cambridge University Press, *New Cambridge Modern History* Vol X Chapter II, by Herbert Heaton;

Constable and Co Ltd, A.A.W. Ramsey's *Sir Robert Peel*;

Co-operative Bank and P A Management Consultants, *Workers' Co-ops, Past Present and Future*;

Co-operative Union, G.D.H. Cole's *A Century of Co-operation*; J.M. Dent and Sons Ltd, Robert Owen's *A New View of Society*, in Everyman's Library;

Victor Gollancz Ltd, E.P. Thompson's *The Making of the English Working Class*;

Hamish Hamilton, H.L. Beales' *The Early English Socialists*;

Industrial Common Ownership Movement, Alistair Campbell's *Mondragon 1980*, and David Spreckley's foreword to *The Co-operative Way*;

The London School of Economics and Political Science, Sidney and Beatrice Webb's *The History of Trade Unionism*;

Longman, Douglas Jay's *Socialism in The New Society*;

Manchester Statistical Society, Peter Jay's paper *The Workers Co-operative Economy*;

Methuen & Co, L.C.B. Seaman's *Victorian England*;

Oxford University Press, Isaiah Berlin's *Karl Marx*;

Penguin Books Ltd, George Woodcock's introduction to Cobbett's *Rural Rides*;

Plunkett Foundation for Co-operative Studies, Professor A.J.

Eccles' paper *Trade Union Behaviour towards Workers' Co-operatives;*

Tawney Society, *Equality And The Ownership Question,* R. Gravil (Editor);

George Weidenfeld and Nicholson, George Lichtheim's *A Short History of Socialism* and Eric Hobsbawm's *The Age of Capital;*

The quotation, as a chapter heading, of lines from 'Little Gidding' is reprinted by permission of Faber and Faber Ltd from *Four Quartets* by T.S. Eliot. The material quoted from Cmnd Papers 4811 *Report of the Committee of Enquiry on Small Firms,* 6706 *Report of the Committee of Enquiry on Industrial Democracy,* 6972 *Report of the Working Group on a Co-operative Development Agency,* 7293 *Winning the Battle Against Inflation* and from the Co-operative Development Agency's *Annual Reports and Accounts for the years ending 31 March 1979, 80, 81* is reproduced with the permission of the Controller of Her Majesty's Stationery Office.

For permission to quote from them, my thanks are due also to:

The *Financial Times,* Rupert Cornwell's article of 28 March 1970 on Industrial Co-operation in Italy, and David Churchill's of 12 June 1984 *A Resurgence of Interest;*

The *Times,* Roger Boyes' article *Spectrum,* 17 October 1984, and a leading article, 20 December 1985;

New Statesman, Patrick Wintour's *Labour in Co-op Plan Row,* 17 April 1981;

as well as to the political parties, Conservative, Labour, Liberal and SDP whose publications are drawn upon. Each is identified in the text.

Pantheon Books, a Division of Random House, Inc., ask me to give full credit to them in respect of the American copyright in E.P. Thompson's *The Making of the English Working Class.* My thanks to them for their permission to quote from it; and to Simon Schuster in respect of Bertrand Russell's *History of Western Philosophy.* The material from 'Little Gidding' in *Four Quartets* by T.S. Eliot, copyright 1943 by T.S. Eliot, renewed 1971 by Esme Eliot, is reprinted by permission of Harcourt Brace Jovanovich, Inc.

I record my thanks to people whose work has helped me: to

Professor Tom Bottomore and Maximilien Rubel, editors of *Karl Marx: Selected Writings in Sociology and Social Philosophy.* I am grateful for their permission to quote from the selection; and to M. Rubel for his kindness in sending me an article *Marx et le mouvement co-opéretif,* published by Thomas Lowit in the *Cahiers de l'Institute de Science Economique Appliqué* (Paris 1962);

Keith Bradley and Alan Gelb whose articles, published in the *British Journal of Industrial Relations*, on the Mondragon Co-operatives are invaluable. The provenance of the articles is given in the text;

Leonora Stettner who had allowed me access to, and to quote from, unpublished work on the performance of industrial co-operatives; and

George Wright, for permission to quote from publications by *Wales Co-op Centre*.

Nor should I leave unacknowledged the help I have had from the Director, George Jones, and staff of the Co-operative Development Agency; and, over the years from debate and discussion with friends and colleagues in the Co-operative Union, in the Industrial Common Ownership Movement (ICOM), and in Job Ownership Ltd (JOL).

Next, may I take this opportunity of thanking Betty Nash, formerly and for many years my secretary, whose typing of my text confers on it an authority the manuscript lacks.

Finally, I would like to thank especially Alida, my wife, but for whom this book would not have been written.

— 1 —

The Third Way

Poverty is a great enemy to human happiness; it certainly destroys liberty, and it makes some virtues impracticable and others extremely difficult.

Samuel Johnson, in Boswell's *Life of Johnson*

Though many still sincerely believe in human equality and theoretical democracy, the imagination of modern people is deeply affected by the pattern of social organisation suggested by the organisation of industry in the nineteenth century, which is essentially undemocratic. On the one hand there are the captains of industry, and on the other the mass of workers. This disruption of democracy from within is not yet acknowledged by ordinary citizens in democratic countries.

Bertrand Russell, *A History of Western Philosophy*

There is a disposition, particularly marked in political discussion, to suppose that the answers to basic questions are to be found at either one or the other of two extremes. Falling in behind the leaders who assert with most persuasion the unqualified rightness of this or that absolute alternative, those of us who are interested enough will rally to one or other of them. Simplistic though it is, that disposition embodies a priceless virtue. It recognises that to almost any question worth asking there are at least two sides; and so holds out the prospect that, from the ensuing debate between them, something better than a ritual dismantling and re-assemby of opposed pre-convictions, something closer to the truth may emerge. For nearly always the truth will lie somewhere between the extremes of the spectrum of possibilities. Almost certainly it

1

will be neither ideological red nor dogmatic blue. So perhaps after all, at the beginning of this attempt to review the history of Co-operation and to assess its relevance to the social and economic condition of the United Kingdom today, it is not wholly disadvantageous to have to admit that the subject is undefined. Not, of course, that ignorance is an insuperable bar to opinion, nor even to conviction; but usually it prompts us to pause where otherwise we might rush in.

Because it lacks exact definition, Co-operation can only be described. For most people, the description starts and stops with a picture of the co-operative store. Nor is it a picture to fire the imagination. Though there are brighter patches, it is on the whole one of dullness; of growing irrelevance; of a slow-moving, out-dated and unresponsive organisation; one motivated by a moral earnestness which, admirable in its time, has now no cause to engage it and so has degenerated from an urgent dynamic to a pointless posture. Embattled with the great supermarket chains, it lacks the single-mindedness of their unconditional commercial purpose; and, since the social purposes it once served are now as well or better met by other means, the structures, procedures and affiliations designed to subserve them have largely lost their validity and have become a burden where once they were a support. It is, in short, an amiable dinosaur, well adapted to the economic and social environment in which it emerged and developed, but quite unsuited to that in which it now finds itself.[1] No doubt some will say that the picture is too sombre. Yet not, I believe, so far exaggerated as to relieve the co-operative store of the need to adapt to present conditions: that is, to find a new and relevant raison d'être to express co-operative principles and a structure to activate them. Failing such an adaptation, the present ills from which co-operative stores in general suffer are only too likely to prove terminal. Nor is it an exaggeration to say that, though the case is not yet beyond cure, time is short and nothing less than an organic change will do. The amiable dinosaur will have to become another kind of animal.

So, though any review of the history of Co-operation, any assessment of its present relevance is bound to refer extensively to Consumer Co-operation, it is upon another kind of co-operation, upon that kind which for other reasons and in other contexts is re-appearing to provide a purpose and a future that attention is increasingly focussing: and that kind is Industrial Co-operation.

Here, it is enough to distinguish the two kinds: (a) the consumer co-operative, a chain of stores with ancillary undertakings, owned by those of its customers who choose to become members and who, in a corporate capacity, employ people to work for them; and (b) the industrial co-operative – or 'producer' or 'workers' co-operative' – the essential characteristics of which are that it manufactures goods or provides services, and that is wholly or very largely owned by and ultimately controlled by those working in it. The distinction is not merely of degree, but of kind; and so sharply contrasted as to be antithetical. There are, of course, other forms of co-operative: agricultural co-operatives, for the joint marketing of produce or arrangement of supply – a form capable of more general application; housing co-operatives; and credit unions. Valuable though they are, however, it is the polarity presented by the sharply contrasted purposes and structures of Consumer and Industrial Co-operation which establishes a major and recurring theme of the movement's history.

Given the diversity and the sharp contrasts within the movement, the virtue in the absence of definition starts to become apparent. Advisedly, the basic law on co-operative societies, the Industrial and Provident Societies Acts 1965 to 1975, pronounces that for the purposes of that law, a society is a co-operative if it satisfies the Registrar of Friendly Societies that it is authentically so. The statute then goes on to say not what an authentic co-operative *is*, but what it is *not*. It is *not* a body which carries on business with the object of making profits mainly for the payment of interest, dividends or bonuses on money invested in it.[2] Subject to this essential qualification, for all practical purposes a co-operative is – for the objects of the statute he administers – what the Registrar says it is. He is to know a co-operative when he sees one.

Condensed as it is, the statutory pronouncement needs analysis if we are to see its full significance. First, a main purpose of the law as it relates to co-operatives is to provide for their registration as corporate entities and so to confer on them legal personality with the rights and privileges, duties and obligations that such incorporation commonly implies; in short, to remove impediments from the conduct of co-operatives as businesses. To this extent it serves the same purposes as do the Companies Acts for conventionally organised businesses. It is by the fact of registration that a society is made a corporation with perpetual succession, a

3

common seal and limited liability; and hence may sue and be sued in its own name. Among the matters for which its rules must provide are its objects; the amount (currently not more than £10,000) that an ordinary member may hold in it; whether it may contract loans or receive money on deposit; whether, and if so, how and on what authority any parts of its funds may be invested; how its profits are to be applied; and the audit of accounts.[3] As to its accounts, it is by statute required to maintain them so as to enable a true and fair view to be given of the state of its affairs and to explain its transactions. Annually, a return of the accounts, as audited, must be sent to the Registrar, together with a copy of the auditors' report; and every member of a co-operative registered as a society, or anyone with an interest in its funds, may obtain as of right a copy of the latest annual return. In summary, the fact of registration constitutes a co-operative as a body such that all who might trade with it, or who might lend money to it, should recognise it as one of a class of enterprise with which they are in principle ready to do business. More particularly, to the concession of limited liability it attaches the concomitant requirement of a sufficient disclosure of the co-operative's commercial condition. Whether in this or that case they will choose to lend or trade must be a matter for their judgment: their judgment of the co-operative's circumstances, on which they may inform themselves; and of its management. But whether in general they are as ready to do business with registered co-operatives, considered as a class of enterprise, as with bodies incorporated under the Companies Acts, is quite another question.

None of this is to say that co-operatives are obliged to register under the Industrial and Provident Societies Acts. Many do not: some because, for reasons we need not go into here, they prefer to register under the Companies Acts; others either because they are unaware of the advantages conferred by incorporation or because they consider that the lack of it will not put them at any disadvantage. Now, to summarise so far: on the authority of the Registrar, registration identifies a body as a co-operative. Non-registration does not necessarily mean that a body is not a co-operative. And lastly, where the Registrar refuses registration on the ground that the applicant body is not a bona fide co-operative, the presumption must be that it is not. Yet, though the presumption is so strong as to admit of virtually no doubt, for reasons which follow later, it is not an absolute.

Not much yet to help us to see Co-operation more plain; nor can the next exposition – what Co-operation is *not* – provide a positive description. However, it does serve to separate co-operatives clearly from the generality of businesses. Since a genuine co-operative is not a business carried on with the object of making profits mainly for the payment of interest, dividends or bonuses on money invested in it, there is no place in it for those whose purpose is to get investment income from shares held in it or a capital gain on an appreciation of their value. For, while a co-operative may borrow loan capital from whomsoever is willing to lend, only members may provide share capital (subject to the £10,000 per member ceiling); and shares are not marketable but may be bought back at their par value by the co-operative. Does that separation perhaps do more? Does it establish an ideological confrontation between Co-operation and Capitalism?

Disappointing though this must be for those of us who know what side we are on and who, if the answer were otherwise, would need neither to dismantle our pre-convictions nor to read further, it cannot be said to do so. As forms of organisation for doing business, co-operatives and joint stock companies alike are concerned to bring capital, natural resources and labour together for the production and sale of goods, or the provision and sale of services. But more, Co-operation is not excluded from that general view of Capitalism as an economic system which sees its essential features as private ownership, freedom of enterprise in the expectation of profit but with an attendant liability to competition and risk, and freedom of choice for the consumer. So, important as the contrast between co-operative and conventional businesses is, it must not be allowed to mask the comparison; and still less to prompt the misapprehension that for co-operatives it is out of character to seek and make profits. True, some co-operators find the word disquieting and prefer the euphemism 'surplus'. But by whatever name we like to call gain on capital applied in an enterprise, the fact that it will seek to make profits does not disqualify it from registration. The disqualification attaches not to intention or fact nor even to the amount of profit but to a particular purpose to which profits made by businesses conventionally organised and financed are commonly applied: that is, mainly (whatever that may mean) for the payment of interest, dividends or bonuses on money invested with or lent to the enterprise. There are two further comments to make. The first is simply to stress that even the statutory disqualification, the pronouncement of what is not a co-operative, leaves much to the judgment of the Registrar. It is for him to decide in the particular case whether the object is to make profits *mainly* for payment on money invested in or lent to the enterprise. The second is to point to a consequence. There is nothing to relieve a co-operative of the need, in a competitive environment, to make profitability the test of its commercial relevance and justification of the claims it makes on the use of resources: nothing, in short, to relieve it of the need to operate in a market economy. It must do this without access to speculative venture capital and in competition with the generality of enterprises not precluded from it in principle.

At first sight an inhibitive and, some may suppose, a prohibitive disadvantage. Certainly, something more is needed to present a credible description of the co-operative as a business organisation, something to establish a purpose which will explain what, with the satisfaction of investors excluded as a main objective, there is in its stead to provide the dynamic, and what countervailing factor sufficiently weighs against the disadvantage. To find it we must turn back to the positive requirement of the Industrial and Provident Societies Acts: that, the body applying for registration must satisfy the Registrar that it is an authentic co-operative. After observing that there is no statutory definition, paragraph 6 of the *Guide to the Law Relating to Industrial and Provident Societies* goes on to identify the conditions he would normally expect to be satisfied. *Normally*: so they are not necessarily his last word. They are these:

> that the business of a co-operative enterprise is to be conducted for the mutual benefit of its members
> that control will be vested on the general basis 'one man, one vote' in members equally and not in accordance with their financial interest in the enterprise
> that the rate of interest payable on share and loan capital will be no more than necessary to attract and keep necessary capital
> that the amount of the distributable profit to be credited to the individual member will be related to the extent of his participation in the business of the enterprise
> that there shall be no artificial restriction on membership

Simplified still further, the essential and distinguishing features of an authentic co-operative are: membership, with the right to active participation implied by the term: mutuality; equality; and reward measured by reference to participation. They are, let us note, the features of democracy, and establish Co-operation as a manifestation of it. So, where the ultimate requirement of a joint stock company is that it should satisfy its investors as such, that of a co-operative is that it must satisfy its members as participants. In both cases, the satisfaction is material benefit. For the co-operative though, it is something more. And it is just that something more which provides the countervailing factor to compensate co-operatives for the denial to them of speculative venture capital and at which, because it goes to the very heart of co-operative principle, we shall look more closely.

For the present, though, this is what a co-operative as the Registrar would recognise it normally looks like. If he does not recognise an applicant body as one, if in his view it is not an authentic – or, as the statute has it a bona fide – co-operative, there is no appeal to the courts against his decision.[4] This is, certainly at first sight, surprising: for it seems to vest an unchallengeable authority in an official, in a civil servant. At first sight only, because as an official the Registrar may be supposed to be acting, even if at some remove, on behalf of the Government. If not, then at least a Minister has appointed him. In the first case, the Minister could be called to account by Parliament for the actions done in his name by the Registrar; while in the second he could be called to account by it for the competence of the person he had appointed. Thus, there being available no check by the judiciary against a bad decision by the Registrar to refuse to register an applicant body on the ground that it was not a bona fide co-operative, his actions in this particular respect are open directly or indirectly to political check in Parliament. And given that, as there is no definition, it is necessary to develop and refer to case law, given further that the function is one of day-to-day administration which could not proceed with enough certainty and celerity if it were liable to challenge and delay at law, the present arrangement is probably to be preferred. Certainly, there is no record of continuing parliamentary interest in, and still less concern about, the Registrar's performance as the custodian of the public interest in the question what is a co-operative. Happy the department that has no history; and blessed by exceptional competence, or an acquiescent clientele.

After all this, is it still advisedly that the law does not define a co-operative? Yes: and the reasons are persuasive. Definition casts in a rigid mould the subject defined. For its certainty, the price paid is virtual finality. It leaves little or no room for desirable variation from the normal, nor for those differences of degree which sensible administration would wish to admit and which are most likely to present themselves at the growing points of development. Nor can it allow for the fact that categories overlap; so that, however convenient exact classification might be to enable us to make a more ordered model of society in the business of producing and providing, the positive distinctions it would have to draw between the co-operative and other forms of organisation would be too sharp. And so it is indeed advisedly that the statute's pronouncement of what a co-operative is not avoids the absolute and leaves a discretion to the Registrar. Advisedly, the Registrar qualifies his description of the positive characteristics of an authentic co-operative. They are, as we saw earlier, what he would normally expect to find. Members' benefits are to stem mainly from their participation in the business. And even the democratic principle 'one man, one vote' is not prescribed as an invariable. It must obtain – in general.

Yet, a view of Co-operation which ended with an account of the case, founded so largely on constitutional practice and administrative method, for recognition by an accountable public custodian rather than definition by statute would lack the essence of the subject. We have seen that, like any other form of business organisation, a co-operative must succeed in a market economy and must do so by tests common to all forms of enterprise, but that, unlike most other forms it finds its incentive to success primarily in the need to give satisfaction to its membership. Now, because men do not live by bread alone that satisfaction will be of morale as well as material. Other forms of organisation need or choose to provide satisfaction of both kinds; but save perhaps for the family business or the partnership, appeal to morale is not inherent in the structure. It is an additive provided for either or both of two reasons: on the one hand human concern; and on the other the compulsion of the labour market. It will vary with the strength of the concern and the compulsion.

For a co-operative to succeed, both the material benefit and the appeal to morale must be real. That the benefit, be it for example gainful employment in an industrial co-operative, or dividend in a consumer co-operative, or economy and increased effectiveness in an agricultural marketing co-operative must be real requires no demonstration: for, though men do not live by bread alone, most certainly they do not live without it. Like other manifestations of democracy, Co-operation does not exist simply to express a principle for its own sake. It exists first by virtue of its claim to be a fully effective means of organising production and provision. This is not to overlook the further claim that, as an organisational form it is morally superior. Rather, it is to say that it is as a manifestation of democracy, in its insistence on the rights and responsibilities of the individual, that Co-operation asserts that further claim; but more, that upon its truth depends the advantage in morale held by the co-operative over the generality of conventionally organised businesses, and, hence, its inherent capacity in the long run to outperform them. On the highest military authority we are told that in warfare considerations of morale make up three-quarters of the game. One might dispute the fraction; but the general sentiment is irrefutable and applies to the better kinds of human endeavour as well as to the worse.

Yet it is precisely this, the assertion of democratic principle, that critics see as disabling. And the criticism needs to be met. In short, the argument is that democracy is to do with government; and that though democratic government is properly of the people, by the people, for the people, it simply does not follow that the principle extends to the conduct of business enterprises. What is more, the argument continues, it will not work. It will not work because the conduct of business affairs needs such a flexibility and speed of reaction as the protractions of the democratic process would deny to management. Not that that process would interest the great majority, anyway, who do not want to have to concern themselves in the affairs of the business. Only the activists would be interested – the very people whose intervention would prove a damaging, if not disastrous, impediment. In summary, the application of democracy to business is in principle misconceived; and, because it would remove a necessary element of discipline from personnel management as an aspect of the conduct of business, impracticable on any general scale.

Except to remove a misunderstanding, the first of these two points must be summarily dismissed as a denial of the essential worth of the individual. The misunderstanding would be to suppose that Co-operation, properly described, seeks to assert the forms of democratic control against the rights of ownership: that is to say, to control or share in the control of resources it does not own Emphatically, it does not. Membership is a condition of Co-operation; and ownership, whether common or individual, is a condition of membership. How ownership is to be secured is a very different and potentially contentious question. Here, it is enough to repeat that Co-operation does not dissociate the ultimate authority in an enterprise from the ownership of it.

To the second criticism, that whatever the theoretical case for doing so the application of democratic principle to the conduct of business would make it impracticable, it seems enough to observe that there are many successful co-operatives, in the United Kingdom and elsewhere, operating in a market economy; and that it would strain belief to dismiss them all as exceptional. But because a look at the assumptions underlying the criticism sharpens our perception of Co-operation, it is useful to consider them. First, the kind of democracy assumed by critics is nearly always direct democracy: that is, the kind in which the individual retains the right to take part personally in decision making, so that all issues for decision are open to general debate and need a sufficient consensus before there can be action. Where co-operatives number only a few members direct democracy may serve well enough, since it need impose no material delays. But democracy may be indirect as well as direct, as indeed it almost invariably is in politics. For it is with co-operative as it is with political democracy. Increase in size and complexity necessitates the indirect form; and while idealism may regret the fact, realism will admit the need. Thus, in response to it, members of a co-operative may elect some of their members to a directing board to which they would delegate authority to formulate and oversee the execution of policy, and which at due intervals and by settled procedure they would call to account for that formulation and oversight. And the board might either integrate the functions of policy formulation and oversight with those of day-to-day management, so that the chairman would also act as managing director and the other members of the board as the operational heads of the organisation's functional divisions; or it might, by appointing a chief executive, keep the two elements, policy and execution, separate. A practical one, the choice would depend upon the size and character of the undertaking. Whatever arrangements may be made in this or that particular case, the essential point remains this: that the indispensable condition of democracy in Co-operation as in its other manifestations, is that those to whom authority is deputed are effectively called to account and may be replaced. Accountability is the key. Co-operative organisation provides for accountability; and a good co-operative the incentive to make use of it. For in such a co-operative, the perceived benefits will have been, and remained, real – and should be realised. Where they are not, the members will have a short way with management. One point more: though the link between efficient performance and benefit to members is of course present in all classes of Co-operation, it cannot be closer, or more apparent, than in the industrial co-operative where the workforce constitute the membership and expect to be beneficiaries. So it is there that the way with unsatisfactory management will be shortest. As indeed it should be.

Next, there is the criticism that in general people do not want to be bothered by the obligations of democracy as manifested in Co-operation, or – to put it more sharply – that people are not good enough for the concept; and that, this being so, it is a fallacy to suppose that Co-operation is a practicable form of business organisation capable of widespread application. This argument should be seen for what it is, the invariable last resort of arrogance and autocracy against democracy. Of course, people who join co-operatives will continue to exhibit all the faults and failings of fallible humanity. The argument is not that they are, on the instant of their joining, washed clean of them. In the end, it is that Co-operation is a particular example of the general case for democracy: that is, that it provides the best check against the corrupting tendency of power, people – and especially people dressed in a little brief authority – being what they are. So, certainly, where the benefits are realised, when all is well, then the membership as a whole will be content and leave it alone. It is no part of democratic duty to criticise for its own sake; and enough that the check will have done its work simply by being available. Where they are not, and the membership remains acquiescent, it will be for one of two reasons. Either the expected benefits are now seen to be illusory, and the members will be sadder and wiser. Or there was never enough volition. Not that either of the two explanations identifies a defect peculiar to Co-operation as a form of business organisation. They simply reaffirm that a co-operative should never be started except where a clear-sighted appraisal of the possibilities shows both that the prospects of material success are good enough, and where the prospective members want of their own conviction to start it. Glaringly obvious though the point is, it is still necessary to make it if only to put a question-mark against the supposition that the main requirement for a general and lasting extension of the co-operative sector of the economy is financial inducement. Co-operation is not induced in, nor still less imposed on, people who remain indifferent to it.

No: it is not in the acquiescence of members in success or in their acceptance of the failure of a misconceived venture, wrongly identified as indifference, that the acid test of the co-operative form of organisation, considered as an example of democratic practice, is to be found. Rather, the test is whether it can respond soon enough to impending but avoidable failure to remove the causes before it is too late. Certainly, there is no reason to suppose that it would be slower to respond than would conventionally organised businesses in general. And in industrial co-operatives, where the owners are the workforce and so always on the scene, one would expect the response to be quicker and more perceptive than that of shareholders in a public limited company.

There remains the question, noted earlier on and perhaps the most important, whether Co-operation is as its advocates claim morally superior to the present alternatives. It is tempting to rely on the pronouncement that it is an extension of democracy as sufficient proof of the claim. Let us not, though, yield to temptation, but address ourselves to a more analytical re-formulation of the question, as follows. Is the general perception in the west of the purposes of human society now such as to lead to the view that those purposes are more likely to be achieved by the extended use in production and provision of the co-operative form of organisation? To answer it, we need first to draw a distinction between, at the one extreme, the elementary co-operation of primitive, or pioneering or other societies, whose control of their circumstances is so insecure as to put them under threat; and, at the other, Co-operation in the special sense of organising economic activity, production or provision, on a mutual basis in the modern industrialised state. It is of course the second that this book is about. Yet again before we dismiss the first it is worth looking more closely into the distinction. For it brings into sharp focus what are, for our purposes, the specific characteristics of society as it has evolved in the industrialised west: that is a society which, at least in political principle, asserts the prime importance of the individual; and in which the industrial revolution has occurred as an irreversible change. It is, in short, a society wealthy and secure enough to permit the view that it exists for man, rather than that man exists for it. By contrast in the society under threat, the kind of co-operation essential to the survival of the group will be such as to suppress individuality to whatever extent necessary. To cite the extreme case, Eskimos used once to leave to die the old person who had become a drag on a group with nothing to spare for the useless member. From each according to his capacity, to each according to his value; and life was nasty, brutish – and shortened. Suppression of individuality could go no further. But the further man is removed from that extreme, the more man has become master of his circumstances, the more the individual is relieved of the need to suppress his individuality and freed to realise it: that is, to develop, each for him or herself, a potential, unique to *Homo sapiens sapiens*, for awareness. Few would deny that such freedom is the prime purpose, the shining moral imperative for society, nor that it depends first upon a sufficient creation and distribution of wealth nor that it increases the opportunity for vitiating selfishness.

For all its imperfections, for all the misery which accompanied its development, nevertheless as practised in the western in-dustrialised states Capitalism must on any general appraisal be judged to have made possible the massive advance during the last century or so towards its realisation. Nor can it be merely accident that it is to those societies which can afford and do assert liberty of thought and action that the explosive growth in intellectual and emotional awareness is so very largely attributable. And since Capitalism is, as a liberator, an immeasurable advance upon the collective and community-related system of production and provision, available to primitive societies, a case for Co-operation equated to simple collectivism would be a case for retrogression, and absurd. But it would be no less absurd to rely upon that equation for a description of Co-operation as a form of organisation for manufacturing or service industry in industrialised states at the end of the twentieth century. The point at issue is this: given the existence of the industrialised state, would the extended use in it of the co-operative form of organisation facilitate the pursuit of the moral imperative. In other words, is it in the here and now a better means to that end than those generally available under the present dispensation?

To establish the point we need to show that Co-operation, for all that it may be comprehended within a description of Capitalism, is more likely by reason of its special characteristics to create at least as much wealth, if not more, as conventionally organised industry;

and that it is more likely to distribute it better. The contrast is this. In conventionally organised industry, the creation of wealth is liable to be impeded by ultimate conflict of interest between capital and labour. In industrial co-operatives that liability does not exist, a fact which must tend to facilitate the creation of wealth. So, if workers work only because they must, in order to earn a living, where in a conventionally organised business they may from time to time have cause enough to disregard that obligation, in a co-operative they can have none. There is no 'them and us'; they cannot strike against themselves. Next, workers may work also because they believe they ought to, or even because they want to. Almost invariably, of course, they work for a varying mixture of all three reasons. It is the last two reasons, though, which provide the content of morale, three-quarters of the game; and they are likely to operate more forcefully in a form of organisation, the co-operative form, which by offering as of right equality of esteem, reward related to participation, and responsibilities which go with ultimate authority, appeals to self-respect and self-discipline. However much attention may be given in a conventionally organised enterprise by good personnel management to morale, and whether it is given out of benignity or under constraint, it cannot provide anything like the same appeal to self-respect nor expect the same self-discipline. The division between 'them and us' remains; and so the morale which, to cite an admittedly extreme case, is available to sustain a strike called by the National Union of Mineworkers against a publicly owned industry, is not available to the industry itself. Lastly, a form of organisation which disburses the surplus available for the purpose to the workforce, rather than to investors and which may buy back its own shares at their par value and so precludes capital gain on the transaction, will distribute wealth more widely. By contrast, the form of organisation which needs to satisfy investors through the payment of dividends and the realisation of capital gains will distribute wealth less widely, and may well tend rather to concentrate it. We may conclude that, as a creator and distributor of wealth, industrial co-operatives will, over a sufficient period, out-perform conventional organisations. From the macro-economic viewpoint, it has been argued further that a totally co-operative economy offers the only prospect of avoiding the dilemma, inseparable from the arrangements now prevailing, that the country faces the potentially disastrous alternatives: either inflation generated by the exploitation by the trades unions of the asset at their disposal; or massive unemployment as pre-condition of a stable currency. Be that as it may – and one might well ponder the practical and political difficulties of managing and maintaining a wholesale changeover in a relatively short term – the more modest inference that industrial co-operatives can create wealth at least as well and probably better than the traditional forms of industry is reasonable and sufficient; and what empirical evidence there is tends to confirm it.[5] We may say that considered solely as a creator and distributor of liberating wealth, Industrial Co-operation stands as a development from and a material improvement on Capitalism; and for that reason only its extended use would help western industrialised societies better to afford and pursue their ultimate purpose. But the co-operative contributes directly to it: for, of itself, membership of an industrial co-operative recognises individuality in people rather than a commodity in labour; it makes one's working life part of a life of one's own, rather than an abstraction from it. By itself that is an act of liberation. And, one might conjecture that a system which is founded on the principle of the equality of man – not in performance which would be a nonsense, but in esteem – will be more likely to respond positively to the proposition that the more general pursuit of the moral imperative through for example education, health and welfare, and aid to the third world, should be a proper charge on its residual resources.

This, to recapitulate, is the broad picture and potential of Co-operation in the United Kingdom today. Multifaceted, it presents two aspects of special interest: Consumer Co-operation, hitherto by far its greatest achievement but now in critical decline; and, contrasted with it both in achievement and structure, Industrial Co-operation, the new and significant growing point. Undefined, and better so, in the statute a main purpose of which is to provide for the incorporation of co-operatives as trading enterprises, a bona fide co-operative is a business showing certain characteristics which an official charged by the statute of knowing one when he sees it would expect to be present normally, but which neither exclude it from a general description of Capitalism nor relieve it of the need to make profitability the test of its commercial performance. Those characteristics do, however, distinguish it in essential particulars from the commonest form of capitalist enterprise, the joint stock company, and again from the state-owned enterprise. They do so by asserting as rights the democratic values of participation and equality of esteem and by imposing the concomitant obligation of responsibility, including the responsibility of deputing – wherever it is necessary or desirable to do so – effective authority to accountable management. The distinction shows most sharply in industrial co-operatives as a class; for it is there, where the interests of ownership and workforce – capital and labour – precisely coincide, that morale expressed as a commitment to the success of the enterprise is present as an inherent extra factor to ensure that, by and large, industrial co-operatives will outperform conventionally organised industry where there are two sides, where the interests of capital and labour are ultimately and inescapably opposed – as indeed they are also in state-owned industry. At the macro-economic level that opposition presents society with a choice between wage inflation or massive unemployment, while in industrial co-operatives the precise co-incidence of the two interests might well, if the form of organisation had been widely enough adopted, operate to avoid it. Most important of all, the widespread adoption of the industrial co-operative form of organisation would not only satisfy, at least as well as and probably better than the arrangements at present prevailing, the necessary precondition for furthering the liberty of the individual: that is the sufficient creation and distribution of wealth. But more, the industrial co-operative form distributes also authority and responsibility where the conventional form concentrates them. In consequence the one integrates life at work into, where the other abstracts it from, 'a life of one's own'. So, Industrial Co-operation may be said, of its nature and in contrast to both private and public sector industrial organisations, to contribute directly to the perceived purpose of western democracy: that is the promotion of individuality of consciousness and conscience; and hence to act indirectly to promote them more generally. It is upon that appraisal that Co-operation in general and Industrial Co-operation in particular may fairly found their claim to moral superiority. Emphatically, it is not the morality of a pre-ordained prescription to which fallible humanity may hope to aspire but never to attain, but of a much humbler kind which asserts no more than that it is best economic policy. Such an economic policy would recognise an industrial co-operative sector as the third-way. The Italians had the name first: *la terza via*, the way that differs from both the private and public sectors of industry as these terms are commonly understood, a way now assuming a new and practical relevance. New, or better perhaps, renewed though the relevance may be, the idea of the industrial co-operative is as old as the history of Co-operation. So, to see why Co-operation is what it now is, and hence better to understand what it might become, we need to look at that history. It is still too soon for us to reassemble our preconvictions

— 2 —
A New View of Robert Owen:
The Vision and the Visionary

By education most have been misled;
So they believe, because they so were bred.
The priest continues what the nurse began,
And thus the child imposes on the man.

John Dryden, 'The Hind and the Panther'

And was Jerusalem builded here
Among these dark Satanic mills?

William Blake, 'Milton'

Robert Owen is widely regarded as the founding father of the co-operative movement and a review of its history conveniently starts with him. Some of the specific features of Co-operation had of course already shown themselves well before the publication in 1814 of his essays *A New View of Society*. Indeed G.D.H. Cole identifies as co-operatives the flour mills and bakeries established by 1760 by workmen employed in the dockyards at Woolwich and Chatham; and goes on to cite as the first consumer co-operatives two in Scotland: the Weavers Society of 1769 at Fenwick in Ayrshire, and the Govan Victualling Society of 1777.[1] None of this need surprise us; for mutuality, the idea at the heart of Co-operation, is as old as humanity. So too for that matter is competition; and a view which insisted that a society must always adopt for its social and economic basis either the one or the other would be mistaken. The interesting question is why and how far at any given time one or the other will better serve society. As we have seen, for the Eskimo still untouched by western culture, the answer is obvious and absolute. The challenge of his environment is so severe that co-operation is, quite literally, the way of life, the quintessential condition of survival; while competition – if he could conceive of it at all – be dismissed as a fatal irrelevance. Nearer to home and to Owen's day, insurance clubs protected men against the risk that, under the Ballot Act of 1802, they might be drafted into the Militia. For them, membership of a club made a marginal use of mutuality as a safeguard against a possible inconvenience, greater or less. It would not have occurred to a member of such a club any more than it did to the docker at Woolwich or Chatham, or to the weaver at Fenwick, that he was contributing, however minutely, to a movement which in the fullness of time and of many contributions might decisively alter the nature of society. No: those in Britain who came to Co-operation before Owen did so to solve a local and immediate practical difficulty, then and there, not consciously to start building the New Jerusalem.

But Owen did think that he was about to change the nature of society, universally and virtually overnight. Now it is an endearing characteristic of the visionary to suppose that, the truth having been revealed to him, he will have only to publish the revelation and it will at once and everywhere be acknowledged and acted upon. Owen is as explicit as he is sure: 'These principles', he says, 'require only to be known to establish themselves.'[2] What principles? Search as you may in the four essays comprised in *A New View of Society* you will find nothing about Co-operation considered primarily as another way of organising the production of goods and the provision of services, a way which extends democratic principle into the factory or workshop and offers protection to the consumer. What you will find is a series of variations on a single theme, introduced at the beginning of the first essay. Its purpose is

> to direct the public mind to the most important object to which
> it can be directed – to a national proceeding for rationally
> forming the character of that immense mass of population
> which is now allowed to be formed as to fill the world with
> crimes.

And again:

> The governing powers of all countries should establish rational
> plans for the education and general formation of the characters
> of their subjects. These plans must be devised to train children

from their earliest infancy in good habits of every description (which will of course prevent them from acquiring those of falsehood and deception). They must afterwards be rationally educated, and their labour be usefully directed. Such habits and education will impress them with an active and ardent desire to promote the happiness of every individual, and without shadow of exception for sect, or party, or country, or climate. They will also ensure, with the fewest possible exceptions, health, strength and vigour of body: for the happiness of man can be erected only on the foundations of health of body and peace of mind.

O brave new world that had such people in it, born noble savages without so much as a touch of the old Adam in them but full of the latent new Owen, who had only to be saved from a corrupting environment, to be educated on benevolent principles, in order to transform society.

Not much yet, then, in *A New View of Society*, that you will recognise as Co-operation, very little about mutuality, about the democracy essential to a genuine co-operative, a lot less about the brotherhood of man than about the paternalism of the considerate proprietor. Privileged people – the description is Owen's – should welcome the plan. 'A very little reflection on the part of the privileged will ensure this line of conduct' – that is 'to co-operate sincerely and cordially with those who desire not to touch one iota of the supposed advantages they now enjoy; and whose first and last wish is to increase the particular happiness of those [privileged] classes, as well as the general happiness of society.'[3] Privilege could sleep sound in its comfortable bed: the plan would not present 'the least danger to any part of society. That plan is a national, well-digested, unexclusive design for the formation of character and the general amelioration of the lower orders.'[4] And what was more, it would pay handsomely. Well-treated workers would 'effectually co-operate to produce the greatest pecuniary gain to the proprietor'.[5] These, incidentally, are the only uses I have noticed in the four essays of the word 'co-operate'; and the reference is to co-operation between the proprietor and his employees. Owen goes on: 'Look after your work people as you would look after your machines.' Here, the appeal is as much to shrewdness, to business acumen, as to a sense of common humanity.

But it is the address prefixed to the third essay that his view, the utilitarian view, shows through most clearly. After recalling that, like this audience, he was 'a manufacturer for pecuniary profit', Owen continues:

> From experience which cannot deceive me, I venture to assure you, your time and money so applied, if directed by a true knowledge of the subject, would return you not five, ten or fifteen per cent for your capital so expended, but fifty, and in many cases a hundred per cent.

This could be read as disingenuous sales-talk; that while Owen's concern was, in reality, to promote the rights of labour as against the rights of property, he knew that a frontal attack must be defeated and that only infiltration could succeed. On such a reading, Co-operation visualised as an alternative economic order might be held to have been his conscious but concealed objective. Such a conclusion is, however, unlikely if only because it would be inconsistent with Owen's behaviour. His disposition was to announce, regardless of expediency, revelation and denounce evil, for what he took them to be. Innocence, not guile, is the mark of the idealist.

The alternative view is that, certainly in 1814 when *A New View of Society* was published, he was not concerned to propose an alternative to what would later be called competitive Capitalism. At this stage of his thinking he saw profitability, unlimited profitablity, as a proper objective of investment: 'your time and money so applied ... would return you ... fifty, and in many cases, a hundred per cent.' If capital was to maximise the return on investment, it should support his plan: and this was, let us remember, to be 'a national proceeding for rationally forming the character of that immense mass of the population', and so for ushering in a new and beneficent world order.

The second point to be noted is this. The relationship envisaged is that between proprietors and employees, them and us. The proprietors, that is to say in the exact sense of the word, those who owned the property, the land, buildings and machinery – who, in a word, provided the capital, employed labour. The relationship remained contractual; the contract that between a buyer and seller, the proprietor to buy and the employee to sell his labour; and the recognised interest of the employee in the business confined to the discharge of his obligations under the contract. He had no right to any say in, nor any responsibilities for, the conduct of the business.

The insurance clubs were a lot closer to Co-operation than this.

Yet, seen with the eyes of co-operative faith, a passage in the third essay may hold more promise. That essay sets out to apply to a particular situation the principles discussed in the first two essays; and the application consists essentially of a description of the practical means by which education and training are to be brought to workpeople and their children. There was to be a 'New Institution'. It was to contain a playground for use by children from the age at which they could walk. Under adult supervision, they would be told that they were never to injure playfellows but to do all that they could to make them happy. Because character was formed in the very early years, it would be important to get children at a very early age away from the sole influence of their parents. One begins to see at this point how a coin showing on the one side the smiling face of the paternalist is only too likely to reveal on the other the severer look of the authoritarian. The virtue and the vice are rarely separable.

Also contained within the New Institution were to be a school, lecture room and church, for – and here again comes the recurrent theme – 'education for the untaught and ill-taught becomes of first importance to society'. Every opportunity is to be taken to press home the point that happiness is indivisible. Adults would attend evening classes. Among the matter to be taught would be 'how to appropriate the gains that will be left to them in order to create a fund which would remove from them the anxious fear of future want'. At the very least, that statement provides for an element of control of business by the workforce. Not, of course, of the business that employed them, the business of manufacturing for pecuniary profit; but still, an assumption by workpeople of corporate responsibility in their own interest.

There is not enough in that, though, to modify the conclusion that *A New View of Society* is not really about Co-operation at all. As E.P. Thompson points out, Hazlitt at once saw well enough what it was about. The view was not new. It was at least as old as 1793; and old birds, who had seen it all before, were not to be caught with chaff.[6] And Hazlitt was right. The first thing to understand about Owen is that he looks back to the eighteenth century as much, or more, than he looks forward to the nineteenth; if his place is in the British Industrial Revolution, his ideas are drawn from those which fired the French Political Revolution. It is from the French *philosophes*, from Rousseau (1712–78) and, more plainly, from

Helvetius (1715–71) and Condorcet (1743–94) that he derives the optimistic conviction that good education was all that was needed to make men good, that if only the environment were right man born into it would automatically produce the good society. To Owen, eighteen years old when in 1789 the fall of the Bastille marked the beginning of the French Revolution, bliss no doubt it was in that dawn to be alive; and to be young, very heaven. The certainty of his belief in the perfectibility of human nature is the certainty of a magnanimous man who, having lived in that heaven, could never fully accept that that blissful dawn had not after all heralded the glorious day. For him, the truth remained that all men were born equal, uncorrupted, and unburdened by original sin. The fault, the grievous fault, lay in the old corrupt order; and the need was to sweep it away and to replace it by a new order founded on his plan. No longer would miseducation mislead, nor the mind marred in childhood impose upon the man.

But, old as Hazlitt rightly declared or new as Owen believed his view of society to be, it is not recognisably about Co-operation. Nor did his address, in 1816, at New Lanark, mark much advance. Benevolent education as the means to good character formation, remained the essential theme. With its introduction 'all our evil passions', he said, 'will disappear; no ground of anger or displeasure from one human being to another will remain; the period of the supposed Millennium will commence, and universal love prevail.' The intention was still

> to effect extensive ameliorations throughout the British Dominions ... First. By showing the master manufacturers an example, in practice, on a scale sufficiently extensive, of the mode by which the characters and situations of the working manufacturers they employ may be very materially improved, not only without injury to the masters, but so as to create to them great or substantial advantages.
>
> Second. By inducing through this example, the British Legislature to enact such laws as will secure similar benefits to every part of our population.

There is nothing here to reconcile the ultimate conflict of interest between employer and employee. On the contrary, the proprietorial interest is recognised as separate and particular, the philosophy remains utilitarian. And the intention is still, at this stage, to proceed through the agency of the State. Through laws

23

which would 'diminish and ultimately prevent the most prominent evils to which the working classes are now subjected' the New Jerusalem would be legislated into existence. Nor does he, in his *Observations on the Effect of the Manufacturing System* (1817), yet introduce Co-operation into his picture of the perfected society. That essay is, however, important for another reason. Published in the same year as Ricardo's *Principles of Political Economy*, which first pronounced the general labour theory of value, it identifies labour as the source of wealth. This provided a powerful argument against Capitalism. From now on it would on this premise be perfectly possible to argue that the retention by the capitalist of wealth created by workers was expropriation. This may be said to mark the beginning of a socialist philosophy; and Owen's use of Ricardo's pronouncement to justify his place as the first in the Socialist pantheon. But if it was a trumpet call, its sound was still very uncertain. The unmistakable call to the battle had to await Thomas Hodgskin and *Labour Defended Against the Claims of Capital* (1825). In the *Observations*, Owen's objections seem primarily to be levelled at the exploitation of labour by 'new competitors against those of long standing'. One may read this as signalling conversion to the view that competition was bad in principle. One may as well read it as meaning that there had of late been too much of it. His *Address to the Working Classes*, in the same year, tends to support the second reading rather than the first. Those, it advocated, who had 'riches, honour, power and privilege should keep them'; and it went on to 'pledge no attempt to remove them. The cause for contest between us', he added, 'will henceforth cease.' Given the abundance which the new means of production and a regenerate society would guarantee, greed and selfishness would have become pointless, and would vanish. Where there was enough for all and each now loved his neighbour as himself, who could want more? Here one can see the marriage of two revolutions, the French Political and the British Industrial; here Helvetius and Condorcet shake hands with Watt and Arkwright. The Robert Owen of 1789 who at the age of eighteen rejoiced at the news of the fall of the Bastille was the same Robert Owen, formerly a draper's assistant, who in the same year started in business on a borrowed £100, and who in 1809 was able to buy out his partners at New Lanark for £84,000.

A millennium needs a messiah. It would be unfair to say that Owen consciously cast himself in that role. Yet in his *Further Development of the Plan for the Relief of the Poor and the Emancipation of*

Mankind (1817), he sounds an unmistakably messianic note – and not only in the title of the essay. 'I came not', he declares, 'among you to establish a name, but to relieve you from the evils and errors of all names.' To so authoritative a declaration, there can be only one reply: 'Hallelujah!' and then, after a moment or two of reverent meditation, 'But what shall we do to be saved?' Owen had his answer. Let us note first, however, that the first element in the further developed plan was now the relief of the poor. To moral regeneration was now added an objective of immediate and practical importance.

On the best possible Biblical authority, the poor were always and would always be with us. Given that pronouncement, poverty was not necessarily deserved or blameworthy, and the moral obligation to relieve poverty plain. Relief was provided by the parish, the burden falling on the rates. The slump which followed the Napoleonic Wars, the displacement of cottage industry by factory production, now added greatly to the number of people wholly or partly unemployed; and the burden on the parish rates seemed to those who paid them increasingly oppressive. Perhaps, after all, the poor were too much with us. If Owen's plan offered a solution to an intractable problem, he was a man to be listened to.

Owen's answer and solution was that new communities should be started, communities which would be 'Villages of Unity and Mutual Co-operation'. To these the unemployed would go. There they would work. And it would pay handsomely. In his *Report to the County of Lanark* (1820) he argued, again echoing Ricardo but now much more forcefully, that manual labour, properly directed, was the source of all wealth and hence of national prosperity. Labour, in effective action, would be worth more than the expense of relieving the unemployed. What was more, despite Malthus, this would remain so 'under any supposable increase of its population for many years to come' – a view, incidentally, that was not to prevent him from becoming in the 1820s an advocate of birth control. More important, in an interesting anticipation of Keynes's *General Theory*, he contended also that it was only the lack of a profitable market that impeded 'the successful or otherwise beneficial industry of the working classes'. Pay them, well enough, and the market would be created. If one agrees with Keynes that anything which stimulates demand in the economy will help to reduce unemployment, that rather than that men should do nothing it would be better to pay them to dig holes and fill them in again, one will find it easy to applaud Owen's plea for demand-led growth as a cure for unemployment and the means of eradicating poverty. But – Villages of Co-operation?

Let us look at the idea. They would, Owen envisaged, be purpose-built to receive the poor, who would work either in intensive agriculture, or – as at New Lanark – in industry, or in both. Each village would dispose of its surplus produce or products by exchange with others, the medium of exchange being not the coin of the realm but 'labour-value notes'. Coin of the realm would not do because it represented 'an artificial standard of values' represented by metals, an arrangement which though it had stimulated invention and released latent energies had also made man selfish and anti-social. In a sentence from which it is a delight to quote, he sums up: metal coinage had 'blindly urged him forward to create but deprived him of wisdom to enjoy'. Getting down to detail, Owen advocated communal cooking – so the dwellings would need no kitchens – and what we would now call district heating. Clothing for boys was to resemble 'the Roman or Highland garb'. More circumspect about women's clothing, he prescribes only that 'females should have a well-chosen dress to secure similar important advantages', that is to say, to 'free the limbs from ligatures and to allow the air to circulate over every part of the body'. Searching for a modern equivalent, one might be forgiven for lighting upon holiday camps, but with these differences: people would go there to work, not play; the mood would be one of moral earnestness, not of carnival; and there would be winter, as well as summer.

He saw four ways in which the Villages might be brought into being: by wealthy individuals – 'landed proprietors or large capitalists'; by established companies with funds available for benevolent and public objects; by local authorities – that is, parishes and counties, to relieve themselves of the rate-borne burden of supporting the poor; and by what he calls associations of middle and working classes of farmers, mechanics and tradesmen who, 'in a spirit of self-help might wish to relieve themselves of the evils of the present system'. Significantly, he distinguishes the last of the four from the others: significantly, because the distinction bears on the crucial question of control. 'Those', he says, 'founded by land-owners and capitalists will be controlled by those who found them. Those formed by the middle and working classes, upon a complete reciprocity of interest, should be governed by themselves.' Those who paid the piper would continue to call the tune. And that tune would include, for those who invested land or capital, a return on the investment. He says, explicitly: 'As land, capital and labour may be applied to far greater pecuniary advantage under the proposed arrangements than under any other at present known to the public, all parties will readily unite in carrying them into execution.' In sum, land and capital would get its reward: and those who provided it would be in control. There might in the Villages they founded be co-operation in its general sense that the spirit of helpfulness and amity were intended to prevail. But there would not be Co-operation in its particular meaning, in the meaning that distinguishes it from other forms of organisation for production or provision. Only those Villages formed by the people who were to live and work in them would be governed by them, for only there would proprietory rights coincide exactly with the rights of the workpeople. They would coincide exactly because the proprietors and workpeople would be the same people. Here, if only here, in the last of the four ways proposed by Owen for setting up Villages, is authentic Co-operation. It is, of course, easy to smile at the more fanciful aspects of the *Report*, to see in them proof of the wildly unpractical idealist, to dismiss the whole as an irrelevance to the resolution then and now of social and economic problems. It is easy, with the benefit of hindsight, to observe that Owen's sanguine expectations of human nature, expectations which depend so largely on the most optimistic opinions of the *philosophes*, were bound to be disappointed; for that hindsight comprehends Darwin, and the survival of the biologically fittest, and so knows to be invalid the assumptions that all men and women are born equal in capacity, that selfishness is a consequence solely of environment and not an inherited characteristic. If Rousseau abolished original sin, Darwin reinstated it – and, as some were to suppose, justified it. It is easy to see now that the idea of establishing a new community would have seemed natural enough to people who, before the general adoption of steam power and, later, the advent of railway transport, located machinery and the people needed to operate it at places where water power happened to be available.

Not that Owen lacked critics at the time. It is, of course, the radical critic of radical proposals who most commands attention, for he must be supposed to sympathise with their intention. William Cobbett detested the system, *The Thing* as he called it, which protected privilege and denied the working man 'the fair fruit of his earnings'. None sought more constantly to bring it down. His views put him once into prison on a charge of sedition; and drove him twice into exile, once to France and once to the United States. The parliamentary reform he demanded went far beyond that conceded by the Reform Act of 1832. As George Woodcock comments,[7] it was no less than the reform sought by the Chartists: universal manhood suffrage, annual parliaments and the secret ballot. As the Member for Oldham in the reformed Parliament Cobbett remained a reformer and, in the minds of working people, a hero in their cause.[8] His credentials as a fighter in the cause of the labouring poor are impeccable. But he would have nothing to do with Owen's Villages of Co-operation. His sarcasm was bitter. For him they would become in the famous quotation 'parallelograms of pauperdom'; and in another' a proper place for the disposal of place-seeking lawyers'.[9]

For a fairer and moving judgment, let us turn to William Lovett, the Chartist leader, moving because it is the judgment of one who is sadder and wiser but who has not lost faith, who knows that he will not see Owen's millennium but that he must still strive towards it.' At one time', he says, 'I was favourably impressed with many of Mr Owen's views and more especially with those of a *community of property*, but through mature reflection as caused me to have lost faith in a community of property, I have not yet lost faith in the great benefits that might yet be realised by a wise and judicious system of co-operation in the Production of Wealth.'[10]

But that judgment lay in the future. For the time being, Owen left the scene. Westward, lo! the land was brighter, or so it seemed. A country which had declared life, liberty and the pursuit of happiness to be its purpose might well be expected to listen with more attention to a man who knew how to achieve them. After all, the declaration was just what his own pronouncement, that the great object of society is to obtain wealth, and to enjoy it,[11] might be said to paraphrase; and stands with it to reflect what was then the most enlightened perception of a society's purpose. So, from 1824 to 1829, while he was promoting his cause in the United States, others in Britain were taking up his ideas and, in the process, modifying them. Though his grand vision can be said to have contained within itself the germ of the ideas that led both to Socialism as an alternative to Capitalism, or to Co-operation as a manifestation of democracy, though in bringing together the labour theory of value and the criticism on humane grounds of the

28

abuse of labour by master manufacturers under conditions of unregulated competition, he provided the foundation for the case which others were to build for Socialism or Co-operation, he cannot thus far be said to have advocated either in any form that we would recognise. Thus far, the vision of a new, benificent society was still to be realised by so training and educating perfectible humanity as to make it perfect in a world where new methods of production would ensure abundance. The vision was of Utopia, the visionary a romantic utilitarian.

— 3 —

A New View of Robert Owen: Owenites and Owenism

Alle Menschen werden Brüder.

Schiller, An Die Freude

Then I asked: 'Does a firm persuasion that a thing is so, make it so?' He replied: 'All Poets believe that it does, and in ages of imagination this firm persuasion removed mountains; but many are not capable of a firm persuasion of anything.'

William Blake, 'Proverbs of Hell'

Westward, lo! the land, if brighter, was not bright enough. Having addressed the President and the Congress, and having conducted what must have been one of the first lecture tours of the United States, Owen set up a village of Co-operation at New Harmony, in Indiana. The name promised much, but only to deceive. Certainly, the village was co-operative in structure. Indeed, in the range of kinds of organisations recognisably co-operative, it must be placed at the extreme. Property was held in common, work was collective, and produce shared. If individual rights in property are an absolute impediment to the institution of Utopia or even, less pretentiously, to the promotion of the good life, then at New Harmony there was no such impediment. All owned everything, none owned anything; and the experiment failed. As Cole records,[1] it settled down finally into an agricultural colony of individually owned and worked farms. It would of course be wrong to conclude that this particular form of co-operative, the community co-operative, is bound to fail. Kibbutzim, to which it bears most resemblance, do not; nor do the traditional Eskimo communities. One is, nevertheless, bound to suppose that it is only in extreme conditions that people can be expected to volunteer the suppression of individuality to the extent that the more extreme forms of co-operative require: only, that is in short, where a life of one's own would not be supportable.

Nor does the failure of New Harmony, as of other villages of co-operation, allow the conclusion that the idea of common ownership is misconceived; and that its application elsewhere – as in many of the new wave of industrial co-operatives in the United Kingdom – is likely to prove mistaken. But it does at least prompt the question whether the suppression in them, not now of individuality but of individual interest in the sense of ownership, is only likely to be volunteered where the amount of that interest is seen by the prospective volunteer as marginal to his other interests, concerns and obligations. For people leading lives of their own, those other interests, concerns and obligations will often be compelling. They will include, most pressingly, doing one's best for one's nearest and dearest. There will, of course, always be those whose motivation in the cause will over-rule other considerations, whether because the motivation is founded in ideological conviction, or because other considerations are weak, or both. But a view of Co-operation which admitted only those who are thus motivated would make it an exceptional and exclusive creed to which could subscribe only those for whom Co-operation was itself the end and not the means to a better life, to one which enhanced what Dahrendorf calls a man's life chances.[2] And that that would not do. If Co-operation is to appeal broadly, it must be a broad church. It is for all people, as people are and as they behave, for imperfect people living lives of their own in an imperfect world.

In Britain meanwhile, precisely because it was imprecise, Owenism could appeal broadly, and Owenites grew in number. To the masses which the French Revolution had made politically aware and on which the Industrial Revolution was imposing new and appalling burdens while increasing exponentially the capacity to create wealth, Owen's new view was of a society which had realised their aspirations. As inspirational pronouncement rather than an operational blueprint, not only did it give expression to and authority for the idea that a fairer, juster society should be created, as the inalienable rights of man required; but more, it asserted that thanks to machinery powered by steam it could be. If liberty and equality were birth-rights, it remained only to establish fraternity: for, fear having been cast out not by perfect love but by plenty, all men could now become brothers and women sisters. Schiller had already written the words, in his *Ode to Joy*; and Beethoven had provided the music. This, at its most exalted, represented the aspiration of Owenism; and though few Owenites would have heard the song, when the time came for the countless host to stream in through gates of pearl, that surely is what they could have sung as they marched. When, indeed: but practical measures were the immediate need; and it was in the absence in America of Owen himself that Owenism emerged as a response to that need and Owenites as those who formulated the response. It took various forms.

Seeking to use the master's own model, some Owenites established co-operative communities. That road to Co-operation proved, certainly in the United Kingdom, as well as in the United States, to be a dead-end; and it is convenient to trace the whole of its course before turning to the more significant developments started in his absence. In 1826 at Orbiston in Lanark, and as a direct consequence of his report to the county, a co-operative community was set up. In 1827, for reasons which had nothing to do with the success or failure of the enterprise, the land-owner sold the estate and the community was dispersed. Other communities followed. Of them, Cole points to two for special attention.[3] The one, established in 1831 at Ralahine in Ireland, survived for two years before the estate was sold to pay the owner's gambling debts. Again, the community was dispersed. The other, at East Tytherley in Hampshire, was called Harmony Hall. That harmonic strain again; and again it was to have a dying fall. Owen himself served at different times as governor of the community. Kept going only by subsidies, it was wound up in 1846 in circumstances which seem to have been anything but harmonious. So Owen's high road to the regeneration of society through the co-operative community petered out to its disillusioning end. Other developments, more modest in their expectations and deriving from the particular perception this or that group might have of the way in which Owen's new view could be related to its own grievance or apprehension or aspiration, proceeded in parallel, propagated largely by the rapidly growing radical press which included a number of journals advocating Owenite ideas. Some co-operative stores were started, with the immediate object of consumer protection but also to accumulate money with which to finance a co-operative community. So, too, were a number of producer co-operatives by workpeople determined to set up in business

32

themselves whether, by competing with master manufacturers, to reinforce the effect of a strike; or to counter a lock-out; or in response to wage-cuts; or simply to create jobs. After the repeal in 1824 of the Combination Acts, neither trade unions nor strikes were illegal. Perhaps the most significant fact to record about the creation so early in their legitimate lives by trade unions of producer co-operatives is that their purpose was so very largely tactical. It was already a specifically trade union response to the single most important question trade unions face: the question of maintaining and improving the wages paid to their members by employers. Thus, though it demonstrates the existence from the outset a common source of inspiration in Owenism for both trade unionism and co-operation, it demonstrates also that trade unionism saw Producer Co-operation not as an alternative and preferable way of organising manufacture and hence one to be adopted generally, not in short as a prime purpose, but as an occasional weapon. And, as the rest of the century was to show, while as a consumer a workman might be a co-operator, at his place of work with rare exceptions he might not: even in the consumer movement's own factories. At work, he could only be a trade unionist.

The evidence is plain, the witnesses are persuasive. By 1829, the year of Owen's return from America, the organisation by John Doherty of workers in cotton spinning into his Grand National Union of the United Kingdom had marked an attempt to make trade union structure national, whereas hitherto it had been local. Almost immediately, Doherty went on to try to make it general and so, of course, capable of calling for a general strike. His National Association for the Protection of Labour sought to organise workers employed in a comprehensive range of trades: mining, building, textiles, pottery and others. In 1830, the National Association held its first conference. Others followed in 1831. Doherty is described by Cole as an ardent Owenite[4]; but though he records him as advocating 'co-operative self-employment far and wide wherever the workers became organised', he nevertheless identifies the National Association as a purely trade union body. And indeed, its function was explicit in its title, its purpose, the purpose at its most modest of trade unionism within a system of production comprising employers and employees, capital and labour, as separate entities which though necessary to one another were yet ultimately opposed. That purpose was, the Webbs record,[5]

33

expressly to resist reductions but not to ask for advances in pay. So it looks as though at the very beginning of the 1830s, trade unionism was already disposed to settle into the primary role which it was fully and consciously to adopt later in the century, a role which would be ameliorative rather than revolutionary. As a leader among the Owenties, Doherty may not have looked so far towards the promised land of Owen's splendid but indistinct new view; but his perception, though narrower, was clearer.[6] Two things happened, however, to divert trade unionism from the adoption of that role and to lead it instead into what has been called its revolutionary period, one which for a time made the ownership and control of industries by the people who worked in them its main objective, which sought in short to displace the organisation of industry on the capitalist model by an industrial co-operative commonwealth. The first was that, with the passage in 1832 of the Reform Bill came the full realisation that parliamentary reform had done nothing for the emergent working class, except to isolate it. The second was Owen's declaration that there was another way, easy and immediate; a message which, in the collapse of the generally uncritical expectations attending the successful struggle to secure the passage of the Bill must have been all the more persuasive.

For it was in 1833 that Owen appeared at the London Co-operative Congress to advocate the creation of the Grand Moral Union of the Productive Classes. He had just persuaded the Operative Builders Union to restructure itself as the Grand National Guild of Builders. In effect the people working in the industry were to take it over and to run it as an industrial co-operative, organised nationally. Now he sought to extend the idea to the whole of industry. Note again the title and functions. The Union was to be 'Moral': that is to say it would look, as Owen had always looked, beyond the immediate need to protect working people against exploitation of the work-place. It aspired to the reconstitution of the socio-economic order on what he regarded as a moral basis: in short, as an industrial democracy. And the new order was to comprehend not only labour, not only working classes, but the productive classes. The difference is significant. It distinguishes the classes of society not by reference to the contrasted roles of employer and employee, but rather by reference to their usefulness. There were those who were productive, or industrious. There were those who were not. The strong probability is that in this, his latest revise of his view of society, Owen continued to place master-manufacturers among the productive and industrious. We may take it that the utilitarian in him could accept with Ricardo's labour theory of value his hostility to landlords, who might be regarded as unproductive and bone-idle, and share with him a reluctance to extend that hostility to master-manufacturers. For so many years himself a master-manufacturer at New Lanark, he might fairly be supposed still to see virtue in those among whom he had been numbered. And since the master-manufacturer also financed the provision of land, buildings, machinery and equipment he was – or had been – also what would come to be called a capitalist. Yet, the institution of the industrial co-operative commonwealth required that labour should take control of the means of production; and for Owen, for whom the violence and destruction such as had attended the French Revolution were calamitous, the change to control by labour must happen peacefully. The wish had to be father to the belief, the belief to the conviction.

We shall consider the outcome in more detail later. Here, it is enough to note that the adoption, largely at Owen's prompting, by the trade union movement of the strategic objective of organising manufacturing industry in industrial co-operatives, of adopting Co-operation for its own sake so as to make a revolutionary change in the constitutional structure of society, ended almost as soon as it had begun. For the opportunity, if it existed at all, to make such a change would have occurred only in the context of a much more broadly based revolutionary movement. Such a context might have presented itself during the struggle to secure the passage of the Reform Bill. In the event it did not; and by the time Owen had led trade unionism to adopt a revolutionary programme, that struggle was over anyway.

So for a short while the two movements, Co-operation and trade unionism, had fused. And, almost at once, they separated. The Grand Moral Union of the Productive Classes reverted to an organisation having the characteristic objectives of a trade union: the Grand National Consolidated Trade Union. Its avowed purposes still extended beyond those of protecting the interests of its members, as employees: that is to say, their wages and conditions of employment. In language which retained the authentic ring of Robert Owen, it still sought far-reaching social and political change, 'a different order of things, in which the really

35

useful and intelligent part of society only shall have the direction of its affairs; in which industry and virtue shall meet their just distinction and reward, and vicious idleness its merited contempt and destruction.' The co-operative element had, however, disappeared. Cole says simply: 'The Trade Unions and the Owenite Co-operators slipped apart; and Owen, full of his new creature', that is, the GNCTU, 'seems to have lost interest in the more narrowly co-operative side of the movement'.[7]

Certainly, the change within a few months from the Grand Moral Union of the Productive Classes to the Grand National Consolidated Trade Union suggests great confusion of purpose. Was it to establish a quasi-religious movement, one of such moral earnestness as would in the minds of the Owens among the Owenites exercise a compelling influence for beneficial change, one which would establish first alternative and exemplary societies where amity and reason would prevail, and hence would point inevitably to the creation of a co-operative commonwealth? Or was it to organise workpeople to fight the most immediate battles? Looking back at the tangled web of confused events we can see that the answer had already emerged. If until 1832 the working class seen in a Marxist perspective as a proletariat was emergent and potential, if it had yet fully to identify itself, the Reform Bill of that year finally distinguished it from the rest of society. For while by enfranchising the new towns it gave the commercial middle class, and with it the master-manufacturers, a say on the conduct of Government, it totally disenfranchised the working man. The working class had been defined, by exclusion; the master-manufacturers, who had Ricardo's blessing, had been assimilated to the landlords, who had not; and so promoted into privilege. The two component parts of Owen's productive classes had been placed on the opposite sides of a divide; and their separation into 'them and us' was now so far completed as to have become irreversible.

And how now are we to see Owen? The change from the propagandist playing his derivative educational theme throughout *A New View of Society* to the leader, however temporary, of a trade union movement already inspirationally Owenite and now ready on his prompting to aspire to the control of the means of production and provision, was profound. Not, of course, that he abandoned that amiable judgment, assumed in *A New View*, of unspoiled human nature, nor that unshakeable conviction that co-operative communities would bring out the best in it. But it is not on that judgment nor on that conviction that his place among the first of the heroes of Socialism or Co-operation depends. The judgment we know to be mistaken, the case it supports too drily utilitarian. And the conviction refers to an ultimately retrogressive form of co-operation: retrogressive because it requires too great a suppression of individuality, too great a forfeiture of a life of one's own; and hence, justifiable only by sheer necessity. So it is upon his perception of trade unions operating as industrial co-operatives and thus reconstituting society as an industrial democracy, that his hero's place depends, a perception which trade unionism was so quickly to abandon. In an age lacking social imagination the persuasion, however firm, of Owenism, could not remove mountains. Still, the struggle within Parliament for the reform of Parliament came near to being a revolution on whose comprehensive and rolling tumbril Owenites and Owenism could have expected to secure, as a preliminary to the reconstitution of the country as an industrial democracy, a terminal passage for the old corrupt order.

It remains to consider why the struggle stopped short of revolution; and why when it did, Owenism lapsed.

— 4 —

A New View of Robert Owen: Reform or Revolution

A state without the means of some change is without the means of its conservation.

Edmund Burke, *Reflections on the Revolution in France*

I have ever been of opinion that revolutions are not to be evaded.

Disraeli, *Coningsby*

The choice, then, between reform or revolution, involved two contemporaneous strands of development, the one towards political the other towards industrial democracy. With the passage in 1832 of the Reform Bill, the first was to achieve a measure of progress which, though in itself partial and disappointing, nevertheless directed the country which had stood on the edge of revolution along the road of parliamentary reform to complete political democracy. The second strand, industrial democracy, had found its advocates in Robert Owen and his followers. In its most heroic and grandiose form, it proposed no less than this: that working people should take over the industries which employed them and organise those industries into nationwide co-operatives, the whole to be in the charge of one, all-inclusive trade union. Revolutionary this certainly was in concept, for it sought to displace what came to be called Capitalism by industrial collectivism, to secure that industry should be run by the workpeople for the workpeople, and through the agency of trade unionism. As we have seen, for a short while the two main instruments of working-class aspiration, Co-operation and trade unionism, were fused together, at Robert Owen's prompting. In the ignominious collapse of the grand scheme the two separated, each to accommodate itself to the developing capitalist system, each to find its own way forward within the system and as part of it. And in that separation, in that accommodation, there was no place for industrial democracy. My present purpose is to try to establish the reasons.

Though there had been in the years leading up to 1832 theoretical choice between these two ways forward, towards political democracy or towards industrial democracy, few would have distinguished the two so sharply before the passage of the Reform Bill. For most of the leaders among the Owenites the distinction only showed itself in their recognition that the Bill had done nothing for working people; that since the prime need, as they saw it, was to act directly to remove the evils of a system which grievously oppressed the lives of working people, the Bill had been at best an irrelevance, at worst a distraction. Yet history was right and they were wrong. The choice was only apparent: for, as we shall see, the assumptions on which Owen and his followers founded their intentions were insecure in themselves. That they were also impossible as a basis for the next and crucial stage of the Industrial Revolution could have entered into the judgment only of the most prescient. So, while for the first of these two failures Owen may be criticised, for the second he must be excused. And there is, of course, another and clinching reason why the choice was apparent rather than real. Because it is the guarantee of the most important freedom, the freedom of expression and representation of opinion, political democracy *ought* to have come first. To the observation that, nevertheless, industrial democracy could have accompanied or even preceded it, the answer is: yes – but only by violent and successful revolution. For, where the advance towards political democracy succeeded against entrenched opposition because opinion insisted, the proposals for industrial democracy were premature. There was never a consensus for them, as there was for political reform, a consensus of middle class and lower class opinion. True, revolution was for a time a strong possibility, if not a probability; and as true, such a revolution would of course have been seen as the means to industrial democracy by those who sought it. But that possibility arose essentially out of the attempt to frustrate the demand for political reform.

Now it is sometimes argued that the Reform Bill was deliberately framed so as to preclude the threat of a revolution founded on such an alignment, one in which a middle-class bourgeoisie would have provided the leadership and the lower classes the sheer mass, the numbers needed to carry it out; and shrewdly calculated to concede just so much as was needed to reduce to a manageable scale the gathering political unrest which might have led to just such a convulsion. Certainly there was the precedent of 1789. None could have failed to recall that it was the lawyers, capitalists and businessmen of the Third Estate of the French States General who led the masses against the privileged orders. Given that precedent, the institution by Thomas Attwood, a banker, of the Birmingham Political Union of the Lower and Middle Classes, to be followed at once by the creation all over the country of other political unions, must have seemed ominous. Strikes by Doherty's National Union of Operative Spinners, and in the coal fields, greatly alarmed Peel, at the Home Office; and, in what were to be the dying days of the Tory administration, he looked unsuccessfully for a legal answer to what he called 'the constitution and acts of a confederacy calculated in its immediate effects to disturb the peace of the manufacturing districts, and capable, if allowed to gain strength and consistency, of being converted at once into an open resistance to the law.' Picketing – or, as he has it, 'picquetting' – he considered an 'abominable tyranny', not yet revolution, even as seen from Peel's Home Office in 1830, but well on the way to it. Peel reckoned with the prospect of violent conflict between the Government and the trade unions; and went so far as to enquire into the practicability of organizing the middle classes against them.[1] So he for one saw a need to separate the middle from the lower classes. But it was the Whigs who won the general election; and they returned to office committed to parliamentary reform, the measure which for all the variety of the causes of social unrest and of the disorders they prompted, came increasingly to be the focus of the general demand for change. As the political assimilative into which were absorbed the opinions, convictions and energies which would otherwise have been available to impel Owenism and so to maximise its chances of attaining its goal, industrial democracy, the struggle to secure the passage of the Reform Bill demands attention. When Peel heard Lord John Russell's introduction of the Bill on 1 March 1831, he realised that where he had meant to divide the middle from the lower classes, the measure proposed by the Whigs would unite them in support of the new Government. For the Tory Opposition, the only hope was that the Bill might be delayed; that, with the delay, the working man would come to realise that, if the Bill became law, he would have been wholly disenfranchised; and that, with the realisation, the lower classes would unite with the aristocracy to secure the rejection of the proposals contained in the Bill and their replacement by others much more modest. But there was no delay. And the main reason was that reactionary and factious opposition led the Government to seek and obtain an immediate dissolution of Parliament. If there had ever been any chance that the Whigs might lose the support of the great mass of the population, the poor, the unpropertied, the emergent working class, that possibility had now gone. The ensuing general election returned a House of Commons in which the reformers were in a large majority. And the effect was not only to strengthen the Reformers' parliamentary position. It was also to assimilate the various discontents and disaffections into the one comprehensive sense of outrage, and further to inflame opinion so that what had already been enthusiasm, to the point of violence, for reform, now became passion. Even so, the Tories continued uncompromisingly to oppose. The Commons might have its reforming majority. The Lords could still throw the Bill out – and it did, on its second reading. Thereupon, widespread political rioting and arson, directed at Tory notables, broke out. But for the fact that the rioters supported the Government, itself widely believed to regard the riots with tacit approval, it could have been said that the country was on the point of revolution. Some indeed, Ramsey recounts,[2] supposed as they saw the fires in rioting Bristol reflected in the night sky, that the English revolution had begun. Re-introduced, the Bill this time got its second reading in the Lords. But in Committee, an amendment was carried against the Government. The Prime Minister, Lord Grey, asked the King to create fifty peers. The King refused; and Grey resigned.

It was now for the Tories to try to form a Government. However, William IV considered his faith pledged to the enactment of a statute similar in essentials to the Whig Government's Bill. Eventually, Wellington undertook the task of forming an administration to this end. Now the agitation in the country and the violent disorder it threatened could be directed against the Government. Little matter that reform would win. It was offensive that a party should be so unprincipled as first to defeat the Government on a matter of fundamental constitutional importance; and, having done so, should then take office on condition that it passed the measure. Anyway, none could have confidence in such a Government. *The Times* advocated revolt. People began threatening to refuse to pay taxes. Francis Place contemplated the steps needed to induce a revolution. In the event, Wellington failed to form a government. The Whigs, the party of reform, were back in office, but now with a promise from the King to create as many peers as might be needed to secure the passage of their Bill. The King was not called upon to honour his promise. The dissenting Tory peers stayed away; and the Bill was passed.

So, was the great Reform Bill of 1832, as some have seen it, no more than the minimal concession to undeniable demand for change? If that is what it turned out to be, it is certainly not what those most concerned to secure or prevent the passage of the Bill thought *at the time*. The Tories saw it as a constitutional disaster without parallel, the Whigs as a famous and hard-won victory for a bold and far-reaching measure against the reactionary defence of an out-dated and corrupt constitution. That Peel, leading the Tory opposition, recognised that the Whigs' Bill would in the short run unite the middle and lower classes in support of the Government is one thing; to infer from this that Grey and his team deliberately set out both to counter the threat of revolution and to do so in a way which would ultimately isolate the working class, quite another. The better view is that the Whigs were for Reform with various degrees of conviction and for a variety of reasons, ranging from that political expediency which saw in it a cause which would get and keep the Tories out, to that of moral principle. When Lord John Russell declared that 'the whisper of a faction could not prevail over the voice of a nation', he was appealing to moral principle; and if, when that appeal was made, it chimed in with political expediency it was only because factious and sometimes unprincipled Tory opposition had made it to do so. When the rioters took to the streets, when the fires in Bristol lit the night sky, when Attwood's meeting at Birmingham resolved to pay no taxes, when, in short, revolution threatened, it was not because the Whig Government wanted reform as proposed in their Bill. It was because the Tory Opposition would not allow it – and that in spite of a general election which, fought on the one issue, had just returned a House of Commons with a large majority in favour. In sum, in the contention which attended or, as some might prefer, the dialectical process which generated the structural change represented by the measures contained in the Reform Bill, the Whigs by proposing and the Tories by opposing them finally identified it as the exclusive issue on which people would stand up and be counted, for or against, yes or no. So, it was in the ordinary conduct of party politics by men in pursuit of power that expectations, aspirations and objectives were reduced to an apparent simplicity, to a crudity of choice for which all that could be said was that it represented the national will. And that, for most people and for the time being, said everything. After all, the Whigs were still acting within the framework of assumptions commonly held by the ruling class then and tacitly accepted by the great majority of a generally deferential lower class, assumptions which attached privilege – and responsibility – to property. Given that framework, the glaring injustice to which the Whigs pointed was that the distribution of seats in Parliament should secure the 'representation of green mounds, of stone wall, even of a pig sty, while many of our most populous manufacturing towns remain unrepresented'; that one propertied class should be overwhelmingly represented while another had so little say in Parliament. The challenge to the settled order of society originated almost wholly in the political aspirations, suppressed in response to the French Revolution and continuing for nearly forty years, of the latter part of the eighteenth century. We can see that it coincided with the beginning of that period when society in Britain was to adjust to the absolutely new conditions of the Industrial Revolution, to develop the political thought that signalled the recognition of the need to adjust, and of the institutions to realise the adjustment. We may not go on to assume that informed opinion then had already recognised the nature of the prospective problem, nor to attribute to the reforming Whigs a reactionary motive which depends on that assumption. They were catching up with an interrupted past, not forestalling a proletarian future. They looked back to Charles James Fox, not forward to Karl Marx.

None of this is to ignore Thompson's evidence that some among the older Radicals saw that the Bill did nothing immediately to secure political democracy.[3] Rather, it is to agree with his conclusion that, while for the articulate elite, like the artisans who constituted the Owenite membership of the National Union of Working Classes and Others and who debated reform at the London Rotunda, the kind of reform they wanted – annual parliaments, universal suffrage and the ballot – was just what Grey expressly denied. It is also to agree that they could not be said to represent the mass of unskilled working people. 'The unskilled', he observed, 'had no spokesmen and no organisations (apart from friendly societies). They were as likely to have followed the lead of a gentleman as of an artisan.' And for gentlemen, for men of property, the idea that the unpropertied working class should be represented in Parliament simply could not arise, any more than the reformers, with few exceptions, could enter into the minds of working people or sympathise with the political aspirations of their leaders. Where the reformers did start to understand, they perceived that those aspirations were to something much more even than that complete political democracy which required no property qualification; and they did not like the perception. As Bertrand Russell points out, it was James Mill, active Radical as he was, who in 1831 wrote of Hodgskin's followers: 'Their notions of property look ugly: . . . they seem to think that it should not exist, and that the existence of it is an evil to them. Rascals, I have no doubt, are at work among them . . . . The fools, not to see that what they madly desire would be such a calamity to them as no hands but their own could bring upon them.' In a later letter, Mill went on to blame Hodgskin for what he calls 'mad nonsense'. These comments, Russell concludes, marked the beginning of the conflict between Capitalism and Socialism.[4]

But for the great mass of the people, for the emergent working class, that lay in the future. It is impossible to read an account of the tumultuous years from 1829, when Owen returned from America, to 1832 without a sense of the high excitement, the passionate involvement which the mass of ordinary people felt as the drama unfolded. Here, following the banner of reform, led by the gentlemen of that most aristocratic Whig Government, led by Lord Grey, Lord Melbourne, Lord John Russell, they saw for a time before them the high road to a better and fairer ordering of society. The Webbs' account of the transformation of the Metropolitan Trade Union is instructive:

> In 1831 a few carpenters met at their house of call in Argyle Street, Oxford Street, to form a 'Metropolitan Trades Union' which was to undertake, besides its Trade Union functions, a vague scheme of co-operative production and a political agitation for the franchise. But under the influence of William Lovett, the last object soon thrust aside all the rest. The purely Trade Union aims were dropped; the Owenite aspirations sank

into the background; and under the title of the 'National Union of the Working Classes' the humble carpenters' society expanded into a national organisation for obtaining Manhood Suffrage. As such, it occupies, during the political turmoil of 1832, by far the largest place in the history of working class organisation, and was largely implicated in the agitation and disturbances connected with the Reform Bill.[5]

Here we can see how the general impulse to a fairer social order, one which would displace Owen's 'old immoral world', became concentrated upon parliamentary reform. And by William Lovett, remember: one of that articulate elite which attended the debates at the Rotunda; one who, knowing full well how partial, minimal and divisive the Whigs' proposals were, was compelled by the polarisation of opinion they induced to a course of action contributing much to the great flood of support for them; one who was a founder of the Chartist Movement formed in the wake of the Reform Act.

For disappointing though the Act was to prove to the great and unpropertied majority whose aspirations had been absorbed into the emotional dynamic needed to sustain the political will to secure its passage through Parliament, nevertheless it had shown that the Constitution could be changed constitutionally. Thus, Chartism was the eldest surviving child of Owenism; and the six points of the People's Charter[6] brought into sharper focus, and as a realisable political objective within the given constitutional framework, the expectations of most of those who had earlier looked, if not for the re-creation of man on Owen's visionary model, at least for a rapid and general application of co-operative practice as the means to a better life: who had, in short, looked for the reconstruction of the state as an industrial democracy. Owen's own first chosen vehicle, the co-operative community, had become an irrelevance and was seen to be impracticable. William Lovett was indeed right to lose faith in 'a community of property'. Nor should we overlook the emotional fatigue that would have followed the achievement of the 1832 Reform. By institutionalising conflict, party politics provides the means by which the accumulated potential of passionate conviction may be so far discharged as to avoid its most damaging manifestations: where the resources available to the forces for and against change are evenly balanced, civil war; where they are greater for those against change, repression; and where they are greater for those for change, revolution. But, the discharge having occurred, it takes time for such another potential to accumulate. Cole observes that the rate of growth in the number of co-operative societies was fastest in 1829 and 1830, when the struggle for Reform was beginning, and declined thereafter; but dismisses as unsupported by evidence the view that Reform drew popular support away from Co-operation.[7] This surely puts the burden of proof the wrong way round: those most actively engaged in promoting Co-operation or, more precisely, Owenism, were involved in the fight for Reform. The need would be to show, against reasonable expectation, that the second did not divert attention from the first. And the fact remains that the People's Charter not Co-operation, not Owenism, became after 1832 the great cause. After 1832, after Reform, in Britain revolution was done for.

Yet not in Owen's view, not the change that was to establish an industrial democracy, not the revolution that this least violent, this most sweetly reasonable of men now sought to bring about. Long since, in 1817, he had argued for moderation, for careful preparation. 'The circumstances of our times', he had then said in his *Report to the Committee of the House of Commons on the Poor Laws*, 'render a change in our internal policy respecting the poor and the working classes absolutely necessary; and the first question to be decided by every man of all ranks is: shall the alteration be made under the guidance of moderation and wisdom, foreseeing and gradually preparing each step, one regularly after another, thereby preventing a single premature advance – or, shall the change be effected by ignorance and prejudice, under the baneful influence of [anger and violence] .... But, surely, the experience of past ages, and particularly of the last twenty-five years, will have taught men wisdom, and prepared the minds of all for a calm and dispassionate enquiry.'[8] And again, in the same year, in a letter printed in the London newspapers, he warned:

> A reform of any of our great national institutions, without preparing and putting into practice means to well-train, instruct and advantageously employ the great mass of the people, would create immediate revolution, and give new and extensive stimulus to every bad passion: violence would follow; every party, whether more or less virtuous, ignorant or intelligent, would equally suffer in their turn: and, in a short

period this empire, and all Europe and the Americas, would be plunged in one scene of anarchy and dreadful confusion, of which the late French Revolution will give but a faint anticipation.[9]

Not the language, not the style to call the people to the barricades, then, but quite the reverse – the language of reform, illuminated by the sweet smile of reason. Even when, sixteen years later in 1833, he saw in trade unionism the instrument through which to establish industrial democracy, the change was to be painless, to steal upon the country unaware, 'like a thief in the night'.[10]

For it was as we have seen, in September 1833, that the delegate conference of the Builders' Union decided at Owen's prompting to constitute the union as an organisation to run the building industry. The prompting was persuasively simplistic; and, but for the fact that Owen believed every word of it, would have been unforgivably irresponsible. Labour was, he told the conference, the source of all wealth; and by means of a universal compact among themselves those who produced it would keep it. At once, the Builders' Union was faced by a lock-out. Among the masters the move to destroy unions spread; and support for the Grand National Consolidated Trade Union, not yet fully organised and unable to sustain its members through the ensuing series of strikes and lock-outs, rapidly faded away. In 1834 the Tolpuddle Martyrs were transported to Australia, ostensibly for administering a secret oath but in fact for forming a trade union.[11] The Factory Act of 1833 had not established the ten-hour day. Thus, so soon after the passage of the Reform Act was it shown to have done nothing to realise the aspirations of working men. Thus, as soon, was Owen's attempt to create a nationwide union of workers to collapse; and with it, his complex of interdependent aims: the assumption by the union of the ownership and control of industry; the adoption by the union of the co-operative form of organisation as the instrument of ownership and control; and hence the establishment, even before political democracy, of a comprehensive and integral system of industrial democracy. Thus, so soon after the pronouncement of the intention to restructure industry, through trade unionism, as national co-operatives and so in effect to deny labour to conventionally organised industry, reality compelled the unions to start fashioning themselves as a response to capital rather than as an alternative to it. A trade union was now to become, in the

Webbs' first definition 'a continuous association of wage earners for the purpose of maintaining or improving the conditions of their employment', a definition later altered so as to refer to 'working lives' rather than 'employment'. The reason for the change points again to the essential dilemma trade unionism faced. The Webbs explain that their original definition, relating the trade unions' function to conditions of employment, implied that trade unions had always contemplated a perpetual continuance of the capitalist or wage system, whereas they had at various dates during the past century at any rate frequently had aspirations towards a revolutionary change in social and economic conditions.[12] Yes, of course: but the change of definition and the explanation advanced in support of the change serve rather to emphasise the reality that, after 1834, emergent trade unionism moved towards a juncture with the system it could not supplant. That movement might be said to have become irreversible with the advent after 1850 of the 'new model' unions. Usually cited as the first of its kind, the Amalgamated Society of Engineers comprised into a national organisation over one hundred unions or branches of union, the whole administered by a central executive. The Union 'eschewed the secret society methods of many earlier unions, welcomed publicity, and persistently reminded the public that it was a peaceful concern, with no desire for Utopia or class war.'[13] The Union had become part of the capitalist system. Even more precisely to the point was the preliminary report to the conference, at Easter 1845, of trade union delegates from all parts of the country. One of the principal objects of the conference was, it declared, 'to cultivate a good understanding with the employers and thereby remove those prejudices which exist against trade combinations, by showing that they only seek by combination to place themselves upon equal terms as disposers of their labour with those who purchase it; to secure themselves from injury, but by no means to inflict it upon others.' Here unmistakably is the language of the market economy, the language of Capitalism. And again, the Flint Glass Manufacturers declared at their first conference, held in 1849 at Manchester, that 'the scarcity of labour was one of the fundamental principles'. It was, the Union affirmed on a later occasion,' simply a question of supply and demand, and we all know that if we supply a greater quantity of an article than what is actually demanded, that the cheapening of the article, whether it be labour or any other commodity, is a natural result.' And what this pointed to was not the brotherhood of man, but to exclusiveness: to the restriction of the supply of labour, by limiting the intake of workers, by abolishing overtime and by actively supporting emigration. So far by then had trade unionism gone to accommodate itself to Capitalism, so far to accept its values, its virtues and vices: on the one hand its realism and practicality, on the other its ultimate selfishness and lack of scruple. No doubt the leaders of the new unionism would have denied with all sincerity that they had, in effect, lined up with the economists who, as Coleridge had long since pointed out, were willing to sacrifice men to the creation of national wealth (which was national only in statistical tables) but had forgotten that even for patriotic purposes, no person should be treated as a thing. The denial would not have convinced those upon whom Capitalism, as practised in the middle of the nineteenth century, bore most harshly: those whom the new unionism excluded so as to make labour a scarcer and more expensive commodity, and those who voted with their feet – those who emigrated.

Yet, none of this is to say that the men who created the new unionism were wrong in their time. It is to say that there was available neither the will nor the means to drive through the revolution which would have established Owen's new order. For it was in the end a revolution only in thought, not in action. It could not steal upon the country unaware, like a thief in the night. It would have come, if it was to come at all, only if a well co-ordinated, centrally directed campaign of strikes, carried out by an immensely disciplined and united workforce, and backed by enough money to support the strikers for as long as necessary, could have been made to prevail against the resolute and more readily co-ordinated opposition of masters who stood to lose everything if the strikers won. There was no possible reason why the masters should acquiesce in the expropriation of the means of production they owned. Why in that case should they wish to help secure the continuance of production? As far as they were concerned, it might as well stop. The revolution would have come, if it was to come at all, only if the demand for industrial democracy through the agency of Industrial Co-operation, could have prompted such a comprehensive tide of sympathetic opinion as had carried parliamentary reform over the barriers of stubborn opposition. But it certainly could not be said of the master-manufacturers that theirs was the whisper of a faction, nor of the unions in their post-1832 revolutionary phase that theirs was the voice of the nation. Quite to the contrary; and it could have been repeated – and no doubt was – that their notions of property looked ugly, very ugly indeed. No: the revolution would have come, if it was to come at all, only if the resources available to the forces for change, the unions, had been enough to enable them to seize and hold the means of production, and if they had had the will to employ those resources; not as a thief in the night but in a scene of anarchy and dreadful confusion of which the French Revolution would have given but a faint anticipation. Not a bit what Owen had in mind, but since the unions had neither the resources nor the will to use them, the revolution did not come at all.

The men who created the new unionism and, in so doing, abandoned Industrial Co-operation (except as a minor and incidental means to trade unionism's ends of improving conditions of employment) were not wrong in their time because, in short, history was not yet ready for Industrial Co-operation. It was ready for the further development of Capitalism as the means of assuring the exponential increase in production which the Industrial Revolution was making possible, the phenomenal expansion which for the next forty years was to be centred on a Britain uniquely the workshop of the world and the engine of economic growth. Certainly, that expansion could never have occurred in a society organised into villages of co-operation; nor would industries run by trade unions as workers' co-operatives and organised nationally have provided a basis for it, for the accumulation of capital with which to finance the crucial, secondary stage of the Industrial Revolution: that is, the establishment of a capital goods sector of the economy. For where the first stage, the mechanised production in factories of consumer goods for an existing colonial market virtually monopolised by Britain, promised and provided immediate and enormous profit on a relatively modest outlay, the second did not. Capital was needed on an unprecedented scale to satisfy the opportunities for investment in the coal mines and, more importantly, in the means of transporting coal. In financing the development at home and abroad of the railways, it made possible the enormous growth in the production first of iron, later of steel, which characterised the secondary stage of the Industrial Revolution and guaranteed it as an irreversible change.

Robert Owen is not to be understood at all except as a man of his time, of the French Political and the British Industrial Revolutions;

nor fully to be understood except as a man of the first stage of the Industrial Revolution. The man who, in 1789, borrowed £100 to start in business as a master-manufacturer was 64 years old when in 1825 the Stockton to Darlington line ushered in the age of the railway. One can see that, fanciful though the idea of the co-operative community is bound to look in the light of the later development of the Industrial Revolution, in 1814 when he wrote *A New View of Society* that idea would have seemed quite credible. It was, after all, founded in his own successful participation in the first stage of the Revolution – but the first stage only. What the second stage needed was not a distribution, such as a successful general adoption of the co-operative form of organisation would have prompted, of the wealth created by the first stage, but rather an accumulation and concentration. So, while in 1814 the prime criticism of the idea was that it expected too much of human nature, too much of the people who were to live in the communities and of those who were to put them there, while then it was in short a social criticism, by 1832 the idea had become an economic nonsense. It was no way to build railways. Profitability or, as some may prefer, greed was the dynamic – plus, to be fair, a romantic enthusiasm for railways as the most vivid expression of man's capacity to master his environment. 'Let the great world spin for ever down the ringing grooves of change,' wrote Tennyson, somewhat later, catching the romance and enthusiasm exactly but getting the detail of his metaphor badly wrong. Better still, for a sense of the triumphant achievement of the Industrial Revolution in its second stage, look again at Turner's *Rain, Steam and Speed*. The triumph and the achievement were Capitalism's. It is difficult to see how at that point in history it could have been otherwise.

Thus it was that the country which, reflecting the convictions of an invincible alliance of the middle and working classes, chose parliamentary reform, limited and partial but irreversibly directed towards full political democracy, and avoided revolution. Thus it rejected Owen's bid, revolutionary in concept but illusory in fact, to appropriate all industry into a nationwide industrial democracy: and, by that rejection, but quite unaware that it had done so, left unimpeded the second stage of the Industrial Revolution, the stage that guaranteed that it too would be irreversible, that the continuance of a phenomenal increase in the production of wealth could occur. In the result, Co-operation seen as an exclusive alternative to Capitalism as the means of organising society for the production of wealth was, for all practical purposes, abandoned; and abandoned with it was trade unionism seen as the means by which capitalism was to be displaced by Co-operation. Their functional link severed, Co-operation and trade unionism went on separately to join the system they could not defeat. The price they paid for admission was the sacrifice of industrial democracy: Co-operation by largely foregoing the promotion of Industrial Co-operation, trade unionism by making the maintenance or improvement of their members' working conditions the prime object. The rights of working men at work remained the rights inhering in the property they owned: their labour, and nothing more. They would sell it at the best price they could get for it. Labour, which in Owen's prospectus, was to become a dominant estate in a reconstituted body politic, remains a commodity. For those who see in this the loss of an opportunity to remould the world more nearly to their hearts' desire, that must be the overwhelming pity. Others who take the view that the outcome was inevitable, and with it the continuing conflict between capital and labour, will find comfort in the fact that the conflict was, after a time, institutionalised. Where the lower orders of life have to make do with conditioned reflexes which so operate on behaviour as to limit conflict to levels that do not threaten the species, man – blessed as he is with free will – must institutionalise or die. Co-operation and trade unionism chose to become acceptable and respectable, to become part of the institutional framework.

— 5 —

Producers and Consumers

What profit hath a man of all his labour which he taketh under
the sun?

Ecclesiastes 1.2

Identified by Hobsbawm as *The Age of Capital*, in the history of
Co-operation in the United Kingdom the period 1848 to 1875 is
marked by the emergence of the Consumers' Movement as a major
feature of retail trade, the exposure of the antithesis between it and
Producers' Co-operation and, as a result, the virtual abandonment
of the latter as an expression of democracy. Not that the Pioneers
of the Consumers' Movement supposed that they were
abandoning Owenite objectives, still less that they intended to do
so. For the men of Rochdale, desirable though the store at Toad
Lane was for its immediate practical purpose, their principal
objective remained the setting up of a Co-operative Community.
As Cole points out,[1] the Pioneers 'were setting out to be at one and
the same time a Producers' and a Consumers' Society; and this
seemed natural to them because all their endeavours were meant to
lead to the creation of a Co-operative Community on the Owenite
model, in which the distinction between producers and consumers
would not exist.' First on the list of their declared objectives was
'The establishment of a store for the sale of provisions, clothing
etc.'; and third 'To commence the manufacture of such articles as
the Society may determine upon, for the employment of such
members as may be without employment, or who may be suffering
in consequence of repeated reductions in their wages.' Cole adds
that what actually happened when the Pioneers engaged in
production was not what they had intended when they started
their co-operative; and goes on to offer a more detailed explanation:

It will be seen that the Pioneers, when they decided to launch out with production on a big scale, did not attempt to carry it on as part of their own activities under the control of the general body of members, but helped to found a separate Society for the purpose. They invested capital in this Society:

The Rochdale Manufacturing Society was set up in 1854,

> and a number of their leaders were active upon its committee.... Similarly, four years earlier, the Corn Mill had been started not as a branch of the Pioneers' Society but as an independent venture .... Why was this? ... It was that the leaders of the Pioneers believed in Producers' as well as Consumers' Co-operation.

Supposing that, as an expression of democracy, Co-operative principles are as valid for the producer working in the factory producing goods for sale in the Co-operative store as they are for the consumer buying them there, a newcomer to the story might find it surprising that the Pioneers' belief is presented, if not itself as a matter for surprise, then certainly one for explanation. Cole continues:

> As long as they [that is the Pioneers] had been thinking in terms of a Co-operative Community as the ideal towards which they were working the distinction between producers and consumers had been hardly present to their minds, and they had set out with the idea of employing as many as they could of their own members productive as well as distributive work. ... As soon, however, as Co-operators ceased to think in terms of community-making and came to think in terms of trade and manufacture, the distinction between producers and consumers necessarily obtruded itself upon their notice. They began to think of the Society of Equitable Pioneers as a Society of Consumers.... Accordingly, the Rochdale Co-operative Manufacturing Society came into being as an entirely separate concern.... The idea was of course that the workers in the mill should be at the same time shareholders and should receive interest on their capital holdings. But, in addition to this, the workers were to receive, as of right, a share in the profit as a bonus on their wages; and this was regarded as giving the Society its distinctively Co-operative character.

That explanation is significant as much for its excusatory tone as for its substance; and the excuse is of the Pioneers' decision to establish a production arm as a separate entity from the consumer society, a decision pointing production for consumer co-operatives along a road to the industrial co-operative form of organisation, along a road it was not to take. The Pioneers did not 'attempt to carry it on as part of their own activities under the control of the general body of members'. By contrast, production by what became in time the Co-operative Wholesale Society is, in principle at least, under the control of the general body of members of the consumers' societies. So, the Pioneers must have been wrong: and to pronounce that judgment upon heroic founding fathers must have been difficult. Still, they were to be forgiven because the course they adopted, of 'setting out to be at one and the same time a Producers' and a Consumers' Society' seemed natural to them. It is here that the explanation falters. It is one thing to recognise that the interests of producers and consumers are likely to be opposed: for the first will wish to sell at the highest, the second to buy at the lowest price. But the assumption, doubtful in itself, that in a Co-operative Community the distinction would have had no meaning does not explain why, when in the real world of Rochdale in the 1850s the distinction became apparent to them the Pioneers chose to set up the production arm as a separate society. Yet it was accordingly – to quote Cole again – that the producers' co-operative was set up as an industrial, or perhaps more exactly, as a proto-industrial co-operative. As revealing is his observation that the rights of the workers in the separate producers' societies were regarded as giving them their distinctive Co-operative character. Again, are we to infer that the appearances were deceptive and that the Societies were not co-operatives? Plainly, in the minds of the Pioneers they were; yet Cole uses language from which we may infer that they were not. In summary, his presentation allows readers to suppose that the Pioneers were wrong in establishing, or attempting to establish, the producers' societies as bodies separate from the consumers' societies, and wrong even in seeing them as genuine co-operatives.

And in 1944 when Cole wrote his book as part of the Movement's centenary tribute to the Rochdale Pioneers, when Consumers' Co-operation could still look back on many decades of unbroken success, it would have been as natural for him to suppose that the Pioneers had in this respect been mistaken and that their mistake stood in need of explanation. Production for wholesale supply to co-operative retail stores was for virtually all practical purposes incidental to the Consumers' Co-operation and had little separate existence. Workers in the Movement's factories were its paid employees. In no sense could they be said to be members of industrial co-operatives: that is, of organisations set up for the manufacture of goods or the provision of services and wholly, or very largely, owned and ultimately controlled by those working in them. As labour employed by capital, in principle they needed trade unions and were organised by them, exemplary employer though the Consumers' Movement generally was. So, in their capacity as workers in those factories they were not Co-operators at all, though they may very well have been members of consumers' co-operative societies owning an interest in those factories. Yet, because nothing succeeds like success, Cole too may be excused; for making the tacit assumption that the Pioneers were mistaken, excused because Consumer Co-operation had abandoned their model, was successful, and had all the authority of success. In 1944, Co-operation was the Consumers' Movement, confident in its achievement; and its self-imposed limitation upon its perception of its purposes was justified by success.

Perhaps more significant are the events in the remaining and short history of the Rochdale Co-operative Manufacturing Society. Cole records that, in the straitened circumstances attending the trade depression of 1857–8, the payment of dividend on invested capital was made a prior charge on profits, payable, that is, before the workers' bonus; and the remaining profits were to be divided at a uniform rate on wages paid and on invested capital. 'The position was', he observes, 'thus reversed, the investors taking both a prior claim and a higher rate in the pound than was allowed the workers.' The main body of the investors was, of course, the Pioneers' Society; and it was primarily in intention and practice a consumers' co-operative. Dissatisfaction continued, Cole adds.

> When the Cotton Famine smote Lancashire in the early sixties, the directors [of the Manufacturing Society] again insisted on maintaining wages in the face of the depression. This led to indignation on the part of the shareholders, who were in may cases out of work themselves; and in 1862 the opponents of the 'bounty' returned to the charge and succeeded in getting the majority needed for abolishing it. The Co-operative

Manufacturing Society was thus converted into an ordinary profit making concern . . . . The leaders of the Pioneers were bitterly disappointed at what they regarded as the shareholders' apostasy, and the news of the defection was a heavy blow all over the country to the cause of Co-operation as it was then understood.[2]

As it was then understood: here again, Cole's problem is to reconcile a course seen by the Pioneers themselves as treasonable, with the fact that it foreshadowed the policy to be followed by successful Consumers' Co-operation, that policy which for its purposes made co-operative production incidental and subordinate to it and which most certainly did nothing to promote the development of an industrial co-operative sector properly so-called. What at the outset in 1854 had been perceived as a bonus, an extra but due as of right to the workers, had by 1862 become 'the bounty to labour', a gift bestowed and so gratuitous. Capital, co-operative but capital nevertheless, employed labour; and capital would whenever expedient exert the employer's authority. The truth is that, as the Co-operative Manufacturing Society was constituted, it was not – for all the Pioneers' intentions to the contrary – a genuine co-operative. For since, just as in any conventionally organised manufacturing enterprise, capital employed labour, its first priority naturally and necessarily was to secure a sufficient return for the investors on their investment. There is, therefore, no difficulty in accepting the inference Cole presents. But only so far as this: that the Pioneers did not in fact succeed in creating the Manufacturing Society as a Co-operative. For that is not necessarily to say that the Consumers' Movement's treatment of production as incidental to its interests was, on a strategic view of the objectives of Co-operation, right. To follow Cole that far would come perilously near to accepting that Co-operation was, as nearly as makes no difference, the Consumers' Movement; and that its future lay in further growth beyond that already achieved by 1939 until, so long as progress continued, it could within its chosen field have virtually displaced all competing provision and all competing manufacture for the purpose of provision. That indeed, though subject to some caveats, is the prospect Cole seems to have seen.[3] However, we need to reserve, against his conclusion, this other possibility at least: that the Pioneers' intention to establish the Manufacturing Society as a separate entity was strategically right, but structurally

57

mishandled; while the Consumer Movement's perception of the place of production in the Co-operative scheme was a strategic mistake, most successfully carried out. And nothing succeeds like success.

Yet, for two main reasons, the demise of the Rochdale Co-operative Manufacturing Society did not finally close the question of how in principle co-operative production should be organised. The first reason was external, the second internal to the Movement. The first derived from the interest of the Christian Socialists in the institution of Working Men's Associations for Co-operative Production. Charles Kingsley and his associates saw the question, Cole records,[4] as a moral issue; and valued Consumers' Co-operation only because it helped to provide retail outlets for producers' co-operatives. The high moral principle, to use his own phrase, of mid-Victorian muscular Christianity, may well have seemed to the agnosticism of early twentieth-century scientific certainty an insubstantial basis for the development of Co-operation; and, as a derivative from the French, from the advocacy by Louis Blanc and Buchez of self-governing Producers' Associations formed by workmen and operating through 'National Workshops', the concept was not only at odds with but alien to that of the British Movement which had come to be dominated by the Consumer Movement. Anyway, the Christian Socialists' Association for Co-operative Production failed; and nothing fails like failure. Moral principle is of course no guarantee of practicality. But again, that is not to say that the Christian Socialists had necessarily got their priorities wrong, nor that the French emphasis was wholly misplaced.

The internal debate was revived as a controversy which 'rent the Co-operative Movement for many years':[5] should there be paid a bonus to labour? The occasion for the controversy was the foundation of a central agency to produce goods for sale by Co-operative stores; and it was to the workers in the agency's factories that the question related. Set up in 1851, the first of these precursors of the CWS was the London-based Central Co-operative Agency. The CCA's constitution provided that one-half of the profits remaining after the payment of interest on subscribed capital should be paid to the Agency's workers as a bonus. No provision was made for the payment to Co-operative retail stores of dividends on their purchases from the Agency. By contrast, the Co-operative Wholesale Agency, proposed in a report to a Co-operative Conference held in June 1851 in Manchester, was to pay one half of the net profits not as a bonus to its employees but as dividends to co-operative retail stores on their purchases from the Agency. Thus, the intention was that the CCA should give the workers in the factories, the producers, a right as against the members of the local co-operative stores, the consumers; while the CWA should give the members of the stores a right as against workers in the factories. Here in that contrast, the antithesis between the interests of Consumers' and Producers' Co-operation is sharply presented. And when in 1863 the Co-operative Wholesale Society was set up, it was on the basis that participating stores should contribute capital and share in the profits. Even now, the controversy was not resolved. To quote from Cole again:

> The problem of the status of employees gave much trouble. The advocates of Co-operative Production were continually pressing the CWS to admit its employees to some kind of partnership, at the least by agreeing to pay a 'bonus to labour' parallel to the dividend on purchases.[6]

They had a short-lived success. In 1872, the CWS agreed to do so; but in 1875 the employees' right to a bonus was abrogated when delegates to a quarterly meeting of consumers' societies 'swept away the entire bonus system after less than three years' trial, and at the same time abolished the United Employees' Association and the privileges' – that is, on the purchases of goods – 'attached to it, decreeing that employees should share and share alike with other members both as purchasers and as recipients of dividends on their purchases.'

There were what Cole calls difficulties, but which might better be identified as disadvantages, for the retail co-operatives in so constituting the production arm as to admit the bonus to labour. For the retail co-operatives, it posed the question whether their employees too were to be paid a bonus, thus reducing the amount available for distribution on purchases, or whether they should be paid the rate for the job. Certainly: yet behind that most immediate question remained the profounder one. Was co-operative store keeping to be regarded 'not as an end in itself but as a step towards the Co-operative or Socialist Commonwealth ... envisaged partly in terms of producers' self-government'?[7] That contrast needs to be focused more sharply. Was Consumers' Co-operation, first conceived of as a means to realise co-operative aspirations of a much more comprehensive kind, to establish the same relations with its employees as would any other employer? Was it, in other words, to adopt a tactic which, however successful in securing the advance of a particular sector at a particular period, would tend to work against that realisation? If a major feature of the Co-operative Commonwealth was to be the ownership and control by the workforce of the particular enterprise employing them, if, in other words, it was to comprehend authentic industrial democracy, then the abrogation in 1875 of the workers' rights and privileges of the workers employed in factories producing goods for sale in co-operative retail stores was a misdirection of the Movement.

Only of course, if the other direction, the road to industrial democracy through the promotion of an industrial co-operative sector, was in reality then open to the Movement. There is a persuasive argument that it was not. That argument is that the dividend was necessary to the successful establishment, from nothing, of the co-operative store. For the great majority of its members this, and not the long-term and grander aspirations of the Movement, was the compelling attraction; and the institution of the dividend on purchases created among members a dominant body of people whose interest was to maximise the amount. This is not to criticise them. For housewives trying to do their best for their families, for whom every mid-Victorian penny counted, of course the dividend was what mattered. Yet once that dominant interest existed, the option of directing available money away from consumers to producers was no longer real if the system were to grow sufficiently in good times, survive in bad. One cannot argue of Co-operation then both that it was the dividend that did it, and did for it. Those proponents of Producers' Co-operation who 'wanted each factory to be established as a separate profit-sharing society' were right in principle: for only thus could it escape from the dominant consumer interest, only thus secure the ground from which to mount its own advance towards the more important objective of Co-operative aspiration. Right in principle, but almost certainly wrong in their appraisal of the practical possibilities. And the Pioneers were right to see in the dispossession by the consumer interest of the rights of the workers in the Manufacturing Society as a fundamental change of Co-operative purpose and as implying the acceptance of a much more limited expectation for it, but wrong not to recognise that that change, that limitation inhered in the idea of a dividend itself: for that, more than anything else, activated the potential conflict of interest created by the differing functions – that of workers making things for sale and that of consumers buying them to use.

So, to the conclusion that the Pioneers' attempt to establish Producers' Co-operation was structurally mishandled, we may now add something more. We may agree with Cole's conclusion that the resolution of the debate in favour of Consumers' control was right at the time, but on ground of practical necessity. We can agree with him therefore that the Pioneers were wrong in their view that the abolition of workers' rights, expressed as a bonus to labour, was a misdirection of the Movement – but wrong only because there was then no other direction for it to take. But we do not have to follow him further, to the view that authentic Producers' Co-operation is to be found in factories owned and ultimately controlled not by the men and women working in them, but by the members of the Consumers' Co-operatives whose capital built and equipped the factories, and employed labour to work in them. The Pioneers need no apologia for insisting that the means were being turned into an end in itself; and that, in the process the Movement was losing sight of, if not abandoning, its great cause. One would have wished for some recognition of the fact that a view of Co-operation which limits it almost wholly to the Consumers' Movement and is satisfied with that limitation, is at least to be regretted.

That limited view had authoritative support. The idea of social security as a proper charge on the State, and of the use in consequence of taxation as a means of distributing wealth more widely, lay well beyond the British political horizon. For Gladstone it was entirely consistent with his ambition to abolish income tax, which he declared to be immoral,[8] that Consumers' Co-operation should be endorsed as an instrument to encourage the working classes to frugality. In a broader context, it can, as ideological preference may urge, be regarded either as part of the exercise in the 1860s of that liberal political wisdom which freely conceded timely advances to the advocates of change and so harnessed their energies and aspirations to the support of the general interest in the maintenance of stability and the creation of wealth in a prospering nation; or as part of the calculated manipulation of events so as to ensure the preservation of the existing social structure against fundamental changes such as the institution of a juster order would require. Those who prefer the second view are, however, in this difficulty: that it was the Movement itself that took the decision to reduce its ambitions to the more narrowly ameliorative and unobjectionable. Though Christian Socialism 'with the old Owenites and idealistic Socialists ... regarded Co-operative Store keeping not as an end in itself but as a step towards the Co-operative or Socialist Commonwealth ... envisaged partly in terms of producers' self-government', the victory had gone to those who stood 'against them, the main body of the working-class adherents for whom the Store Movement was a reality and Co-operation mainly an agency for mutual thrift and the procuring of unadulterated goods at fair prices.'[9] It was entirely consistent with liberal social and economic philosophy.

So, too, was – and remains – the title of the legislation empowering the Registrar of Friendly Societies to register a co-operative as a corporate entity. To this day it is the Industrial and Provident Societies Act; and none in 1852 would have denied the need to encourage the working classes to provide for themselves. The irony is that the Act came before Parliament at the instance of the Christian Socialists, whose concern was to promote the industrial co-operative form of organisation; and the further irony that the legislation was put through Parliament under the Tory administration formed by Lord Derby in that year. Lord Russell's Liberal administration had refused facilities. Cole explains the refusal as a consequence of the strike in that year by the Amalgamated Society of Engineers. The union had sought to frustrate the lock-out by the masters of its members by engaging itself in co-operative production. So it may be said that the legislation was promoted by a pressure group whose perception of Co-operation was decried by the Consumers' Movement; and passed under a Tory rather that a Liberal Government because a trade union tried to make a tactical use of just that form of co-operative preferred by the promoters and decried by the Consumers' Movement. Nevertheless, except in one regard, the Industrial and Provident Societies Act of 1852 provided the basis on which co-operative societies of whatever kind could establish themselves as corporate entities. In doing so, it secured for co-operatives what the first of the modern Companies Acts had done in 1844 for joint stock companies. To neither form of business undertaking had the privilege of limited liability yet been conceded. For this, companies had to wait until 1855; and co-operatives until 1862. Thus rapidly, and with support on all sides, did Co-operation become accepted as a means of doing business, and at much the same time as did the joint stock company in essentially its modern form.

It is tempting to see the role of the Tory administration, which included Disraeli, as an anticipatory theft of the other Party's clothes. But the Conservative conversion, at Disraeli's prompting, to the cause of reform, had to wait another fifteen years. The better view is that classical liberal economic thought, which propounded that the market allocated resources satisfactorily, that unimpeded private enterprise guaranteed growth and progress, and that intervention by governments was unnecessary and undesirable, had already become common ground. As a form of enterprise entirely consistent with that thinking and with the given social order, Co-operation could command the support of John Stuart Mill just as much as it responded to the exhortation of Samuel Smiles. So, manifested as the co-operative store, Co-operation was bound to be acceptable. Gladstone, Cobden and Bright were for it. And so too were the Earl of Shaftesbury and Sotherton Escourt, Tory Home Secretary in 1859. What had in the early 1830s been, in Robert Owen's perception, an instrument of revolution, for the reconstitution of society as an industrial democracy, had now become an expression of Victorian values. As we saw earlier, the period which marks the emergence of Consumers' Co-operation as virtually the sole objective of the Movement, and its rejection of authentic Producers' Co-operation, coincides with Hobsbawm's *Age of Capital*, that period which marked the phenomenal growth of a global economy of industrial capitalism and so held out the prospect of unlimited and unfailing progress – and nowhere more than in Britain which held a *de facto* international monopoly in trade in manufactures. If, for that reason, 'the (British) industrial revolution had swallowed the (French) political revolution',[10] then as part of the process, successful Capitalism digested Co-operation as the Owenites had envisaged it. The coincidence was not mere chance. The quarter-century of sustained growth, broken only by minor interruptions, provided a favourable climate for the growth of self-help Consumers' Co-operation operating in a buoyant and free domestic market:[11] Producers' Co-operation, the self-governing workshop, remained a means of protest against the generally accepted order, an out-of-fashion remnant from the hungry forties.

By contrast, trade unionism through which Owen had intended to organise the Country as an industrial democracy stayed out in the legal cold. Cole says, first and simply, that after 1850, 'Co-operation became respectable but that trade unionism remained much longer an outlaw. So the two movements drifted further and further apart.'[12] Too simple a judgment perhaps: it might better be said that, manifested as the Consumers' Movement, Co-operation had become an alternative presentation of the rights of ownership against the rights of labour, while trade unionism existed to assert the rights of labour against those of ownership. Insist though trade unions might that their purpose was not to subvert the market economy but to sell labour at a fair price as a commodity in it, the fact remained that successful trade unionism implied reduced dividends on investment, just as organising the production of goods for sale in Co-operative stores as a function of independent industrial co-operatives implied reduced dividends on purchases from them. The movements did not so much drift apart as come to represent opposed interests. Later, Cole comes near to conceding the point: 'in the eighties, Trade Unionism and Consumer Co-operation went on their several ways, each shedding much of its earlier idealism and each settling down to consolidate its position within somewhat narrowly delineated fields', which will do as an anodyne description but which, in suppressing the pain, obscures the diagnosis. And again:

> By 1900, Co-operation and Trade Unionism had slipped a long way apart ... from the Owenite period right up to the seventies, the trade unions were actively interested in various forms of Co-operative Production. ... As this interest died out and Co-operation became more and more decisively a Consumers' Movement, engaging its labour in the ordinary labour market and rejecting such notions as the 'bounty to labour' and the self-governing workshop, there was much less to bring the two movements together as well as something – the problem of wages and conditions in Co-operative employment to hold them apart.[13]

Even this concession is too kind a description of the divorce. It misses the significance of the points: first, that the occasional engagement of trade unionism in the promotion of industrial co-operatives had been tactical and opportunistic, rather than principled; and second, that Co-operation identified as the Consumers' Movement had opposed any significant role for the industrial co-operative, properly so-called. The significance is that, together, the two operated to remove an essential feature from the full description of Co-operation; and in so doing to deny to the movement that function which it was uniquely able to discharge and which was, therefore, most likely to guarantee its growth and survival in perpetuity. That function was not the provision of wholesome food at fair prices. It was, and remains, authentic industrial democracy.

Yet, though in the early years almost certainly there was no alternative, there is still the question whether Consumers' Co-operation, once firmly established, could have reverted to the Pioneers' intention to establish independently controlled producers', or industrial, co-operatives. And the question was raised, though with little success. In 1874 J.T.W. Mitchell became Chairman of the CWS, and 'under his strong hand its activities were,' Cole writes, 'rapidly developed; and it was largely due to his personal influence that the "federal" principle of consumers' control came to be the accepted principle of the main body of the Movement.'[14] He was not, one gathers, a man to brook opposition. 'Often at loggerheads with Holyoake, Greening, Hughes and other advocates of the "bonus to labour" and the development of Co-operative Production by means of independent Societies under producers' control, he was able to impress his personal philosophy of Co-operation upon the Movement and to win for himself a position of recognised leadership.' Some sense of the conflict and confrontation generated by the difference on fundamental principle, the antithesis between Consumers' and Industrial Co-operation, comes through Cole's flat account, some sense of Mitchell as a man who saw things narrowly but very clearly, was sure of his objective and of the means of its achievement: the development of the CWS into the very large, multifarious and highly successful undertaking it became. In that development there was to be found during the twenty years of his chairmanship no place for industrial democracy such as the admission of self-governing producers' co-operatives would have admitted. And by then, the mould was set. The CWS, and later the Scottish CWS, had become big business.

One other attempt to revive the Pioneers' intention requires a mention, that of the Co-operative Productive Federation (CPF). The Federation established industrial co-operatives with the intent that they should not be absorbed into or controlled by the Consumers' Movement. Cole grants them a grudging accolade. It

65

was, he says, only a small movement. It did not match the growth of what he calls Producer Co-operation under Consumer control. Those who find in that formulation a description of authentic Co-operation will be content with his verdict. Those who wonder whether the hire of labour by capital can ever be a feature of authentic co-operation may not be, even though the employing capital is owned by the Consumers' Movement. Both may find a certain irony in the fact that some of the CPF industrial .co-operatives founded in the 1880s are still trading successfully,[15] while many retail co-operatives have failed, and have in the process of rescue become assimilated into other societies, so losing their individual identities and the reality of the democratic practice they are meant to activate. From well over 1,000 retail societies in the 1930s, the number has dwindled to 100; and the possibility of reducing it to 25 has been discussed (see Chapter 1 above). The democratic form remains; the function is failing.

So, this at least is indisputable: that however it may have seemed to Cole in 1944, justification by success has lost its validity: and the loss prompts the question whether the Movement should re-appraise its purposes so as to establish Co-operation on a broader and securer footing. For the practical appeal of Consumers' Co-operation – wholesome food at what, through the payment of dividends on purchase, amounts to lower prices – can ultimately be matched or bettered by competing non-co-operative stores, and so puts the Movement's existence at risk. There is now no exclusive ecological niche for Consumer Co-operation to occupy as a guarantee of its survival and growth nor any reason to declare its stores, those aimiable dinosaurs, deserving of special protection, endangered though the species is. If it could still be shown that it remains an effective expression of democracy, that would indeed be a reason; for any diminution of democracy is deplorable. But there is no use in preserving the form when the function has failed; and it is difficult to see the democratic form of the consumers' co-operative can have much meaning for the generality of members – nor, of course, any for non-members – who use the stores. Enlightened self-interest is, for those of us who are not saints, the necessary condition of social behaviour. Take away the self-interest, and the residual appeal is enough only for the wholly unselfish. And that is why democracy is to be understood as a practice before it is conceived as a set of abstractions; why it is a system of checks and balances before it is a set of principles; why, as has been said, it is worth just two cheers, and no more. Only the kingdom of love is worth three.

By contrast, the appeal of the industrial co-operative remains unchallengeable, its ecological niche exclusive to it. No other form of industrial organisation can, of its nature, do what the industrial co-operative form does. None of them is, nor can be, structured as to require that those in charge of enterprises in which people invest their working lives and expectations should account primarily and principally to them for the uses they make of those lives. None is, nor can be, so structured as to ensure that the individual is not treated as a thing, as a commodity for use in the process of production or provision. So, where for the great mass of its members, the success of a consumer co-operative is now no more than a matter of marginal interest to them, for the members of an industrial co-operative it is quite otherwise. For the latter, the self-interest lies in being fully and finally in charge of one's working life, in recovering it as part of a life of one's own. The enlightenment derives from the need for commerical success, from the necessary recognition by members that their business cannot succeed if they take more out of it than it can stand. There is, in short, a conjuction of ultimate authority with ultimate reponsibility.

Yet, something more than the previous success, and consequent authority, of the Consumers' Movement is needed to explain the apparently complacent appraisal of the Co-operative scene as Cole portrays it, the unregretting acceptance of the failure of Co-operative principle implicit in the virtual abandonment of the promotion of authentic Producer Co-operation, the strategic mistake of continuing, after Consumers' Co-operation had so firmly established itself, to commit its resources solely to its own further development, and the failure to realise that where its attractions were not exclusively its own, industrial democracy attached uniquely to Producer Co-operation and so was an inalienable advantage. If this seems too severe, there is no denying that the development of the industrial co-operative sector has had little reason over the years to feel grateful to the Consumer Movement. On the contrary, its successes have been won in spite rather than because of that Movement. Read Cole, speculating on the possibility of a revival, after the Second World War, of Producer Co-operation:

the Consumers' Movement is unlikely, however much capital it may dispose of, to become the financier of future productive ventures unless they are to be conducted under its own control. The CWS has its own factories, its own building department. It would sooner expand these and enlarge the influence of Consumers' Co-operation than give aid to ventures which embody primarily the rival doctrine of producers' control.[16]

That is an authoritative pronouncement of the view, prevailing for many decades, of the Consumer's Movement's attitude towards Producer Co-operation: the rival doctrine, not quite anathema, but something very like. It may be supposed that Cole's comments refer only to the production of goods for retail in the Consumers' Movement's own stores, and are not to be read as relating to the more general development of the industrial co-operative sector. No doubt the first was much in his mind. But certainly not exclusively so. And the general tenor of his appraisal of the history of the Movement after the Pioneers is that Producer Co-operation had been a vexatious distraction and would have little worthwhile future.

So dismissive a judgment requires further explanation. Perhaps it is this. Cole writes as a proponent of British Empirical Socialism: that is to say, of that view of Socialism which sees it as state, or municipal, ownership of industry and the planned economy, but as preserving political freedom and democracy in the western, liberal tradition. But Capitalism was to go. And developments which did not contribute to, nor necessarily seek that objective were for that reason defective. Let Cole speak for himself:

> For many of the supporters of Co-operation in the Victorian era the 'bounty to labour' rather than anything else was regarded as fundamental. These supporters hoped to humanise and liberalise the relations between employers and workmen rather than get rid of these relations altogether. They did not greatly distinguish between a Co-operative Society which accepted the 'bonus to labour' and a capitalist form which instituted a system of profit-sharing and co-partnership.

Nor, we might interpolate, should they: for the relationship between employer and employee is essentially the same in the two cases. Unless the workers employed in a producers' co-operative are the final custodians of its affairs, the bonus – or better, the bounty – remains a payment made as an act of grace; and the co-operative is not properly so-called. Cole continues:

> They regarded the Consumers' Stores rather as mutual thrift agencies and as a means of marketing the goods produced by co-partnership firms and Producers' Societies than as the forerunners of an alternative economic system based on consumers' control and the elimination of private profit. They were social reformers, not socialists of any sort; and the idea of co-partnership particularly appealed to them because it held out the prospect of amending capitalism without doing away with it.[17]

Socialism is seen here as an alternative and exclusive economic system, among the identifying characteristics of which two must be present: consumers' control and the elimination of private profit. On that severe view no Socialist could support the promotion of producers' or workers', or industrial co-operatives, call them what you will, if they are described as organisations for the manufacture of goods or for the provision of services, and wholly or very largely owned by and ultimately controlled by those working in them. For, so described, they deny consumers' control and admit private profit. They might be Capitalism with a human face. It is that, the dissonance between the industrial co-operative form of organisation and the economic prospectus presented, when Cole was writing, by British Empirical Socialism, that completes the explanation of his dismissive judgment of Producer Co-operation.

Both of the main factors contributing to that judgment, the one the reality of the success of the Consumers' Movement and the certainties of the future growth and achievement, the other a perception of Socialism which cannot accommodate authentic Producer Co-operation, were fixed by the end of the nineteenth century. And though, of the two, the first is no longer available to support the judgment, the second – whether the Socialism perceived is dogmatic or diffident, Marxist or empirical – is operative still to provide, for better or for worse, assumptions about the form of industrial democracy and about the roles, contrasted or opposed, to be played in it by an industrial co-operative sector and the trade unions.

For better or for worse? We shall see.

— 6 —

Dogma and Diffidence

This shows how much easier it is to be critical than to be correct.

Disraeli, House of Commons, 24 January 1860

So, by the end of the nineteenth century, there was little in Co-operation, or in trade unionism, that Owen could have identified directly with his proposals to reconstitute the state as an industrial democracy and to create the productive classes, master-manu-facturers and work-people, into a great estate of the realm. And the lapse of interest in those proposals had been matched by the growth of a body of criticism. Certainly, he does not lack for critics; and they are mainly to be found on the left of the political spectrum, amongst those who subscribe to Socialism in one or other of its varying forms. Acclaiming him as one of the chief progenitors, the critics come not to bury but to praise him with faint damns. Nor are the damns always so faint, though they are of course almost always uttered with that tendentious hindsight which devalues protest unless it proclaims class warfare and anticipates the emergence by the twentieth century of political parties created to prosecute it. Also, their vehemence varies from one school of Socialism to another. Thus, Marxists blame him for not anticipating Marx, war between classes as they define them; and the need, as they see it, for a frontal attack upon rights in property. In their earlier period, those who preferred the inevitability of gradualness blamed him – as they did Marx – for the inadequacy of an economic theory which stopped at Ricardo; and for proposing an instant change to a national and co-operative structure for industry which would, they considered, in the event have failed to abolish competition and Capitalism, and would have left the class structure of society unchanged except perhaps in detail. The two, Marxist and Empirical Socialist, unite in their criticism of the utopian promise of his schemes and of the impracticability of his proposals for carrying them into effect.

The Marxist criticism is magisterially put by E.P. Thompson.[1] 'There comes', he says, 'through his writings, not the least sense of the dialectical processes of social change, of "revolutionising practice".' He goes on to quote Marx's comment that the materialist doctrine that men are the product of circumstances and upbringing forgets that it is by men that circumstances are changed. So, Owen's view that social character could be changed by education is a nonsense; for the kind of education needed could not occur unless circumstances changed first: no egg because there was no chicken, no chicken because there was no egg. Some other agent of change was needed. For Owen, whose materialist doctrine was rigorously environmental and mechanical, but not dialectical, that agent could only be millennial, a kind of secular second coming after which we should all in a moment, in a twinkling of an eye, be changed. And thus is Owen's prospectus reduced to absurdity. Thompson's purpose here is to contrast the eighteenth century's passive materialism, reflected in Owen's views, with the active, the dialectical materialism advocated by Marx: that is the materialism that would not be content only to interpret the world, but would alter it. Thompson does not say here, in terms, that dialectical materialism has its answer, the class struggle carried to the extreme of revolution – unless we are to read 'revolutionising practice' as implying it, while sounding something less and, therefore, less disturbing. That that implication is intended finds support in his summary of his objections to Owen's attitude. There he pronounces Owenism's insistence on the right of property to be its vitiating weakness and contrasts it unfavourably with those who 'could see that Socialism entailed the expropriation of the great land owners'; and goes on to conclude that because Owen refused to face the problem of ownership and power, he was able to remain quite indifferent to political Radicalism and to lead the movement astray. Elsewhere, Thompson[2] relates Marxist thinking to what he called industrial syndicalism and describes as one of the great themes of Owenism. When Marx, he observes, was still in his teens, the battle between a capitalist and a socialist political economy for the minds of English trade unionists had been (at least temporarily) won. One may read the observation as meant to imply that the victory was something more than temporary. It was not: for, as we have seen, organised labour very soon and consciously became the necessary reciprocal to employing capital and so constituted with it the developed system which had yet to be called Capitalism. If the point of the reference to Marx is to show that emergent English trade unionism had anticipated his conclusion that workers must take control of the means of production, that, to re-iterate his contemporaneous quotation from A Member of the Building Union: 'labour and capital will no longer be separate but they will be indissolubly joined together in the hands of the workmen and work-women'; and again,[3] this time from Bronterre O'Brien to the effect that the object of combination was 'to establish for the productive classes a complete domination over the fruits of their own industry .... An entire change in society – a change amounting to a complete subversion of the existing "order of the world" – is contemplated by the working classes'; it is right to recall that the workers very soon abandoned the strategic option of displacing Capitalism. Perhaps they were wiser in their generation.

But the more immediate comment is this: that whether the victory was at least temporary or only temporary, Thompson does not name Owen among the victors, as he does O'Brien; and where he reduces Owen's millenarian prospectus to absurdity, he is kinder to O'Brien. 'It is easy', he says, 'in retrospect to see this spirit as naive or "utopian" but there is nothing in it which entitles us to regard it with academic superiority.' Of course not: nor, given the same fair-minded approach, is there in the spirit of Owen's prospectus – unless we consider that the millenarian aspiration which envisages 'revolutionary practice' is in some sense superior to one which does not. Those who believe, or rather, know that the dialectic in its predetermined movement requires the appropriation, by wage-earners and as the outcome of their victory in the class war, of the means of production, and know that it is historically right to be on the side of that movement, will know also that the first is superior. Those who suppose that a millennium is a millennium is a millennium will see that the distinction between Owen's and O'Brien's to be one without a practical difference; and put a question-mark against the doctrine on which it stands. At the very least they will regard as over-severe that judgment of Owen which condemns his failure in his fifties to act upon Marxist doctrine before Marx, still in his teens, had formulated it. And if, whether from an examination of the assumptions on which the doctrine depends, or from an inspection of the results both when it is acted upon and when it is not, they conclude that it is mistaken anyway, they will also dismiss the Marxist criticism. They will not necessarily suppose that Owen was right. But, most certainly, they will not suppose that he was wrong because Marx knew better, because the future for society would inevitably be Marxist. Nor, more importantly, will they be able to suppose that there could therefore be no lasting future for an industrial co-operative sector operating in a market economy, as an extension of democracy as the term is understood in the west and, hence, as an evolutionary advance from Capitalism. We have, therefore, to consider the objections to the doctrine. They are founded on three over-lapping grounds: usually, economic and philosophic; more rarely, biological.

Deployed often enough already, the objection to the economic element in Marx's thought needs no lengthy rehearsal. It is enough to recall that Ricardo's labour theory of value, on which it depends, is generally held to be fallacious in its assertion that the price of goods or services is solely determined by the amount of socially necessary labour required to produce or provide them, and so ignores the cost of other inputs and the effect of demand. Yet it is of course the labour theory of value which justifies the conclusion that the whole of the proceeds from the sale of goods or services should accrue to the workers: and hence, that income accruing from property – that is, from land and capital – to the owners is misappropriation; that the remedy is to abolish rights in property; that, since property owners are bound to resist abolition, a class war between the workers or proletariat, and the property owners or bourgeoisie, is inevitable; and that it will be resolved by revolution. The occasion of the revolution would be a culminatory economic crisis of a kind to which the bourgeois mode, or Capitalism, was inherently and incurably liable: that is, of over-production and under-consumption. For then, the burden of misery imposed on the proletariat by the alienation of labour and the crisis would have become unbearable.

That the revolution must succeed does not, of course, follow from the economic argument alone, even if Marx has got it right. The guarantee of success must be sought elsewhere. For him, it resided in the philosophy of history he derived, although in an amended form, from Hegel, and which sees history as a dialectical process; that is, one of perpetual conflict between polarised opposites leading as by a law of nature from a less to a more perfect condition – in short, a trial: thesis, antithesis and synthesis. Where Hegel sees national or supra-national civilisations as the instrument or the perfecting dialectic, Marx sees classes of society; and where Hegel sees history as the account of the development of the abstract spirit of humanity – or, perhaps better, of the development of human consciousness – Marx relates his view to the mode of production which he sees as comprehending within itself all the factors affecting the formation and attributes of a society. Where Hegel sees three stages, oriental, classical and germanic, in the progressive development of the spirit of humanity, Marx[4] identifies four successive modes of production. 'In broad outline', he says, 'we can designate the Asiatic, the ancient, the feudal and the modern bourgeois modes of production as progressive epochs in the economic formation of society.' Within each mode, its attendant conditioning factors operate to stratify society into two, and only two, classes. In the bourgeois mode, those classes are the workers and the property-owners, 'two antinomies' as Marx calls them. That stratification would occur as a necessary consequence of the alienation of labour. We shall need to return to the idea of alienation. For the present, let us note that in Marx's view of history as a dialectical process, just as in a society whose mode of production was feudal, with its 'contradictions', a ruling class of landowners had been overthrown by an exploited peasantry, so too in a society whose mode was bourgeois would the capitalists be overthrown by the proletariat. Let us note, too, that coming as Marx did to English economics after he had studied Hegel's philosophy of history, he could come with a mind predisposed to fit the first into a grand dialectical scheme such as the second propounded. English economics provided him with the two antinomies he needed, proletariat and bourgeoisie, as the polarised, opposites of the dialectic. And it was the necessarily progressive movement of the dialectic that was to ensure the victory of the first over the second, the success of the revolution.

Only, of course, if the philosophy itself is unquestionably right. The case against it is precisely that it purports to explain the whole of history and, for that matter, of pre-history, by reference to a total system, and so denies to any of its implicated parts (social, economic, racial, geographical, religious and so on) as well as to the actions of its great or good men any separate authenticity. Given the system, neither those parts nor those men may be said to have conditioned or influenced history. Rather, history has conditioned them. The claim, in short, is that history is programmed; and programmed as progress. The objection to the claim is that it is mere assertion or, more kindly, an act of faith. More, that even if it chances to be true, the further claim to have discovered the programme is incredibly courageous, the courage that of enormous intellectual conceit. And when the programme as exposed by the discoverer is seen to have been falsified by history, what in Marx was bravery becomes in latter-day Marxism mere bravado. For an unrepentant Hegel, called back to Earth and observing that the two most conspicuous antinomies were the opposed superpowers, might well persist in preferring his perception that nation-states were the vehicle of the dialectic. He might add that, if there had ever been any prospect that the class war would provide its movement, that prospect had patently disappeared except, ironically, in those eastern European countries bound to submit to Russian supervision. There, the opposed classes were on the one hand the government and its apparatus; and on the other, the governed. There in the German Democratic Republic in 1953, in Hungary in 1956, in Czechoslovakia in 1968, in Poland in 1980, the governed had risen against the government, workpeople against the apparatus. The risings had been repressed by Russian military intervention, actual or threatened. Quoting from *The Times*,[5] he would agree that, as applied in Poland, Marxism had created a proletariat disposed to 'revolutionising practice' inspired by those who could not take advantage of the widespread corruption through which a black economy, supported by western currency, operates to mitigate the sheer harshness of a regime of scarcity. 'It was', he would read, 'inevitable that the Solidarity revolution was sparked off by the Gdansk shipyard workers. Nobody bribes such workers... nor do they have access to hard currency'. To our interjection that on the evidence from Poland and other European countries under Russian domination, applied Marxism had neither created the wealth nor allowed the freedom to enable the purpose, as it is perceived in the democratic west, of the State to be realised – that is, to provide the circumstances in which the individual may most fully live a life of his or her own and so fulfill his or her potential for awareness and creativity, he would reply that that perception was mistaken; and go on to remind us that he had attached supreme importance to the State. It was still his view that it did not, as the Liberals apparently continued to contend, exist for the interest of individuals.[6] The intervention by Russia, one of the two super-powers through which the dialectic would operate, to suppress uprisings irrelevant to the operation, was only to be expected – and morally justified. In summary, his view that the State was the instrument through which the dialectic operated was evidently right; and Marx's view that it operated through class warfare as evidently wrong.

But if, having served a term in purgatory, if having had the chance to try his arguments on other philosophers, Hegel was not unrepentant, he might agree that there was perhaps something in the alternative view: that each of the factors affecting historical development does have its own authenticity; that they act upon and react to one another; that from time to time this or that factor will take on a greater or lesser importance; that of course – with a nod in the direction of Marx – at least since the neolithic age and the development of agriculture the mode of production has been a major factor; and that the actions of particular men, Marx among them, have in fact been formative, changing not merely the degree of development of a kind already prescribed by a programme of social evolution, but the kind of development itself. He might even agree that, perhaps after all, in the formation of opinion, of the choice of the direction in which a society is to move, the moral unit is the individual; and, therefore, that a kind of organisation which accounts to opinion and responds to the consensus is more securely founded than one which rests moral perception and authority in the organisation itself. He might, in short, agree that democracy was to be preferred and its extension to be sought.

That the actions of particular men have determined the character and not merely the pace of the development of human society introduces the biological objection to Marxism. Darlington[7] argues persuasively that Marx believed the process of evolution to be by direct Lamarkian and not by indirect Darwinian, or selective means: that is to say, that the environment in which individuals found themselves operated directly upon them to adjust them to it and that the adjustments were transmitted by them to the next generation; and not that, fortuitous mutations having occurred in the genetic package, they would when favourable equip the mutant for greater success in the given environment than the unmutated form could achieve. Hence, for Marx the biological laws governing the evolution of society were similarly simple and direct; and, in consequence, he failed to show 'an awareness of the causes and consequences of individuality, an awareness conforming entirely to the genetic understanding of today'. And on Marx's notion of the class struggle, Darlington adds:

> we now understand what was not clear to Marx, Darwin, or to Tennyson, that nature red in tooth and claw told only half the story of the relations of classes and races of men and animals. All working together of human beings therefore demands a compromise between the largely instinctive urge of self-interest and the largely rational understanding of joint interest.

No support here then for the necessity of the class war between proletariat and bourgeoisie, to be fought to its revolutionary finish. On the contrary, the conclusion is that co-operation between mutually dependant classes is the long-term condition of the survival of stratified societies. And further:

> To be sure, all social co-operation, even within the family, involves also competition and conflict. But, as we have seen, animal species as well as paleolithic man, have found various means of compromise as a substitute for life-and-death struggle.

We can, in summary, at the very least draw this conclusion: that it is, by reference to modern biological thought, a tenable view of society which – so long as its component classes are not exclusive – sees advantage to it in the variety of aptitudes and attitudes implied by class structure in a mixture of co-operation and competition between them.

So, the economic, philosophical and biological criticism of Marxism all point in the same direction: that though 'muddled Mr Owen'[8] was, of course, wrong in supposing that sweet reasonableness and an appeal to the best in human nature would, following the organisation into general unions of workers in productive industry, enable them to take control of it; and further, by thus reconstituting society as an industrial democracy, remove its evils and usher in an era of plenty and universal happiness, he was not wrong because a clear-sighted Mr Marx's alternative was right. It is one thing for Marx to have seen that Owen's vision was millennial. It is another to suppose that Marx's was not. A contrary view is that 'Marx united Romantic and working-class protest with the Jewish Messianic tradition to make them powerful elements in his "scientific" socialism'.[9] The truth, both for Owen and Marx, is likely to be this: that in the pervasive optimism of the time, it was natural for the revolutionary to suppose that the change to usher in the new order was at hand, whether prompted by an Owenite vision of human perfectibility or by the culminatory movement of the perfecting Marxist dialectical materialism. Since both were wrong, it is of little practical significance that where the one saw the change stealing upon the scene like a thief in the night, the other envisaged the proletariat oppressed beyond further endurance rising in response to the call to the class war to enforce the change. For if, as we have seen, the vacuity at the heart of Owen's prospectus was the tacit assumption that owners, having seen the light, would agreeably acquiesce in the expropriation of their property in order that it would be beneficially used by the workers, that at the heart of Marx's was that the proletariat would as the movement of the dialectic ordained, seize the means of production. In this, as much as in its expectation of the proximity of the event and of the brave new world that the event would introduce, Marx's vision was as millenarian as Owen's. It was as millenarian because there was no tension in the mainspring of the mechanism, in the idea of the alienation of labour.

Let us look at the idea. In present everyday usage the phrase could be understood to mean quite simply that capital, or more precisely, the people disposing of it, treats labour, or more precisely, the people employed, so badly as to create resentment. The word in Marx's German text is *die Entfremdung*. A literal translation would be *estrangement*. No real difference from alienation, then; and given that the outcome whether of alienation or estrangement is to be the class war carried to the point of revolution and expropriation, perhaps the simple understanding is good enough. Yet this would be to miss the essence of the point Marx seeks to make: for bad treatment by employers of employees is open to correction by moral conviction whether that of the employers themselves acting in pursuance of enlightened self-interest, or that of legislatures acting to prevent abuses; and the simple understanding would, by introducing the possibility of an extrinsic and corrective moral factor, threaten the inevitability of the class war. Whether they did so because they ought to or because they were obliged to, so long as employers treated employees only just well enough, there need be no struggle between them. So, some other understanding of alienation is required to validate it as the dynamic which establishes a proletariat and a property-owning bourgeoisie as Marx's two antinomies predestined to engage in that life-and-death struggle;

and Marx seeks to provide it by postulating alienation as intrinsic. On that view, institutional forms created by men to suit their common or social needs at a particular point in time take on a being of their own. They come to be seen as existing in their own right; so that, even when they have ceased to serve their original social purpose and have become an impediment to the progress of society, men continue to defer to them. Thus, under the capitalist dispensation, the social values of work – common objectives, common interests, the communion of shared experience and achievement – are lost because that dispensation requires the concentration of the means of production into the hands of one class, the property-owners; and the exploitation by them of another, the proletariat. Work, or labour, the activity which, in Marx's view, governs social relationships and provides the means of the individual's self-fulfilment, has become 'alienated' – or perhaps better, dissociated – from men and its values attributed to the system of production.

His detailed description of the identifying characteristics of alienation is instructive. They are:

> that it is external to the worker, that it is not part of his
> nature, that consequently he does not fulfill himself in his work
> but denies himself, has a feeling of misery not of well-being,
> does not develop freely a physical and mental energy, but is
> physically exhausted and mentally debased. The worker
> therefore feels himself at home only during his leisure,
> whereas at work he feels homeless. His work is not voluntary
> but imposed, *forced labour*. It is not the satisfaction of a need but
> only a *means* for satisfying other needs. Its alien character is
> shown by the fact that as soon as there is no physical or other
> compulsion it is avoided like the plague. Finally, the alienated
> character of work for the worker appears in the fact that it is
> not his work but work for someone else, that in work he does
> not belong to himself but to another person.
>   Just as in religion the spontaneous activity of the human
> fantasy, of the human brain and heart, reacts independently,
> that is as an alien activity of gods or devils, so the activity of
> the worker is not his spontaneous activity. It is another's
> activity, and a loss of his own spontaneity.[10]

It all depends on what you mean by work. The objectionable characteristics Marx finds in alienated work are, almost all of them, as much present in work done by a self-employed person as in work done by an employee for an employer. Drudgery, monotony, fatigue, mental frustration, physical discomfort – all are the same in either case. Self-employment is by no means the guarantee of self-fulfilment, nor of the satisfaction of a need rather than the means of satisfying other needs. And what, too, of the work done by one half of the human race ever since the species emerged: the work of the housewife? Is that alienated labour? Presumably not: but it would be a very bold man, a Karl Marx indeed who would assert that, for each and every woman and always, housework is her spontaneous activity, that it is the satisfaction of a need; or that she fulfils herself in it; or that through it she develops freely a physical and mental energy and will not be physically exhausted and mentally debased. The truth is that there are disagreeable aspects to nearly all work; that what is regarded as disagreeable in work will vary from person to person and, within one person, from mood to mood; and that, in the end, the distinction to be made is simply but none the less crucially that the disagreeable features are more readily tolerated when the worker is working for himself than when he is working for someone else. The give-away in Marx's description of alienation is the reference to leisure. Only, he says, during his leisure does the worker feel himself at home. Are we to understand that all work, when not alienated, is to provide the same freedom for the creative development of mind and feeling as do those pursuits we may choose to follow when our time is our own? If so, the only rational response is plain disbelief. Or are we to suppose that Capitalism having been displaced by Socialism in the Marxist version, work with all the disagreeable characteristics which turn it into toil or boredom will have been reduced to the bare minimum necessary to sustain society and that a consequent and vast increase in the leisure will enable us to fulfil ourselves? If so, the point for attention is not alienation at all. It is too much work: or, more precisely, too much time spent by too many people on work of a kind which contributes insufficiently to their fulfilment and which may tend to diminish their capacity for fulfilling themselves, too much soul-destroying toil or boredom. Isaiah Berlin has pointed to the uncertainty in Marx's attitude to this 'the most central of all the concepts of his system'[11] and to his failure to reconcile the two views he expresses: the one, that in unalienated labour there is perfect freedom for the fullest realisation of human potential and happiness; the other, that 'the need for this minimum of toil is an inescapable fact of physical nature which it is mere Utopianism to hope to conjure away'.[12]

Yet, among its symptoms listed by Marx in his description of alienation, one – the fact that the work is not done for the worker but for someone else, that 'in his work he does not belong to himself but to another person. . . . It is another's activity and a loss of his own spontaneity' – remains of special relevance. For it is one thing to deny the significance Marx attaches to alienation as the prime impulse to class struggle; and quite another to identify it, cleaned of its Hegelian war-paint, as we have identified it already: as the abstraction of one's working life from a life of one's own.[13] The condition to which this particular symptom relates is the collapse of morale, the ingredient which is three-quarters of the game. And the most complete cure, the structural cure, is the adoption in manufacturing and service industry of that form of organisation which extends the application of democratic principle into industry; which, by offering as of right equality of esteem, reward related to participation and responsibilities which go with ultimate authority, appeals to self-respect and self-discipline: the adoption, in short, of the industrial co-operative form.

That cure is not, of course, available east of the Iron Curtain. For it was precisely such a measure of reform, heralded in the Prague Spring of 1968 as 'Communism with a human face' and containing the germ of the industrial co-operative idea, that was denounced as 'revisionism'. And, in the twentieth century, revisionism occupies much the same place in the Soviet Russian construction of Marxism as did heresy in the medieval church. The revision proposed that works councils should be set up in order to vest in the workers a measure of control as against the bureaucratic command of the central planning authority. No one considering the outcome could continue under the illusion that the co-operative form of organisation, as it is recognised in the west, can exist in any country the political constitution of which is modelled on the Soviet Russian derivative from Marxism. For there, control over the means and amount of production vests by doctrine in a central authority; and the idea that the ownership of particular factories or plants by the people who work in them, of accountability to those people, and of ultimate control by those people, is grossly incompatible with that doctrine. And more: the political bureaucracy, the 'Nomenklatura' as Voslensky calls the three million or so people he numbers in the Soviet ruling class[14] has the

81

most powerful reason of self-interest for opposing 'revisionism'. It might well revise them out of positions of privilege and power.

Proceeding as it does from dogma, the Marxist pronouncement on Owen and the idea of the industrial co-operative considered as an extension of democracy is a verdict from which there is no appeal. By contrast, the pronouncement of empirical Socialism on him is diffident. Not that the Webbs, to whom we must first turn for an authoritative opinion, think that well of him. It was some fifty years after the short-lived high point in Owen's career that they started their work, when in the 1880s and 1890s much of the constitutional reform sought by Owenism's eldest child, Chartism, had already been secured. In response to a pervasive loss of faith in mid-Victorian economic liberalism, a string of measures had been put through Parliament by Conservative and Liberal Governments in concession to the case against unregulated *laissez-faire* and for intervention on social grounds by the state. Sir William Harcourt had declared 'We are all Socialists now'; and in 1894, as Chancellor of the Exchequer in a Liberal Government had introduced graduated income tax and death duties, so activating the principle of redistributive taxation. In short, though not yet fully attained, political democracy had become respectable, and Socialism had become arguable. The Webbs and their fellow Fabians were able to present democratic Socialism as the vehicle of evolutionary and moderate reform and as an extension to national administration of a practice already prevalent at municipal level. Seaman comments that that presentation

> has usually been seen as a piece of brilliantly successful
> propaganda designed to convert those to whom Socialism was
> otherwise still as fearful a word as Jacobinism had been a
> century earlier. It would be more realistic to see it rather as a
> manifestation of middle-class intellectual complacency. At its
> widest, Fabianism was mostly a matter of a tiny middle-class
> minority demonstrating its intellectual and statistical
> superiority before a (largely indifferent) middle-class audience;
> the humanitarianism it displayed was usually perfunctory; the
> contacts it made with the working class at this stage were few.
> It worked, if at all, in influencing administrators, civil servants
> and the occasional politician and, via Sidney Webb, the LCC.[15]

Another and concordant view is recorded by Lichtheim:

They adhered to democratic procedures and orderly methods but had no objection to a certain degree of enlightened authoritarianism. Their fundamental assumption was that Socialism would be introduced not through class conflict, but by way of democratic welfare legislation administered by the civil service, of which some of them were members.

Lichtheim goes on to quote Pease, then Secretary of the Fabian Society, as saying: 'We were thus in a position to welcome the formation of working class Socialist societies, but it is certain that they would never have welcomed us'; and to add, perhaps unkindly: 'Beatrice Potter – a rich, spoiled, arrogant young woman with more beauty than brains – was determined to have as little as possible to do with the working class.'[16] It is not unfair, then, to see the Webbs and the other early Fabians as they seem to have seen themselves: as philosopher-kings concerned to persuade people of sufficient education and standing to see Socialism through Fabian eyes and so to behold its full beauty. It would be unfair not to recall that they did, in the long term, have a formative influence on the social history of the United Kingdom. Among their criticisms of Owen they placed his failure, as they saw it, to anticipate the economic centrepiece of Fabian thinking: the theory of rent. This sought to demonstrate a concept of surplus which, taking besides labour other inputs – land, skill and ability, capital – into account, did not rely upon Ricardo's labour theory of value; but went on to conclude that, under Capitalism, the inputs are not rewarded by reference to the parts they play in the creation of wealth and that labour in particular did not get its fair share. Thus fortified, the Webbs decried both Owen and Marx for depending on the labour theory of value. Owen was, they declared:

> disabled by that confident sciolism and prejudice which has led generations of Socialists to borrow from Adam Smith and the 'classic' economists with erroneous theory that labour is by itself the creator of value, without going on to master that impregnable and much more difficult law of economic rent which is the very corner-stone of the collectivist economy. He (Owen) took his economics from his friend William Thompson who, like Hodgskin and Hodgskin's illustrious disciple, Karl Marx, ignored the law of rent in his calculations, and taught that all exchange values could be measured in terms of 'labour time' alone.[17]

Did they, one wonders, ponder on the words 'illustrious disciple' as they dismissed Marx to the second rank of the misled and misleading who had got their economics so grossly wrong? And did they reflect that they, who had not merely mastered but discovered the much more difficult law, who had got their economics so impregnably right, would be seen to stand shining brightest of all in the very front rank? However that may be, Marxists are said to regard the theory of rent as 'a quaint attempt to bypass the analysis of capitalism as a dynamic system propelled forward by its own internal contradictions'.[18] And, if they have read the passage, they might well be forgiven for entering it as further evidence, if evidence were needed, in support of their view that evolutionary Socialism is anathema and its proponents the prime enemy.

But that was not the whole of the Webbs' criticism of Owen's grand project for the reconstitution of the economy as a set of nationwide industrial co-operatives, one for each trade or industry. They contrast his intention to supersede capitalists and managers by the elected representatives of voluntary and sectional associations of producers with 'the modern Socialist proposal to substitute the officials of the Municipality or State' which would, they recognise, have been 'unthinkable at a period when all local governing bodies were notoriously inefficient and corrupt and Parliament practically an oligarchy'.[19] Having thus identified the right way to do the job and explained why it was not practically possible for Owen to adopt it, they then proceed to attack the substance of his proposal. It would not, they say, have abolished competition: his 'Grand Lodges', each directing its own industry, would in effect have been the head offices of huge joint stock companies owning the entire means of production and subject to no control by the community; and they would have been able to revert to the capitalist form of enterprise, admitting fresh generations of workers only as employees and not as shareholders 'thus creating at one stroke a new capitalist class and a new proletariat'. More, shareholders would have been able to dispose of shares whether in order to spend their capital or to buy into more profitable businesses, thus creating a speculative stock market. The summary of the Webbs' view is that, by contrast with their model of Socialism, Owen's scheme – if it could have been carried out – would have done no more than redistribute the capital of the country without altering or superseding the capitalist system in the least. After noting that, in Owen's expectation, passive resistance –

that is, the 'sacred holiday month' or, in modern parlance, a general strike – would bring his new order of society painlessly into being, they next regret the persistence of the idea that Trade Unions, as Associations of Producers, should recover control of the instruments of production, an idea which they call 'Joint Stock Individualism' and which, they note, has scarcely been eradicated from the minds of the idealists of the trade union movement. And that, we are to understand, will never, never do. Finally, the Webbs distinguish stigmatised 'Joint Stock Individualism' from the 'demonstrably successful Co-operative Production of the Associations of Consumers which constitutes the Co-operative Movement of today'.[20] So there we have it. Trade unions should confine themselves to the business of wages and conditions. Co-operation is the Consumer Movement. Production incidental to it is identified as 'Co-operative Production'. Demonstrably successful – at the time – yes: but demonstrably co-operative? And how far is their insistence on the complete separation of the functions of trade unionism from those of Co-operative Production conditioned by the earlier Fabian conviction that the principal prerequisite for the beneficial restructuring of society was public ownership, municipal or national, of the means of production and provision?

For in fact, Co-operation does not fit comfortably into the Webbs' conception of Socialism. It can be regarded as private ownership at least as readily as it can public ownership. What it most certainly is not, is ownership by national or local public authority: and because it does not look to the Government as its banker and so imposes no liability on the public sector borrowing requirement, it provides no levers for a hypothetical State economic planning agency to handle. Nor, more modestly, does it provide any reason why the Treasury, responsible for the ultimate public obligation to pick up the bill for public bodies which cannot be allowed to default, should exercise a prudential interest in its performance. Incompatible therefore though a Co-operative sector would be with the Webbs' version of the fully Socialist economy, the incompatibility has not so far become obtrusive in the United Kingdom because Labour Governments, which incidentally have had the support of the Co-operative Party as the political arm of the Co-operative Consumer Movement, have carried western Socialist Empiricism to the point of settling for the mixed economy; and any central planning has been indicative – and, some would say, ineffectual – rather than mandatory. So, in its relations with

Government, Co-operation as practised in this country functions as part of the private sector. As for the Webbs' insistence on the separate and restricted role for trade unionism, the practical effect was, once again, to abandon industrial democracy, to accept that the rights of working people at work remained the rights inhering in the property they owned: their labour, and nothing more. The prescription was to offer them no reason for distinguishing between employers who, as custodians for the State, managed those centre-pieces of Socialist attainment, the nationalised industries; and those who managed privately owned industries. Also, it was bound to implicate Government deeply. A role for trade unionism which continued to confine its main purpose to the sale of labour at the best price it could get for it was bound to prompt unions first to seek and then to exploit a monopoly of it; bound to make incongruent two prime objectives – full employment and a stable currency; and bound to present Government with reasons of national interest or excuses of ideology for intervening. It is no surprise, therefore, that the history of the relations between Government and the trade union movement has consisted so largely of intervention to harden or soften the market for the commodity at the movement's disposal.

Not that this is to say that no industry should be owned by the State, not even when, for example, a service to be provided is a natural monopoly; and the presumption is, therefore, that those who provide it should be accountable to users who cannot register dissatisfaction by taking their custom elsewhere, rather than to private owners whose interest is to exploit the monopoly. It does, however, put the onus of proof, case by case, on those who would nationalise industry. Perhaps this marks the single biggest difference between Marxist Socialism, and Empirical Socialism as it is now practised. For the first, public ownership is a virtual absolute, the derogations from it minimal and the necessity for them requiring proof. For the second, public ownership has become a question to be settled on the merits of the particular case.

Nor is it to say that none of the Webbs' criticisms of Owen is valid. But some of them have worn badly. Thus, to put the point at its mildest, it is by no means clear that the general abolition of competition is desirable, that the alternative of centrally planned provision and allocation will offer a more sensitive and efficient response to consumers' demands and wishes, or a better means of deploying resources. So even if we agree that abolition was his intention and that that intention would have failed, if we consider also that it was mistaken anyway, we need pursue the point no further, except to add this: granted that the evil of insufficiently regulated competition is that it leads ultimately to the vicious exploitation of employees, the point can hardly be made of industrial co-operatives. The people working in them choose whether or not to 'exploit' themselves.

It is even less clear that industry, in general, should be 'under the control of the community'. A less ominous formulation would be 'accountable to the community'; yet, formulate it as we may, the notion cannot confidently be said to afford a guarantee of efficiency, if the control or the accountability is to relate to its performance as business in operation. Only on the assumption that public ownership, defined as ownership by the State or by the local authority is in the particular case an overriding need, does the requirement of accountability to the community arise. And since that assumption is implicit in the Webbs' criticism of Owen, it cannot be understood too clearly that on their argument there can be no place at all for industrial co-operatives, properly so-called: no place, because the ownership, whether individual or collective, of an industrial co-operative rests in the people working in it. And so, too, does the ultimate control. In principle, there is the same incompatibility between the Webbs' prospectus of general public ownership and Consumer Co-operation as an aspect of private ownership; and since the Webbs' approval of consumer co-operatives makes them an exception, we need to know why. A two-fold explanation suggests itself. First, by the time that they were writing, Consumer Co-operation with its own production arm had been firmly established and was growing strongly. It could be seen therefore as its own safeguard provided by the people against a particular form of exploitation of the people; and hence as something to be excepted on pragmatic grounds from the general case for nationalisation or municipalisation. Second, within the Consumer Movement, the long-standing question whether its producer capacity should be developed as independent industrial co-operatives and hence under the control of the people working in them, or whether it should be treated as incidental to the consumer co-operatives and accountable to them, had, as we have seen, been decided once and for all in favour of the latter alternative.

How, then, are we now to see the Webbs' appraisal of Owen? First, as a criticism of the sheer impracticability of the grandiose project Owen had in 1833 put to the Grand Moral Union of the Productive Classes and which still survived in the objectives though not in the activities of its even shorter-lived successor, the Grand National Consolidated Trade Union, the Webbs' case succeeds. It succeeds, too, as a condemnation of his messianic presentation which inspired in those, having little cause for hope and much for despair, an all-too-ready belief in an easily-obtained and immediate millennium. But as a general attack upon industrial co-operatives as a means of organising production and provision, it is ill-founded and ill-considered: ill-founded, because it proceeds from the unproven principle that the public ownership of industry was a necessary pre-requisite of the good society; and ill-considered, because it ignored the democratic virtues – accountability to and responsibility from the workforce – of the industrial co-operative form. It pointed instead to a new meritocracy indistinguishable for all practical purposes from the old autocracy, but writ sometimes smaller, sometimes larger. In that meritocratic future, working people would remain the proletariat, managed in their lives by meritocrats whose intentions would, of course, be benevolent. Confined to their present role, trade unions would remain a response to the exploitation, actual or hypothetical, of employees by employers – a response which meritocratic benevolence would, if performance matched intention, progressively reduce to a satisfied silence. Work-people would not be expected to reason why, but to go on doing until they retired. The world would have become one fit for philosopher-kings to manage.

It has not turned out that way, of course. Nor was it likely to have done. For, in its guise as the Parliamentary Labour Party, British Empirical Socialism cannot be said to have intended, when governing the country, to have replaced private ownership of industry wholly by public ownership. And just as well: because, however persuasive the case for the public ownership of particular industries, experience since 1945 can hardly be said to bear out the general case, the proposition that public ownership is the necessary precursor to the realisation of the rights of man. There is, too, the appalling possibility that the corrupting tendency of power would operate to turn a meritocracy into a *Nomenklatura*.

My main point is, though, not simply that the Webbs' own general prospectus was wrong, nor even that it misdirected their appraisal of Owen. Rather, it is this: that in its failure to comprehend the essential quality of the industrial co-operative or, as they put it, Producer Co-operation, that appraisal displays a vitiating absence of imagination. It does not comprehend that the case for the co-operative form is its respect for the individual man or woman, a respect that is intrinsic to the form because the mainstay of its structure is equality of esteem. 'One man, one vote' is not merely a slogan. It is an assertion of the dignity of humanity. And the man in question is not a philosophical or statistical abstraction from reality, but the reality itself; not a theoretician's concept to play a mechanical part in a Marxist phenomenology of history or a philosopher-king's model of ideal society, but flesh and blood; the thinking and feeling individual whose right it is to make his life, including his working life, as fully as possible his own in a society the essential purpose of which should be to maximise his chances of doing so. Further, the Webbs' gross failure of comprehension is complemented by their advocacy of an apparatus of state and municipal ownership, and of a bureaucratic management such as might have been deliberately designed not to maximise those chances.

So, the Marxist and the Empirical Socialist prospectuses according to the Webbs both point to State ownership, in general, with its attendant bureaucracy, and to the separation of society into two classes, the governors and the governed. But between the practice of the two, the difference of degree is so great as to amount to a difference in kind. In those countries where it prevails, Marxist absolutism has led to the suppression of individuality to the point where dissent and criticism are crimes against the State and punishable by imprisonment or by internal exile, or madness to be treated in mental hospitals; where art and science must conform to the State's perception of their supportive purposes; where the measure of morality is no longer 'what if this day thy soul is required of thee?' but 'does it serve the system?'

By contrast, empirical tentativity need not pursue objectives beyond the point where they cease to produce their expected social benefit. Nor will it do so in countries where genuine political democracy is firmly established and the electorate will no longer support the objectives. Empirical Socialism may be supposed to have judged that that point had been reached in western Europe by the 1960s. Douglas Jay[21] quotes the Swedish, Dutch, Swiss, West German and Austrian Socialist parties as admitting the desirability of privately owned production, competition and the market economy. And he quotes eminent British Socialists to show that competition and, by inference, the price mechanism are admissible features in a socialist landscape. There is not, however, among those he quotes the same unambiguous acceptance of the private ownership of the means of production as appears in the pronouncements by the continental Socialist parties. There is a clear consensus that the case for the public ownership and management by State corporations of whole industries was limited; and, further, that the objective was not nationalisation for its own sake, but the need to bring economic enterprise under social control – whatever that means. In a statement made in 1952, Aneurin Bevan comes closest to the continental view. He is quoted as saying:

> A mixed economy is what most people of the west would prefer. The victory of socialism need not be universal to be decisive. I have no patience with those socialists, so-called, who in practice would socialize nothing, while in theory they threaten the whole of private property. They are purists and therefore barren. It is neither prudent, nor does it accord with our conception of the future, that all forms of private property should live under perpetual threat. In almost all types of human society, different forms of property have lived side by side. Where the frontier between the public and private sector should be fixed, is a question that will be answered differently in different nations.

This formulation left it open to those in the electorate who were disenchanted with nationalisation to suppose that there would be little if any more, and to those on the left wing of the Labour Party to expect that there would still be a lot. Still, set it beside the earliest of the quotations, from the Webbs' *A Constitution for the Socialist Commonwealth of Great Britain*, dating from 1920, and we can see how far the Empirical Socialist view had changed. Thus the Webbs:

> Thoughtful Socialists ... far from heaping up all Government on a centralized authority, propose the widest possible variety in the forms of socialization ... a vast extension of the consumer's co-operative movement, a great development of local government .... What we visualize is a community so variously organised, and so highly differentiated in function, as not only to be invigorated by a sense of personal freedom, but also constantly swept by the fresh air of experiment, observation and verification.

Splendid stuff, especially for the experimenters, observers and verifiers: but stuff, nevertheless. For since the pronouncement is not about debatable ends but unexceptionable means, no one should find difficulty in applauding its purport – that well-ventilated administration is a condition of healthy government. As evidence for the empirical attitude of British Socialism as exemplified in the Labour Party, it may perhaps be allowed to stand. But its greater significance is as a bench mark serving to show how far the Labour Party, influenced by experience in government and by the pressure of opinion in a political democracy, had revised its prospectus. For empiricists, revisionism is no heresy; and heresy no bad thing, anyway. What, however, the revision shows no sign of at all is any advance from the Webbs' dismissive view of Industrial Co-operation.

It remains first to say that neither Marxism, nor Empirical Socialism in the Webbs' versions of it, anticipated Keynes's *General Theory of Employment, Interest and Money*. If, as Marxism postulates, the final catastrophe of Capitalism is to be triggered by a crisis of under-utilisation of capacity and of over-supply of goods, then the *General Theory* provides the remedy: a positive investment policy by the State and deficit financing in certain circumstances. And since the effect would be to put off the catastrophe indefinitely, since Capitalism could now continue by reason of policies which provided also a solution to the problem of unemployment, Empirical Socialism need no longer distinguish itself from the Marxist version solely by the method and pace of change, by being evolutionary rather than revolutionary. Where in 1931 early Fabian economics, with its 'impregnable' theory of rent, had no answer either to the crisis or the problem, in the twenty-five years from 1945 the application by Governments of Keynesian principles led to an unprecedented creation of wealth and a remarkable rise in living standards. We had never had it so good. The necessity for the complete displacement of Capitalism by public ownership having gone, Empirical Socialism could well embrace the mixed economy. That the embrace was electorally opportune must be admitted. That it was mere opportunism may be denied.

Yet, Empirical Socialism did not have to wait for Keynes to propound the idea of demand-led growth as the solution to the recurrent crises in Capitalism. After all, Owen had proposed something of the sort a century before. The Webbs' failure to pick up the proposal would have been forgivable but for one thing; and that is their criticism of his failure to comprehend before they were born their theory of rent – a theory which, whatever might be its academic merits, provided no practical help to Governments. Or to the unemployed.

And it remains finally to ask what place there was for trade unionism in the Labour Party's revised prospectus. The answer is: industrial democracy. In the 1960s, the idea had resurfaced – though not in a form that Owen would have recognised as remotely related to that that he had advocated. There is the irony: that, just when British Empirical Socialism had come to terms with the idea of a mixed economy, when it had accepted that for the indefinite future a public sector and a private sector would co-exist, when the tangle of objections which the Webbs had seen to the development of a privately-owned industrial co-operative sector had been so far cleared away as to open the path to a natural growth of industrial democracy by a means which, because it reconciled the rights and interests of labour with those of ownership, would have been sustainable, the Labour Government ignored or overlooked the opportunity. It preferred to insist that industrial democracy should be imposed by a means that had to be in principle unsustainable: that is, by the appointment of representatives of trade unions to the boards of directors of industrial enterprises. Thus, falling into the technocrats' natural sin, it mistook administrative device for organic substance. It proposed a shot-gun marriage between two parties who, so far from having anticipated the bliss of that honourable estate, had ventured nothing much more than the frozen smile of recognition that passes for politeness between opponents who see in one another much to dislike and little to love. It wrote the terms of reference of the Committee of Enquiry on Industrial Democracy.

— 7 —

The False Start

'No! No! Sentence first, verdict afterwards.'

Lewis Carroll: *Alice in Wonderland*

'Contrariwise,' continued Tweedledee, 'if it was so, it might be; and if it were so, it would be: but as it isn't, it ain't. That's logic.'

Lewis Carroll: *Through the Looking Glass*

As is customary, The Committee of Enquiry on Industrial Democracy, chaired by Lord Bullock, opened its Report by reciting its remit. It had been set up 'to advise on questions relating to representation at board level in the private sector' with the following terms of reference:

> Accepting the need for a radical extension of industrial democracy in the control of companies by means of representation on boards of directors, and accepting the essential role of trade union organisations in this process, to consider how such an extension can best be achieved, taking into account in particular the proposals of the Trade Union Congress report on industrial democracy as well as experience in Britain, the EEC and other countries. Having regard to the interests of the national economy, employees, investors and consumers, to analyse the implications of such representation for the efficient management of companies and for company law.[1]

Here, then, was a proposal to promote industrial democracy in a particular specification. By the fortunes of politics, it has been dismissed from the scene. By the same fortunes, it might be recalled. For that reason, as well as for the attention it requires of any interested in the subject, it needs to be considered. And since the case for the development of an industrial co-operative sector stands primarily on its merit as the practice of industrial democracy, we have now to ask whether the proposals contained in the majority Report of the Bullock Committee are a valid and, if so, a preferable alternative.

There are two things to note at once about the remit. First, it excludes the public sector, that is to say, the nationalised industries. Whether intentionally or not, the effect of the exclusion was to dodge for the time being a major constitutional problem. This we shall return to. The second notable point is the one which, when the remit was published, led to much criticism of it, and which is registered in paragraph 1 of the minority report signed by three of the nine members remaining from the ten who at the outset composed the Committee:

> The Committee's remit required it 'to consider *how* such an extension' (representation on Boards of Directors) 'can best be achieved': it did not ask the Committee to consider *whether* 'a radical extension of industrial democracy' should be achieved by the representation of employees on Boards of Directors. The proposals in this Minority Report therefore represent, in our considered view, the best ways of fulfilling what we regard as a far from satisfactory or even wise remit.[2]

Certainly, the terms of reference specified industrial democracy as an extension of the activities of trade unions into the control of enterprises, other than public sector enterprises, by which the members of those unions were employed. The defence and advancement of the interests of their members as employees, traditional functions of trade unions, were to remain their principal *raison d'être*. What the remit conspicuously ignores is the possibility that a change, as radical as the intended extension of industrial democracy, but in the essential character of trade unions might also be a need if they were to play the new part written for them. The new wine might need new bottles. So, for the remit's specification of industrial democracy, the rationale has to be this: that officials or, for that matter, ordinary members of the union, elected or deputed to represent it on a board of directors, would be accountable to the membership which would replace them if it judged their performance to be unsatisfactory.

But unsatisfactory in what respect: as representatives of a body established to negotiate on behalf of employees with management acting on behalf of owners; or as representatives of the union but charged, along with representatives of the owners, with the corporate responsibility for the performance of the enterprise? The two kinds of responsibility do not coincide. They are liable to be, and often are, in conflict. There is no escaping the fact that a trade union will, in pursuit of its purposes as they are commonly understood, have its own corporate policies; and that the authority of members of a trade union appointed in that capacity to boards of directors of joint stock companies will derive from the trade union. And it is to the trade union that they would have to account for the exercise of that authority. A board of directors could not exist and act as a corporate entity if it were composed of two groups of people, each deriving its authority from and answerable to a different principal body, the one liable to be in conflict with the other; for it would in fact be a negotiating committee. Of course there would be some non-contentious business, perhaps quite a lot; but even then, there must also be the reservation that nothing should be disclosed by the one group to the other which might prejudice its case when the business was contentious. It is no good insisting that, so long as you look at it with your eyes closed, a pig's ear is a silk purse after all. So, only if the trade union representatives were not, whether actually or in effect, appointed by the union or, if appointed by it were neither accountable to it nor liable to be dismissed by it would that difficulty be avoided, at least in principle. But then it is hard to see how that arrangement could be described as, or even contribute to, industrial democracy.

The reality that there are rights of ownership and that they are liable to, and do, conflict with those of labour cannot be exorcised by pretending that they are not there; and it is the exclusion of the public sector from the Committee's purview which admits that reality. A nationalised industry is owned by the State. The public corporation in which its assets are vested and which is charged with the conduct of the business, is accountable to Parliament. The Secretary of State at the head of its sponsoring Department of State must lay its annual report and accounts before Parliament which may debate them and which may, if it thinks fit, call the Chairman and others before a select committee, examine them and report on their performance. Thus, Members of Parliament may be said to occupy much the same position with respect to the nationalised industries as do shareholders with respect to a joint stock company. And though, by a well-established convention, Members do not ask Ministers questions about the day-to-day conduct of the industries' affairs, since that is by definition not government business, they may very well ask him about a matter that most certainly is: about the appointments Ministers make to the boards of nationalised industries. If there is continuing disquiet about the way an industry is being run, Members can express their disquiet by questioning the fitness of the persons appointed by the Government to run it. Because the Government appoints the board, Members can if they are not satisfied with its performance, seek changes in its composition. So by this means, the interest of ownership in the performance of the business owned can assert itself. If, however, the authority to make appointments to the board of a nationalised industry did not reside solely in Government, but in part in trade unions as the instruments of industrial democracy, the Secretary of State could no longer be held responsible for the fitness of the board to discharge its functions; and it would no longer be meaningful for Members to ask Questions, nor possible for Government to answer them constructively. In short, the ownership by the State of nationalised industries requires accountability to Parliament. Accountability to Parliament requires the appointment of persons to the boards of nationalised industries to be, in law and in fact, the act of Government. If a power of appointment, either in law or in fact, is vested in trade unions, the effect is not only to arrogate to them rights attaching only to ownership, but to establish them in this particular matter as the constitutional equals of Parliament. The issue is indeed a major constitutional one. In practice, the result at best would be the confusion which must result when two bodies serving different purposes and interests are equally the ultimate custodians; and the large probability is that there could be no effective accountability at all. So it was advisedly that the terms of reference excluded the public sector. Nevertheless, behind the constitutional difficulty that its inclusion would have imported, the substantive and quite general point remains: industrial democracy as specified in the terms of reference of the Bullock Committee is not compatible with the rights of ownership.

However, what an owner sees as his due rights may be seen by others as undue privilege; and where the general interest is material enough to insist on the second alternative, it may with whatever necessary degree of consideration and justice, seek to override the first. Given the terms of reference, those who signed the majority Report might well have supposed that that part of the argument had been decided. The question was 'how' and not 'whether'; and what was required of them was not a justification of the ends, but a formulation of the means. So it is especially a matter for satisfaction that the signatories nevertheless provided a chapter in support of the specified objective. It is Chapter 3, 'The pressures for change'. And if in places it reads tendentiously or relies overmuch on rhetoric, it could hardly do otherwise than echo the tendentiousness and rhetoric of the terms of reference themselves. Anyway, it is in Chapter 3 that is mainly to be sought any justification for the conclusion, in advance of the Committee's work, that industrial democracy in the particular form specified by the remit was necessary or desirable in the general interest.

The chapter opens by recalling that the term 'industrial democracy' was first used by the Webbs in 1897 as the title of their book on the structure and functions of trade unions. But, it continues, since the Second World War there has been 'a shift of emphasis in the use of the term'. What it is about now is 'the need to involve employees to a greater extent in company decision making'.[3] A shift of emphasis? Here the expression may, as so often, be read to blur the fact of a change of substance, to present a difference of kind as though it were only a modest difference of degree. For the Webbs' prescription for Socialism was ownership and control by the State or municipality of the means of production or provision, the control to be exercised in the general interest. For them, the sovereignty of the consumer was the over-riding consideration. Even in industrial co-operatives, that consideration ruled out control by employees, and so confined the trade unions to their traditional concerns. Most surely, the Webbs would have seen the omission of the industries of the public sector from the Committee's terms of reference as evidence of the flaw in them. Anyway, the perceived need since 1945 is said in the Report to have been 'to involve employees to a greater extent in company decision making'[4] whatever involvement involves or a greater extent extends to. The general sentiment is so unexceptionable as to be positively sedative. It is only when the reader wakes up that he wonders what it means. But he may yet be enlightened.

For the chapter[5] goes on to record the developments which had prompted a recognition of the need for that involvement, starting with those it identifies as industrial and economic changes. They are: first, the growth of giant industrial enterprises and the concentration of economic power in fewer of them. In the result, decisions affecting the lives of thousands are taken by people remote from them. Next, quoting the Confederation of British Industries, the chapter rehearses the view that companies have a duty to take account of the interest of employees and should develop effective systems of employee participation. Then it turns to the effect of the 'managerial revolution'; that is, it says, to concentrate power in the hands of directors and to withdraw power from ineffective and acquiescent shareholders who only exercise it at times of crisis. There follows the observation that the need for responsiveness to rapid technological change and fluctuating economic climate requires management to involve employees in the process of making decisions, if only for the practical reason that there will be great difficulty in carrying through decisions against resistance by trade unions. The comment that all of this prompts is first, that it amounts to no more than the well-understood case for good personnel management in conventionally organised manufacturing or service industry. And except in one particular, it applies with equal force to nationalised industries. The exception is, of course, in the pronouncement that shareholders have in effect surrendered their power to professional management, a pronouncement which does not so much face the central question of the rights of ownership as to try to pass it by. For it invites the view that the powers attaching to the rights have largely fallen into abeyance and may, therefore, the more readily be disregarded. As a case, therefore, for the extension of industrial democracy defined as the kind of consultation practised, the worker-participation sought by good personnel management, it is to be applauded. But as a case for a 'radical extension' of industrial democracy by means requiring the assumption by unreformed trade unions of rights which had hitherto attached only to ownership, it merits at this point no more than a suspended judgment at best.

Under the heading 'Social changes' the chapter says, in brief, that the deferential society is dead; and that 'the coming of age of democracy in our society is a process that inevitably affects the whole of people's lives; it cannot be excluded from the workplace.' This has something of the smack of a 'like it or not' pronouncement of the kind commonly declaimed by those who would have us suppose that opposition to things we do not like would be pointless. More persuasive perhaps is the quotation from the EEC's Green Paper *Employment Participation and Company Structure*, to the effect that 'the pursuit of goals other than economic growth, such as the improvement of the quality of life and working conditions, the protection of the environment and the interests of the consumer ... can probably be secured only by the existence of decision-making processes in enterprises which have a broader, more democratic base than such processes often have at present.' Well, yes: but much depends on what 'a broader democratic base' means. Finally and, since it is presented as a statement of fact, unobjectionably, it records that there 'has been an increasing desire among employees to control their working environment and to have a say in decisions which affect their working lives'. Once again, what case is being supported? It is easy to read it with approval as support for the view that management should be considerate of the well-being and interests of employees, and would be well-advised to promote their participation in the discussion of them. If the purpose of this part of the chapter is to provide a platform for the proposition that, to use the Report's own words, management generally should 'involve employees in decision-making, rather than impose decisions on them without consultation', then it is as persuasive as is any declaration in favour of obvious good. But if it is to serve as the platform for a conclusion that something else and qualitatively different is required, something to place authority, at least in part, for the conduct of a business owned by others in the hands of employees, then by itself the statement is not strong enough to bear the weight of the proposition. The presentation is, once again, persuasively for extension. It does nothing for 'radical extension'.

Next in its review of the pressures for change, Chapter 3 turns to the growth of the functions of trade unions. It refers first to the widening of the scope of collective bargaining to include subjects other than pay and conditions, citing as examples: the provision of time and office services for lay trade-union representatives; manpower planning; job and income security; and disclosure of information. This it sees as evidence of the shop-floor pressures for greater industrial democracy. There is some already. There should be more – even if, on inspection, the examples cited can again be seen as part of or an extension of the practice of good personnel management. To this, however, it adds a further proposition. Recent legislation, on employment protection by making provision for disclosure of information and advance consultation on redundancy, and on health and safety by bringing the subject into the sphere of joint regulation, is advanced as the basis for this declaration: 'It can be argued indeed that the basis for a legislative framework designed to encourage industrial democracy at shop floor level already exists'. Indeed it can: but whether the argument would carry any weight is another matter entirely. To be fair, the majority report does not in so many words advance the argument. It is content to let us follow it, if we want to do so. And, last in this section comes a reference to the 'emphasis of the industrial strategy on union involvement in company level planning together with new concepts like planning agreements.' These are, the chapter says, creating new pressures for the extension of joint regulation which 'inevitably raise the question whether existing institutions can be developed to provide for employee involvement at this level, or whether new institutions are needed.' Well, at least this pops the question even though rather coyly. New institutions might include boards of directors containing trade union members as such – just as the terms of reference, in 'accepting the essential role of trade union organisations', assumed. But, what industrial strategy, whose industrial strategy? What that reference does is invite the reader to compare unlikes. Thus, we are prompted to suppose that an unspecified industrial strategy on the one hand is so like matters of health and safety for the purposes of the Health and Safety at Work Act 1974, or like employment protection for the purposes of the Employment Protection Act 1975 on the other, as to amount to much the same kind of thing as they are; and so to accept the view that, just as the second is a subject for joint regulation by management and unions or of prior discussion between management and unions, so too should the first. But the two are unlike. For while the health and safety, and the prospective redundancy of its members, are the union's business as of generally recognised right it is by no means clear that an industrial strategy that was anything more than a slogan would be. For such a strategy must eventually require that resources at the disposal of people who own them will be applied in one way rather than another. And it cannot be said that that is the union's business as of generally recognised right to decide, or to share in deciding, that application. To influence, to seek to persuade, yes: to decide, no. The distinction is borne out by the Report's own reference to the disclosure of information, and prior consultation on redundancy. Unions are to be given information; and consulted in advance. Consulted: not invited to share in the decision whether redundancies are to be declared. And it is hard to see how unions retaining the functions of protecting and advancing the interests of employees could be expected, or wish, to do so. Whose side are they on? Nor does the reference to planning agreements help the case; for an agreement is negotiated between two parties representing different interests. Management accountable to owners cannot be expected to enter into meaningful agreements, planning or otherwise, which limit their freedom under the law to act in the best interests of the owners. Few, if any, lasting planning agreements were made. The fact is that all the examples adduced to support the proposition that there should be a qualitative – or 'radical' – extension of the role of trade unions into the management of the business employing their members fail at the crucial point. None concedes the massive change of principle that such an extension would require. On the contrary, they stop short of it. They stop at consultation. So far under this heading 'trade union and legislative development', as under the earlier headings, the case effectively stated remains the case for extension, within the existing dispensation, of the role of trade unions.

So far: but now it sounds a different note. By reference to the TUC'S report on industrial democracy, it states the movement's own position as follows: that the development of participation at national and local level has left a gap at company level which can only be filled by employee representation on the company board. Important though collective bargaining is as a method of extending employee influence at local level, there is a range of important decisions which it cannot by itself reach. Then, quoting directly from the TUC's report:

> It is clear that this leaves a wide range of fundamental
> managerial decisions affecting workpeople that are beyond the
> control – and very largely beyond the influence – of
> workpeople and trade unions ... Major decisions on
> investment, location, closures and take-overs and mergers, and
> product specialisation of the organisation are generally taken at
> levels where collective bargaining does not take place, and
> indeed are subject matter not readily covered by collective
> bargaining. New forms of control are needed.

Here then is the quantum leap: not consultation, but control. Representation at board level of the workers is declared, in effect, to be a natural right. In a true political democracy, such a declaration is of course perfectly allowable; and none the less so for being sectional. To be persuasive, however, it needs to show at least that the general interest will not suffer from the exercise of the right; and that the loss or diminution of any other opposed rights can be justified. This the quoted passage does not seek to do. The persuasion rests on the assumptions that the forms of consultation practised and of participation prompted by the best employers are a measure of industrial democracy, but not enough: that the representation of employees on company boards is necessary to establish complete industrial democracy; that total industrial democracy, in this prescription, will so far improve industrial efficiency as to benefit materially the general interest; and that the implicit loss or diminution of the rights of ownership should not be allowed to preclude the realisation of that benefit. Each of these assumptions is so questionable as to put the onus of proof very heavily on the trade unions. And the conclusion must be that the unions failed utterly to make the case out. They failed to persuade the electorate. 'The coming of age of [political] democracy in our society' was, in the event, marked in 1979 not by the return to office of the Labour Government which had written the terms of reference for the Bullock Committee, and to which the trade union movement might look for the advancement of industrial democracy as the movement had specified it. It was marked by the election of a Conservative Government committed to reduce what it saw as the excessive powers and privileges of the movement.

Nor does the last reference in the chapter, the reference to continental European and, in particular, to Western German practice, help. The Report observes: 'It is now 25 years since *Mitbestimmung* (Co-determination) was introduced in the Federal Republic of Germany'; and again: 'As long ago as 1972 the EEC published draft proposals for a Fifth Directive on Company law, proposing employee representation on the supervisory boards of all companies in the Community with over 500 employees' – a rhetorical presentation that pictures the United Kingdom as dragging its reluctant feet well in the rear of a party marching briskly along the path towards a bright new future entrusted not wholly but largely to trade unions. Put the reality next to the rhetoric and the case looks very different. The winter of 1978–9 was the winter of discontent, the discontent of trade unions generally with the guidance contained in the White Paper, published in July 1978, on pay policy. Paragraph 12 pronounced the key requirement: the Government's duty was, it said, to advocate a policy which would provide the best possible foundation for a further reduction in inflation, already reduced in the previous year from 17 per cent to around 8 per cent; an increase in jobs and output; and an improved standard of living. To this end: In the Government's view, the total increase [in pay] for any group compared with the previous year . . . should not be more than 5 per cent.

Thus the Government proposed; but the trade union movement disposed. Either it would not or it could not observe the policy. If it would not, then it was irresponsibly careless of the general interest. If it could not, then its claim to be one of the great estates in the land was greatly reduced. Whichever alternative is right, the trade unions' bid for a share in the control of industry and, implicitly, to stand as an equal with Parliament as a body to which the nationalised industries should be accountable, could no longer be entertained. They continued to be seen for what they continued to be: organisations concerned to get the highest wages and the best conditions they could for their members. And when put to the test, they were nothing more. If they would not or could not, at the request of a Government sympathetic to them and their aspirations, give sufficient support to the economic policy advocated by that Government in the general interest, it could not with confidence be supposed that trade union representatives on the boards of companies would give sufficient support to the policies of those companies. The conclusion can only be this: that if a 'radical extension' of industrial democracy means the appointment of trade union representation to the boards of companies, then the case for it – always improbable in principle – has been shown by events to be insupportable.

Even if it had been otherwise, it still would not have followed that the unions should as of right share in the control of those resources they did not own: land and buildings, plant and equipment, and finance. Their case would have been vastly more plausible; and a decisive electoral victory for the Labour Party might have been seen as a mandate for the promotion of industrial democracy in the trade unions' model of it, and as an implicit declaration of public opinion in favour of the consequential abridgement or even abrogation of the rights of ownership. Whether in the event owners would have consented is quite another question. It must be very doubtful indeed whether, in a free society, property can be used otherwise than as those with title to it will allow. They would be bound to see such a use as virtual expropriation, without compensation.

In the end, the account in Chapter 3 of the pressures for change amounts to an effective review of the recognition of the right of trade unions to be fully informed and consulted, in good time, by management about its intentions where they will or might affect the interests of employees organised by unions; and so may be said to provide a firm footing for the argument that the practice of providing full information and of engaging in full consultation should be extended and adopted generally, in order that unions may better consider, and act in pursuance of, those interests. However, except in the reference to the TUC's report on industrial democracy, it provides no evidence of opinion in support of the recognition of a right for trade unions, acting on behalf of employees, to share with management, acting on behalf of owners, in the control of companies: that is to say, no evidence of opinion in support of a case for a 'radical extension', as prescribed by the terms of reference, of the unions' role. Indeed, it can almost be read as inviting the supposition that industrial democracy, in that prescription, differs only in degree from current practices of consultation; is to that extent already customary; and is therefore unobjectionable and, as a 'democratic imperative', inevitable. But, read the chapter this way or that, if there was ever a case for recognising that unions have a right to share in the management of companies, that case depended critically upon a general expectation – amounting to a near-certainty – that, rather than give primacy to their sectional interests, unions would and could act in the general interest whenever it was necessary or desirable for them to do so. And events since the Report have exposed the emptiness of any such expectation. Two final points: first, except to imply that, because the rights of ownership in joint stock companies are rarely used, they can be discounted, the chapter offers nothing to support a conclusion that the reduction or abrogation of those rights, such as the 'radical extension' of the unions' role would require, would command general support, and second, it gives no guidance on the question whether that 'radical extension' would create genuine industrial democracy.

But both points are referred to later in the Report. The first, the implications for, and of, the rights of ownership, are not examined. When it comes, in Chapter 6 'A review of some major issues', to this point it simply declares:

> to regard the company as solely the property of shareholders is to be out of touch with the reality of the present-day company as a complex social and economic entity subject to a variety of internal and external pressures, in which the powers of control have passed from the legal owners to professional management.[6]

There is in this assertion more sound and flannel signifying not very much than there is substance. Thus: are we to read 'solely' the property of shareholders as implying that it is in fact that, or can be, someone else's property? Then again: 'a complex social and economic entity' – how does this alter by one iota the hard fact that ownership, the title to property and the right to use it and to dispose of it, vests in the shareholders? And how do 'the variety of internal and external pressures' alter that fact? They may well limit the uses to which property may be put and hence affect its value, even to the point where owners may prefer not to allow it to be used at all;[7] but they do not alter the fact that ownership confers the licence to use, or not to use. And finally, the statement that 'the powers of control have passed from the legal owners to professional management': are we to infer that besides 'legal' ownership there is a kind of *de facto* ownership; that management appointed by owners are *de facto* owners; and that, because their members are employed in this or that particular company, trade unions should similarly be regarded as *de facto* owners? What, anyway, does 'control' mean here? It is so presented as to invite us to see no difference between on the one hand management appointed by, acting for, and accountable to owners, and on the other union representatives appointed by, acting for, and accountable to employees. A neutral presentation would expose the difference and show that the delegation of authority does not imply the forfeiture of ultimate control. It is not good enough to use language which blurs the sharp reality, as for example: 'the ultimate control of the Company is seen in law as residing with the owners or shareholder'[8] as if to suggest that there is some other and valid way of seeing it, a way which may put the ultimate control, at least in part, elsewhere. It is not as though the law adopts, or still less, creates for its own peculiar purposes and processes a special view of ownership, one which is worth as much or as little as any other view. Rather, it is an expression of the rights and liabilities generally held to attach to ownership: more exactly, the right subject to the general law to determine whether and how the assets and resources owned will be used, and the liability in certain circumstances to answer for the consequences of that use. If this is to labour the obvious, it is because the formulation quoted above serves to anticipate the conclusion that a statute should attach to non-owners the same rights and liabilities. It looks towards a statutory requirement that representatives of trade unions should be appointed, in that capacity, to the directing boards of companies. And that is a nonsense. Either there is ownership and the rights and obligations that go with it, or there is not and neither are there nor can there be those rights and obligations.

Nor does the fact that, so long as they consider that the affairs of the business they own are being conducted well enough on their behalf, owners do not choose to exercise their ultimate authority, provide any reason for supposing either that companies would be better managed if trade unions were implicated in management or that owners would acquiesce in the assumption, in whole or in part, of their rights by any other party – let alone by one whose essential interests are often opposed to their own. In a free society, if trade unions want the rights of ownership, they cannot expect to get them as a free gift and call it industrial democracy. They will have to buy out the owners. And with the rights, they would get the obligations, too. The signatories to the majority Report of the Committee of Enquiry on Industrial Democracy are as misled and misleading in treating property as a negligible factor as Robert Owen was in ignoring it. So great a change does not enter upon the national economic scene unnoticed, like Owen's 'thief in the night' nor even conspicuously to the trumpetings of statutory provisions and the flourish of bureaucratic apparatus. It does not enter because the entry assumes the willing compliance of people who consider that they have nothing to gain and much to lose by complying. It takes two to tango; and if one of them will not, there is no dance.

But if there could be no *pas de deux*, perhaps there could be a *ménage à trois*. There could be 2x + y, where x is the number both of the members appointed to a board of directors by the owners of the company, and of the trade union members; and y the number of directors to be co-opted.[9] The majority report concluded that there should be equal representation of owners and trade unions; and then proceeds straight to the view that a third group of co-opted directors should be appointed, adding as their first reason that those directors would bring special experience to the board room, and a broader and more detached view of the company's affairs. It then comes to the practical point. Citing German experience to show that 'there was a tendency for employee and shareholder representatives to vote and act in distinct groups', they add that the presence of co-opted directors on the board would mean that either group would at the very least need to gain the support of the majority of the directors before they could carry or veto a proposal. This is almost to concede, if it does not in fact do so, that a board deriving its authority from two opposed sources cannot constitute a corporate body such as decision-taking requires. The concession, near or complete, is denied in the statement 'we do not see the co-opted directors primarily as a means of resolving deadlock'. But put their function as arbiters where one will in the numbered sequence of reasons for their appointment, that is the most obvious and necessary purpose they would serve. The denial does not so much refute prospective criticism as pay danegeld to it. Like the Dane, the criticism does not go away. Further, the majority report is silent on the question: to whom would the co-opted directors be accountable? They were to owe their appointment to the trade union's and the owner's representatives on the board; and, if they could not agree, to the binding decision of an independent commission. The case is quite unlike that which prevails at present when non-executive directors are appointed to a board. As part of the board, they share in its collective accountability to the owners of the company. In a $2x + y$ arrangement, there would be no such collective accountability, to a single ultimate authority, for the y directors to share in. It seems, therefore, that they would be accountable to no one.

So, to summarise our findings on the proposals contained in the majority Report. First, a presentation founded so largely on the view that equates the development of industrial democracy to the growth of the process of consultation by management of unions intent on retaining their traditional role which opposes them to management, does not provide a credible basis for the qualitative change, envisaged by the Report, in that role: a change to one of shared responsibility for management. There can be no confidence that unions, existing to serve a sectional interest, will or can suppress that interest in order to support the wider interest, whether at company or national level. The majority's assumption or, as they put it, 'persuasion'[10] that industrial democracy as conceived in the terms of reference will lead to increased industrial efficiency is, therefore, too insecure to form a basis for policy. Next, even if it were secure in itself, it would not work. It would not work because it assumes compliance by those who own the assets and resources, other than labour, of industry; and that assumption ignores that there inheres in ownership an inalienable right to determine whether, and if so how, to use those assets and resources. If the trade unions want to exercise that right, they will have to get the legal title to them whether by purchase or by what has been called euphemistically, and in criticism of Robert Owen's failure to see the significance of ownership, 'revolutionising practice'.[11] Compliance by owners would not be induced by administrative device, such as the formula $2x + y$, the practical need for which amounts – despite the majority Report's disclaimer – to an admission of the validity of the criticism of the intention that responsibility for management should be shared by trade unions. And, it would not work because the arrangement $2x + y$ does not provide a means of bringing accountability to bear on the performance of management: for it is highly improbable that a group of people which is primarily a derivative from two opposed and unreconcileable interests can effectively be called to account by either; and the addition of a third group accountable to no one further confounds the confusion. Finally, it is therefore the more difficult to see how the proposals can have anything to do with genuine industrial democracy, that is to say, with the accountability of the board of directors as a corporate whole to the individual men and women who constitute the workforce and who would have the ultimate power to replace an unsatisfactory board. There must, too, be the gravest doubts about a system which excludes those who prefer not to join a union. It is not self-evident that membership of a trade union should be a condition of participation in industrial democracy; nor enough for the majority Report to assert, simply as a statement of belief, that 'if employees wish to be represented on the board, they must be prepared to organise' – that is, to join trade unions – 'to make representation on the board effective'.[12] For the essential characteristic of democracy is its insistence that all men are equal in esteem. Emphatically, it is

108

not this: that all men are equal in esteem – but those who are members of the union are more equal than the others. The fact that such a proposition could be presented a industrial democracy exposes the reality: that the exercise was about the extension of the powers of unreformed trade unionism. This is not to say that those who signed the majority Report were disingenuous. The disingenuity was in the misconceived terms of reference. Well, *la politique a ses raisons que le raison ne connait point.*

The greater pity is this: that because the terms of reference misidentified industrial democracy, the chance of getting a better perception of it, of its value and of the possibility of advancing it, was missed. Because that misidentification insisted on making trade unions the vehicle for it but insisted also on the continuance of their traditional role, the outcome was bound to be primarily about an extension of their power in the performance of that role, the role that implicates trade unionism as the reciprocal to the ownership of the means of production and provision within the total system, Capitalism, as it evolved in Victorian Britain. It was this role that the new model unions had consciously adopted in the eighteen fifties and that the Webbs had emphasised in the eighteen nineties. A 'radical change' within that total system and in the name of industrial democracy, to the advantage of the trade unions, could only be secured by attributing to them rights inhering in ownership. But attribution could only be meaningful if trade union representatives on company boards everywhere and always accepted wholeheartedly the duties of ownership along with the rights, so changing the role of the unions fundamentally and abandoning any pretence to industrial democracy. Or, and this is the near-certain probability, constrained by their accountability to the membership, the trade union representatives would not accept the duties of ownership along with the rights, could not 'change sides'. The new-style boards could not have worked as they were meant to; and the misplaced expectation that they would have established industrial democracy would have collapsed. The proposals contained in the majority Report of the Committee of Enquiry are not a credible alternative to the promotion of industrial democracy through the extension of an industrial co-operative sector of the economy. They are not about industrial democracy at all. By contrast, industrial co-operatives are wholly about industrial democracy.

A different set of questions would have avoided the false start on the wrong track. They would have been something like these:

> Given that industrial democracy, defined as the ultimate right
> and duty of the men and women working in an industrial
> enterprise to call management to account for its performance,
> and, if that performance does not satisfy them, to replace
> management, is desirable in principle and as a means of making
> the efficient conduct of the enterprise their natural concern;
> recognising that the rights of use attaching to ownership,
> whether in the private or public sector, are inalienable;
> recognising the value in general of competition as a means of
> keeping production and provision sensitive to public needs and
> tastes, and as a means of relating the distribution of resources
> to them; to consider
>
> (i) in what sort of industrial organisation would industrial
>   democracy be feasible;
> (ii) how far and in what circumstances would the adoption of
>   such a form of organisation be feasible;
> (iii) by what means should its adoption be promoted and how
>   long would it take to establish it as a characteristic
>   feature in the industrial scene;
> (iv) what part should trade unions play in its promotion and
>   adoption and what changes would that part require in
>   their functions as they are commonly understood; and
> (v) where in the case of a particular industry, or
>   organisation, the general interest requires that
>   accountability should be to the public at large, considered
>   for example as consumers or users of goods produced or
>   beneficiaries from services provided, what compensatory
>   measures should be introduced so as to make good as far
>   as possible the permanent denial to employees of a right
>   which is in principle generally desirable?

Such a formulation would require those asking the questions to
confront the real problems: the need to understand that the
aspiration to the exercise of democratic right and the discharge of
democratic responsibility must arise from those who would
exercise the right and discharge the responsibility and is not to be
thrust upon those who do not want it or induced in those who are
indifferent to it; the need for a form of organisation such that the
interests of ownership and labour would be congruent; and the
need to recognise that since accountability, above all, is the test of

authentic democracy, then by that same test there will be some circumstances in which the general case for industrial democracy is over-ridden. It would recognise, too, that industrial democracy cannot be conjured into being overnight, no more than was political democracy, no more than was the joint stock company as the common expression of industrial capitalism. It may be an exaggeration – though not by much – to observe that industrial democracy stands now where political democracy did before the Great Reform Bill of 1832. This is not to say that we need take so unconscionable a time to establish industrial democracy, but only that it would be naive to suppose that there will be no doubts and difficulties – and that it would be a great mistake to let them deter us from starting from present worse to go to prospective better.

— 8 —

The Awkward Corner

It is proper to state that I forgo any advantage which could be derived to my argument from the idea of abstract right, as a thing independent of utility. I regard utility as the ultimate appeal on all ethical questions; but it must be utility in the largest sense, grounded on the permanent interests of man as a progressive being.

John Stuart Mill, *On Liberty*

New opinions are always suspected, and usually opposed, without any other reason but because they are not already common.

John Locke: *Essay on Human Understanding*

If, like honesty, morality is best policy, it will pay us to do the right thing. So far, the case discussed in this book for the extended use of the industrial co-operative as a form of organisation for production or provision has stood primarily upon the proposition that it is an expression of authentic industrial democracy, that such an extension would help to fill a debilitating gap in the practice in the United Kingdom of western liberal principles, to mend what Bertrand Russell calls 'this disruption of democracy from within'.[1] The discussion has been a moral one. Now it becomes a practical one. It addresses the question whether it would in fact pay us to do the right thing.

The proposition that industrial co-operatives can create and distribute wealth at least as well and probably better than the traditional forms of industry had already been argued from cause to probable effect.[2] In empirical support of that argument we can now cite the case of the much studied and often reported-upon

Mondragon group of co-operative enterprises; much studied and often reported upon because, as Bradley and Gelb observe, 'It represents the largest, possibly the most successful example of a manufacturing co-operative group'.[3] Here it is enough to recall that Mondragon, an industrial town of about 40,000 people in the Basque region of north-west Spain, has since 1956 become the centre of a growing group of highly successful industrial co-operatives with supporting banking, advisory and social services. In 1980, the group employed some 20,000 people, of whom nearly 16,000 worked in a total of 76 industrial enterprises variously engaged in the following kinds of production: foundry and forge 7; capital goods 22; components 27; consumer durables 15; building 5. Of the 76 co-operatives, 10 employed over 400; 11 from 200 to 400; 11 from 100 to 200; 23 from 50 to 100; and 21 under 50.[4] At constant (1976) prices, the sales of all the industrial co-operatives rose from 5,200 million pesetas in 1965 to 28,750 millioin pesetas in 1979; and their share of the domestic market rose from less than 1 per cent in 1960 to 10.6 per cent in 1976.[5] There is, of course, the immediate possibility that an ethnic factor, 'Basqueness', identifies the group with Basque aspirations and so provides a dynamic rarely if at all available elsewhere; and that this factor makes Mondragon a special case and not of any general relevance. Bradley and Gelb find against that possibility:

> 'Basqueness', is not seen as an over-ridingly significant feature of Mondragon either by its workers or by those in other local firms ... The most distinctive feature is seen to be its co-operative nature. Security of employment is generally ranked second. Far behind comes the ethnic nature of the co-operatives and their level of payments.[6]

Not, then, a special case; successful not because it is Basque, but essentially because it is co-operative.

Those for whom one Basque swallow cannot make a British summer may be more impressed by the record of the plywood factories owned and operated by their employees and located on the west coast of the USA. L. Stettner quotes Sachs:

> As a group these employee-owned enterprises have become the most productive and efficient in the industry, with the most progressive records for instituting technological and other modernising innovations. While figures vary from firm

to firm and for the same firm over time, the worker-owned plywood companies as a group have consistently averaged a productivity per worker that is about 30 per cent higher than the mean for conventionally operated plywood manufacturing businesses. Similarly by all other measures such as profitability, growth, share-prices, wages, steadiness of employment and log-recovery ratio, the record of the worker-owned plywoods is remarkable when compared with the rest of the industry.

She quotes also from other studies to show that these co-operatives are better able to survive under adversity than are conventionally organised plywood manufacturing firms, and why: in a phrase, higher productivity, so much higher as to result in some cases in value added per labour-hour of more than twice that of those firms.[7] And there is this also to say. Here we have operating in the same geographical area, in the same economic environment and manufacturing the same product, on the one hand enterprises organised as industrial co-operatives and on the other as conventional firms. So comparing alternatives which are alike save in the form of organisation, we see that the theoretical expectation that superior motivation, the plus-factor available to the co-operative form, should enable it to out-produce the conventional form is borne out in practice. It ought to. It does. And more: in both of the cases cited, the success of the co-operative form has been secured in a market economy.

For further empirical proof of the theoretical pudding, let us look first at the French, and then at the Italian achievements. At the beginning of the decade, there were affiliated to the French Confederation of Producer Co-operatives (SCOP) some 670 active industrial co-operatives, organised in eleven regions each with a full-time staff of organisers and advisers, and having a combined turnover of £500 million.[8]

The Italian example is evidence not only of the effective and widespread use in a western democracy of the industrial co-operative model but also of the rigorously businesslike and wholly unromantic attitude of LEGA towards it. Controlled by the Socialists and Communists, the *Lega Nazionale della Co-operative e Mutue* (the National League of Co-operatives and Mutual Benefit Societies) is not the only national organisation on the Italian industrial co-operative scene. There is also the rival Confederation of Co-operatives, dominated by the Christian Democrats and serving primarily rural and artisanal interests. But of LEGA, the *Financial Times* reported in 1979 that 'the 12,000-odd co-operatives operating under [its] umbrella generated sales of over L.5000 billion (£2.9 billion)'. The article went on to record a growth rate of 20 per cent per annum in real terms; annual exports to the value of $1 billion; and a three-year investment programme of £800 million. And more: 'LEGA ... represents en bloc the fourth or fifth grouping in Italy, behind IRL, ENI and Fiat, but more or less on a par with Montedison.' Indisputably, the industrial co-operative sector is a major economic factor in Italy. Next, and perhaps more significantly, the article recounts the historical perspective in which LEGA's leaders see its development:

> For the Socialists ... it is the key to a new economic model, based on the principle of self-management. While firmly governed by the discipline of the market place, this would offer its own third way between the glaring inefficiencies of state capitalism, Italian style, and the short-comings of classic private enterprise where the interests of employees can be so easily trampled upon.

LEGA emphasised the need for an objective appraisal of a prospective co-operative's commercial prospects: and was critical of the attempt made on Mr Anthony Wedgwood Benn's insistence when he was Secretary of State for Trade and Industry, to rescue the *Scottish Daily News*, Kirkby Manufacturing and Engineering Ltd (KME), and Meriden; and to make the co-operative form the instrument of rescue. 'Politely but comprehensively', recorded the *Financial Times*, Signor Ornelli Prandini, the Communist President of LEGA dismissed the British way of doing things: 'I dont't agree at all. It's as if everyone else had given up and the Government then said, "Oh, give the workers some money and let them have a go."' He draws some encouragement from the fact that the British are at least thinking about industrial, as opposed to consumer, co-operatives. 'But they can't just be an end resort, when the venture has no chance anyway.' 'Not for the first time', the article concluded, 'Italian communism appears economically much harder-headed than British Socialism.'[9]

On the matter of the notorious and failed rescue attempts certainly so; and the events of the day, 28 March 1979, on which the article appeared add point to the conclusion. That day, the Labour Government led by Mr James Callaghan was defeated by one vote. And if there was any one reason which, more than any other, ensured his defeat at the ensuing general election, then surely it was the inability of the trade union movement to assume during what had therefore become the winter of discontent, the responsibility required of them as a justification of the power and influence they claimed. The contrast between British Socialism, as then exemplified by trade unionism, and LEGA, could hardly be sharper; the first, insistent on its traditional and conservative role, the role dispensed for it in the Victorian era by evolving Capitalism – to purvey labour to employing capital; the second, looking towards a synthesis to accommodate and resolve the opposed interests contained in that dispensation, looking towards 'the third way'. Nor, if we are willing to see our co-operative selves as other co-operators see us, should we fail to note Signor Prandini's implied criticism, pointed though polite, of the British concept of Co-operation as restricted almost exclusively to the Consumers' Movement.

A restriction which, whatever the success of the industrial co-operative elsewhere, many in Britain would have judged to be wholly desirable; for the recent British view had been distorted by what it saw as the examples of the *Scottish Daily News*, KME, and Meriden. In its Report, presented in 1977 to Parliament, the working party set up by the Labour Government to develop further the idea of a Co-operative Development Agency, and broadly representative of the whole of the Co-operative Movement, declared of the three attempted rescues:

> The so-called worker co-operatives have, of course, also been the focus of public attention. A main reason for their conversion from companies in the conventional form has been the maintenance of employment. But there is some danger where co-operatives are created out of economic adversity, for the situation is then one of commercial crisis and, important though the rescue may be on general grounds, it is far from an ideal basis on which to promote the reputation of co-operatives generally, or of Co-operation as an alternative form of organisation. It is attempting to use Co-operation to turn failure into success but against heavy odds.[10]

In the first of its annual reports the Co-operative Development Agency (CDA) returned to the theme. Observing that the public interest had fixed almost entirely on the co-operatives set up to rescue failed enterprises organised as companies in the conventional form, the Agency commented first that it was questionable how far those enterprises when reorganised, satisfied co-operative principles; and next that the recent closure of KME might have revived doubts about the effectiveness for industrial ventures of the co-operative form. To remove those doubts and declare its own policy on proposed rescues, the Agency distinguished two possible objectives: the restoration of the failed undertaking to viability, or the preservation of a number of particular jobs. Yet a loss of jobs was often the pre-condition of restored viability. Where that was so and the workforce was invited, or itself proposed, to set up an industrial co-operative, but understood the preservation of every job to be the prime objective, the necessary conditions for effective management were absent from the start. So, the first question the CDA would always have to put was: which of the two objectives did those advocating rescue want? Almost certainly, they could not have both. Because its prime concern had to be the restoration of viability, then where that implied a loss of jobs, the Agency would only recommend rescue if the workforce understood and accepted the implication, would arrange for the selection of those who were to become members of the co-operative and, by exclusion, decide who would lose their jobs. A more general consideration followed. If there were not sufficient expectation that a failed, conventionally organised enterprise could be restored to viability as an industrial co-operative, the injection of resources into it would divert them from more promising projects. Lasting employment would not be created by re-inforcing defeat, but as a result of the creation of viable industrial co-operatives. For completeness, the Report appended under the heading 'Project Appraisal' a questionnaire listing the considerations that any appraisal, whether of a proposed rescue, or conversion of an existing organisation to the co-operative form, or an entirely new start, would have to weigh. The questions provide the framework for a close commercial assessment. No one reading them could conclude that the Agency would allow anyone to suppose industrial co-operatives were in any way exempt from commercial discipline.[11]

The declaration of policy was more than a statement of priorities and objectives, designed to disavow as misdirected Mr Benn's essay in Industrial Co-operation and to restore credibility to the idea – and, incidentally, to meet Signor Prandini's dismissive criticism. It was also an implicit protest at what many in Co-operation had seen as an exercise which at best fundamentally misconceived the Movement's nature and aspirations, at worst misused them for the purposes of a political performance. However the episode is judged, one thing is clear beyond any doubt: the damaging examples of the *Scottish Daily News*, KME and Meriden brought the idea of the Industrial Co-operative into disrepute. That the burden of scepticism imposed by those apparent examples continued to impede the Agency's promotional work shows through successive annual reports to Parliament. Thus, in the Report for the year 1980–81, the CDA commented that the industrial co-operative was still often regarded as characterised by them.[12] A recent study of them makes melancholy if instructive reading. It fully bears out both the disquiet expressed in the working party's Report, and quoted above; and the CDA's dissociation of its policies from those in pursuit of which the three cases in question were projected into disaster. Of the *Scottish Daily News*, the study finds that it was inadequately financed from the outset; was poorly equipped; so applied the principle of workers' control as to make 'executive decision taking impossible if not farcical'; and produced an unacceptable product. 'It is difficult', the study concludes, 'to see how such an ill-conceived, ill-equipped, under-funded project could ever have been successful.' Of KME, it recalls that, in the face of advice that a proposal which made job-preservation the paramount consideration was likely to fail, Mr Benn decided to advance £3.9 million by way of assistance provided under Section 7 of the 1972 Industry Act. Further, KME failed to act on the advice it was given by consultants and academics. Commercially, the consequences were tragic. And it never became an authentic co-operative. 'KME differed little from conventional organisations and fell well short of co-operative ideals'; and again, 'the worker directors apparently adopted an autocratic style and barely communicated with their fellow members.' The study's findings on Meriden are kinder. Few enterprises, it says, could have been faced with such a daunting task. It had to overcome a fundamental lack of capital. It had to succeed in selling, against Japanese competition, the product left to it by a conventionally organised British motor cycle industry which had already admitted defeat; and sales were not keeping pace with production. Yet, productivity rose by 50 per cent over the levels previously achieved.[13] Certainly, Meriden was much more nearly an authentic industrial co-operative than were the other two; and, as certainly, realised the potential in morale, in practical commitment to the objectives of the enterprise, which is the special feature of a co-operative.

There are lessons to be learned from the tale of the three attempted rescues. They may be regarded as having been, at central government level, ideologically inspired: that is, undertaken either on the view that the possibility of rescuing a failed, conventionally organised enterprise would serve to promote Socialism in a neo-Marxist version of it absolutely opposed to Capitalism, and that the occasion was one which must not be missed even though the odds against success were heavy; or in a spirit of uncritical idealism, sure that the ideology guaranteed success, that the gloomy appraisal was therefore wrong and the distinction between co-operative means and socialist ends a carping irrelevance. Alternatively, the attempted rescues may be supposed to have owed nothing to ideology, but as having been purely a misjudged essay in job-preservation. And finally, and the most likely, that a mixture and muddle of all these considerations – political opportunism or opportunity, naive expectation, and well-meant but ill-judged intention – entered in central government's motive. However that may have been, there is no doubting that at plant level and in two cases (the *Scottish Daily News* and KME) an ideological perception of workers' control precluded the effective delegation of executive authority to management. If there had been any chance ever of the rescues' succeeding, that perception would have destroyed it. As it was, it simply advanced the demise of two organisations already terminally ill. And it fortified the widely held misapprehension that an industrial co-operative was of its nature unmanageable. Presented as an essay in Co-operation, they were more nearly an experiment in anarchy.

So the lessons are these. To the extent that the rescues were ideologically inspired and the businesses ideologically managed, then at best the ideology distracted attention from the true nature of the problems to be faced, and at worst served as an excuse for purporting to resolve them by decisions which were patently perverse. It mistook excuses for reasons. And secondly: no one, neither Minister at the head of a Department of State, nor local trade union leader of a workforce at imminent risk of unemployment, nor anyone else, should for purposes which are essentially ideological invite or encourage men and women to invest their hopes and expectations in projects only incidentally and doubtfully concerned to realise them. And neither should they for those purposes make play with the values and ideals of Co-operation. For that would indeed be to misuse the men and women, the values and ideals. If however the attempted rescues were purely an ill-judged attempt to preserve employment, we need only resolve not to make the same mistake again. A donkey does not kick the same stone twice. And if the motive mixed ideology and good intentions, then we may draw both conclusions: that the first perverted decision making and the second, as always, was not good enough. And we may refer again to the CDA's first Annual Report. It concludes the statement of its policy on rescue cases with this observation: that industrial co-operatives need no less organisational care, managerial competence and commercial realism than do conventionally organised enterprises.[14]

Fortunately, there is much more to the recent story of the industrial co-operative sector in the United Kingdom than the depressing account of the *Scottish Daily News*, KME and Meriden. It is not a story of spectacular political initiatives, nor one of unvarying success; and for those who mistrust simplistic answers to complex problems, perhaps therefore the more persuasive. But it is a story of accelerating growth and solid achievement. In its Annual Report for the year ended 31 March 1985, the CDA recorded that whereas, in August 1980, 305 industrial co-operatives had been identified, the number was now about 1,200. The death rate among small industrial co-operatives was still significantly lower than among small businesses generally. Among the 911 co-operatives active in June 1984, 128 engaged in manufacture, 562 in the provision of services, and 221 in wholesale and retail trading.[15]

By themselves, these facts do not stand as a complete answer to the challenge: if the industrial co-operative form of organisation is more efficient than the conventional form, why is it that the first has not displaced the second but has remained until recently a negligible feature of the economy and, even now, can hardly be said to have become so far of more than marginal importance? That is, in effect, to argue that the market, left alone, has deter-mined that the application of resources to the creation of wealth is better undertaken by the conventional form. But, as the CDA has argued, the satisfactory operation of the market requires a suffi-cient general knowledge of the choices available to the buyer. People cannot be expected to buy the co-operative alternative if they do not know of it, or if they misunderstand it. The Agency continued:

That knowledge is not available. For, though there has been useful progress in bringing Co-operation to attention as a credible option, it remains in the United Kingdom, far more than in some western democracies, an exceptional way of undertaking an industrial venture. It has to succeed, not in fair competition, but in the face of ignorance and misunderstanding: ignorance, because whereas professional knowledge and informed advice on the incorporation and conduct of conventionally organised companies are generally available, whereas education and training relating to them are commonplace, this is not true for co-operatives; misunderstanding, because the industrial co-operative sector is still often regarded as characterised by the three well-known rescue cases ... and hence as supposing itself to be exempted from test by commercial criteria and the rigours of the market economy. In short, as an industrial form, Co-operation has to make progress in the face of a massive inertia, against the virtually automatic commitment to doing things the known way.[16]

That was written in mid-1981. Since then, the burden of scepticism imposed by the three cases had lightened; and there has been more progress. There are some 1,200 industrial co-operatives now. There were about 400 then. But it is still true that most members of the professions, accountancy, the law and banking, to whom people intending to start a business might turn for advice on how to constitute or finance it, will propose a company incorporated under the Companies Acts, or perhaps a partnership. The idea of a co-operative will simply not occur. Where it is suggested to professional advisers, the suggestion will commonly be met with the caution and dubiety they naturally bring to a proposal lying outside their experience or practice. This is not at all to say that there is among the professions an animus against the industrial co-operative as incorporated body for doing business. Rather, it is to emphasise that their members are in general uninformed about it; and that even where they are not uninformed, they are for the most part unversed in it. For the great majority, the industrial co-operative is just not the done thing. That is how inertia operates and will continue to operate until the industrial co-operative sector has acquired enough mass and momentum to overcome it. And that is a large part of the answer to the question why the industrial co-operative has not, despite its promise, been much more widely adopted here. If, when it was in a position to do so, Consumers' Co-operation had reverted to the Pioneers' intention to develop independent and self-governing factories and workshops, the story would of course have been different. But, as we have seen, regarding authentic Producers' Co-operation as 'the rival doctrine' the Consumers' Movement did little then to help, and so contributed to the inertia against which the industrial co-operative form has had to contend. In short, the marked growth recorded by the CDA in the industrial co-operative sector has occurred in spite of the special impediment to which it is subject. That recognised, its achievement is answer enough to the question why, given the attributes claimed for it, the place it has so far established for itself in the economy is still no more than marginal.

That much then for the state in recent years of the sector in the United Kingdom. Properly discounting the three notorious rescue cases, we can cite its performance along with the Spanish, American, French and Italian examples as evidence to bear out the theoretical expectation that industrial co-operatives should perform at least as well as conventionally organised businesses; and that the extra that Co-operation has to offer as an ingredient necessary to full success, a potential in motivation, is indeed available to help industrial co-operatives out-perform conventional businesses.

The citation does however leave unexamined one further consideration; that there might within the range of manufacturing and service industries be some which, for whatever reason, whether of the nature or of the size of the business, make them unsuited to the industrial co-operative form of organisation. We have already disqualified industries such as the natural monopolies comprised in the infrastructure of public services: the railways and the postal and telecommunications services are obvious examples. The disqualification stands on the proposition that, where there is no market so that the user cannot by taking his custom elsewhere, discipline the provider, it is wrong to adopt any form which creates a right and duty to use the monopoly so as to satisfy the interests of an exclusive group of owners, as against those of the users. And there would be no more reason for establishing the membership of a co-operative than the investors in a joint stock company as such a group. But besides that wholly justifiable disqualification, two others are sometimes advanced: first, that the form is only suitable

122

for small businesses; and secondly, that it is not suitable for capital intensive businesses.

What is large, what is small? With the reservation, following Bolton, 'that a small firm could not be adequately defined in terms of employment or assets, turnover or any other arbitrary single quantity, nor would the same definition be appropriate through the economy', we can adopt with him an upper limit of 200 employees for small manufacturing firms; and note that, in 1963, when he adopted that limit, the average number of people employed in such a firm was 25.[17] Now, the specific objection that, as a manifestation of democracy, large industrial co-operatives are impracticable has already been found fallacious because, mistakenly, it assumes direct democracy and overlooks delegation of authority to accountable management as a normal characteristic of indirect democracy. We are left with the unspecific practical objection, the objection that is as much to say that only seeing is believing. And it is answered by the fact that there are some pretty big ones to be seen: in the Mondragon group which, considered as a conglomerate, employs some 20,000, and within which each of 10 co-operatives employs over 400; and in the United Kingdom, where Scott Bader employs some 400. Those who, in face of those facts still insist that the industrial co-operative is suitable only for small businesses, contribute to the inertia with which its promotion must contend. They would however presumably agree that since the great majority of manufacturing firms are small businesses and employ only a small number of people, there would still be scope in manufacture for a considerable extension of the industrial co-operative sector. They might also accept that some, if only few, among the many would grow; and that when it had become operationally necessary or desirable a growing business could divide itself and in such a way that the divisions were suitable 'constituencies' for the democratic purposes of the co-operative. There is nothing here that organisational care and experience, some no doubt hard-won, could not attend to. In short, we may conclude that there is no need to suppose that industrial co-operatives in particular cannot become large, or even very large, and remain successful businesses and authentic co-operatives but that the need to accommodate within them satisfactory constituencies may well affect their structure. I make no attempt to define satisfactory; for apart from the truism that it must not be so large that the individual member of it is lost in the crowd and hence in his own view and in that of those who lead, instruct or represent him, reduced to an impersonal average, what makes a satisfactory constituency will vary from case to case.

There remains the proposition that the industrial co-operative is particularly unsuited to capital intensive business. It is, of course, easier to start a new business, whether co-operative or conventional in organisation, which does not demand the investment at the outset of large sums but can build up its capital assets from a modest beginning. However, the recent study by PA Management Consultants Ltd found that in themselves the analyses of the cases examined had not produced hard evidence to support the hypothesis that co-operatives would find it very difficult to compete in capital-intensive production:

> Although it is tempting to hold up Meriden as a co-operative which was at a substantial disadvantage compared with its Japanese competitors, it is difficult to argue that its inability to finance capital-intensive production methods were solely responsible for its problems.... It must certainly be true, however, that any Company competing in product markets requiring significant technological inputs to product development needs to be able to set aside funds for this purpose. Meriden was not able to do this.[18]

Not, though, because it was, or was meant to be, a co-operative. One further point of possible confusion: because venture capital from investors looking for capital gains is not available to co-operatives, they are likely to find it more difficult to raise the larger sums of money needed to start capital-intensive projects. Here again, though, this is not by itself to say that where a co-operative can get properly started in a capital intensive business, it would find it more difficult to compete than would a conventionally organised firm. In summary, the proposition is unsubstantiated. A co-operative may have more difficulty in raising a large initial sum of venture capital and hence be at a greater risk of starting with too big a burden of interest on loan capital; but, having got started on a sound financial footing, it would be under no special difficulty in doing as well as ordinary firms. So, to the conclusion drawn from European, American and British examples that the industrial co-operative is demonstrably a fully effective form of organisation, we can add that it is not necessarily subject to any special limitations of size or kind.

It remains for us to consider the macro-economic case for the widespread and general adoption of the industrial co-operative form. In short, it is that it offers a way of by-passing 'the awkward corner'. Nearly twenty years ago Professor Joan Robinson observed that the predictable consequences of the attainment of near-full employment must, if institutions and attitudes did not accommodate themselves to the new circumstances, be so far to strengthen the power of the trade unions as to prompt a vicious spiral of wages and prices; and that it would become chronic. This was the awkward corner that the British economy was seen, by the mid-1960s, to have reached. Predictable though it was, it had taken 'about fifteen years of experience for the point to really strike home'.[19] But not, even after another fifteen years or so, culminating in the winter of discontent and in the fall of Mr Callaghan's administration, experience enough to induce institutions and attitudes to accommodate themselves. The leopard did not change its spots, its instincts or its appetites. As we have seen, the trade union movement either could not or would not show the forbearance required, in the national interest, of a great and powerful institution; nor, for that matter that sense of enlightened self-interest which would have told it that the morality of forbearance was its own best policy. And that at a time when, as was realised, the stakes were particularly high, when the country's prospective self-sufficiency in oil would provide an incoming Government with a stronger economic base. Read what the movement's spokesman had to say at the time. In early January 1979, a leading article in the *Financial Times* observed:

> The undignified tussle over wages has been sourly described
> by one trade union leader as 'a return to the philosophy of the
> pig trough.' Present troubles are not so much an outbreak of
> anarchy, as a return to normality, with all its faults ... Groups
> who have normally felt able to assert a strong bargaining
> position did voluntarily restrain themselves for three years of
> evident national emergency. The decline in inflation and the
> recovery of real incomes was read, quite naturally, as a sign
> that the emergency was over and that they could safely assert
> their 'rights'.

Just so. Mr Scargill urged the miners to prepare for battle: they must stand firm over their wage claim. Writing in the *Yorkshire Miner* he declared: 'The day of the exploited miner must come to an end now. Our living standards are not going to be eroded any further.' Mr Moss Evans's union, the Transport and General Workers, had called the lorry drivers out on the strike that a reading of contemporary newspapers suggests was the event, seen as characteristic of the abuse by trade unions of their power, that most vividly exposed the vacuity at the heart of policy and so most damaged the Labour Government's prestige and prospects. The union settled, in the face of the Government's public criticisms, for a fifteen per cent pay rise. Remember: the Government had set for the growth of earnings a guideline of five per cent; and looked towards a long-term approach in which collective bargaining would be based each year on a broad agreement between Government, union and employers about the maximum level of earnings which would be compatible with keeping inflation under control in the following twelve months.[20] How sweetly reasonable; and, given the trade unions' function as an implicated part of Capitalism, how impossible. What the country got instead was the return to normality with all its faults; and a general election.

A general election is the occasion for the pronouncement of great expectations. Mr Evans did more than expect. He demanded. As reported in the *Financial Times*, he said that the trade union movement would be demanding and, he hoped, achieving the implementation of the proposals for industrial democracy; and that the next decade would offer the unions a better chance than any other to bring in the desired change. Did, one wonders, did Mr Evans really believe that, having observed the movement's dismissive rejection of the Labour Government's plea for moderation in the general interest, the electorate would return the Labour Party, the vehicle for trade unions' political aspirations, to office? Did he really believe that it would vote for the introduction of industrial democracy in the Bullock Report's dubious prescription for it? Did the trade union movement really fail to grasp that the two pre-conditions were: first, that its sense of responsibility must be seen not to be limited to a commitment in the shorter term to contribute to recovery from immediate crisis, but to extend, at the expense of short-run advantage, to the longer term commitment, to the revival of British industry and to its successful competition in world markets; and secondly, that a Labour Government would have to preside over the management of the country's affairs? Mr Evans seems to have recognised that the prospective decade of self-sufficiency in oil promised a unique opportunity for such a revival and hence the conditions in which a sympathetic government could satisfy the movement's ambition. But for the rest, either his judgment was wildly at fault or his declaration mere rhetoric. For it is not as though the trade unions had gone unwarned. In a television interview on 8 January 1979, Mrs Thatcher said that they had been 'put above the law'. True, this remark was later said to go beyond the consensus in her shadow Cabinet; and Mr Prior sought to moderate it. So, a possible explanation of the unions' behaviour is that they judged a Labour victory uncertain, if not unlikely; that they preferred to make hay while the setting Labour sun still shone; and that they felt secure against whatever weather a Conservative dawn might bring. But if that were the explanation, it would imply that the movement was only willing to act in the general interest when the Labour Party formed an assured Government, and having decided that its defeat was impending, abandoned any sense of responsibility save for the unions' immediate, sectional interests. And that surely would be too unprincipled. The better explanation remains that the policy pursued by the trade unions during the winter of discontent did indeed mark a return to normality.

It is not too pessimistic to see in these events and in the unfolding economic history since 1979 of the United Kingdom, a general corroboration of the prognosis contained in Mr Peter Jay's 1975 Wincott Memorial Lecture. There was, he argued, a fundamental contradiction in the country's political economic system; that, unless that contradiction were corrected, the system would within the foreseeable future collapse; and that the collapse would be catastrophic. In summary, his argument is this. The essential elements of the political economic system are: first, that the Government is accountable to an electorate composed of all adult men and women and so liable, if the electorate judges unsatisfactory the account rendered, to be dismissed from office and replaced by another administration; and secondly, that wages are determined by free collective bargaining in the labour market. Two conditions have to be sufficiently satisfied by a Government if its accounts of its performance is to satisfy the electorate. It must so conduct affairs so as to secure full or near-full employment and that the rate of inflation will be stable and low enough to be tolerable. If any Government fails to meet either of these conditions then it will be replaced by another expected to meet both. And if no Government could do so, then the necessary foundation to government by consent of the governed would crumble and, sooner or later, the country would have become unmanageable as an authentic democracy. And that would imply either anarchy or autocracy. Yet, as things stand, no Government can satisfy both conditions: near-full employment and a low, stable and hence tolerable rate of inflation. No Government can do so because – and here the argument extends Professor Joan Robinson's – as monopolistic suppliers of labour trade unions will charge more for it than would be necessary to exhaust the supply, and supply less of it than would be supplied if there were perfect competition. If, in response to the threat thus posed to full employment, the Government stimulates the economy, the effect will be to accelerate the rate of inflation.[21] The point here is not merely that full employment creates a scarcity of labour and so automatically puts up its price, not such that the unions negotiating with already willing and, indeed, anxious buyers would remain relatively passive as buyers bid against one another. Rather, it is that the active exploitation by trade unions of their monopoly requires a higher rate of unemployment than any acceptable notion of full employment will admit; and hence, that attempts by the Government to create employment by stimulating the economy will not only be inflationary but will fail. If repeated often enough, the stimulus will lead to uncontrollable inflation. Then, both of the conditions on which authentic democracy depends, near-full employment and a stable currency, will have gone.

This presentation is schematic; and it will, of course, be possible to show this or that particular instance as a departure from the proposition advanced by Mr Jay. But this is not to deny its validity in general. The corner is awkward, much more awkward than was recognised when, in 1965, Professor Robinson coined the phrase. It is not to be negotiated by the conclusion of social compacts or contracts between the Trade Union movement and the Government. For reliance upon a voluntary undertaking to observe wage-restraint implies a recognition of the movement's right to resume the full exercise of its powers. It implies that there will be a return to normality, to the philosophy of the pig-trough.

Nor is the corner to be negotiated by reductions in the privileges enjoyed by trade unions which leave largely untouched their function as monopolistic suppliers of labour. The Bank of England's quarterly bulletin (19 December 1985) declared that, unless there were an unexpected and big change in attitudes, excessive growth of pay would prevent the United Kingdom from taking advantage of an improving world economic environment. A leader in *The Times* commented:

> We have heard something of this from the Bank before. In fact, roughly once every three months. However, previous warnings have been accompanied by the hope that good sense will prevail, and the level of pay settlements tumble. This time, even with a forecast that the rate of inflation will halve to 3.5 per cent by the middle of next year (1986), the Bank cannot offer any hope that the growth in earnings will slow in response.
>
> In other countries, the Bank notes ruefully, prices and wages tend to follow one another quite closely. 'UK wage behaviour is out of line with other countries', the Bank says, citing three years of average earnings growth of 7 per cent to 8 per cent a year, despite high and rising unemployment. The blame attaches to both sides of industry. The Bank admonishes the blimpish directors of British companies, 75 per cent of whom, in a recent survey, said that the pay settlements they had conceded were not too high.[22]

So, twenty years after Professor Robinson's observation that institutions and attitudes would have to change, the Bank sees as necessary, but does not expect to get, a change of attitudes. Seven years after Mrs Thatcher's warning to the unions and nearly seven years of government under her direction during which time the trade unions' privileges have been reduced, the growth of wages continues strongly at a time of very high unemployment. It remains a prime cause of inflation. Because a decline in the value of the pound against that of other currencies would aggravate the condition, the Government is constrained to try to maintain that value; and to do so by the inducement of very high rates of interest. Overseas creditors, we might almost say, have never had it so good. In short, wage inflation operates not only to divert resources from investment in the country's manufacturing capacity but also to make borrowing and exporting more and more difficult. In face of all this, it is difficult to deny Mr Jay's proposition: that it is the active exploitation by the unions of their monopoly of the supply of labour which is at the heart of the country's chronic economic malaise. By 'blimpish' *The Times* presumably means that the directors it so describes show an obstinate and blinkered lack of concern for the national economic interest, and persist in pursuing what they judge to be the more immediate interests of the companies they direct. Blimpish or not, they can hardly be expected to do otherwise. In negotiating this or that pay increase, they must be supposed to be settling for the best terms they can get in all the circumstances of the negotiation. That the Government, and the Bank considered as an instrument of the Government's policy, will blame them is to be expected. For the alternative view can only be that the assumptions on which that policy is founded are unsound, if only in supposing that employers can and will deliver wage restraint. They cannot and will not in 1986 any more than the unions could or would in 1979. The essential mistake lies in supposing that there can be an accommodation of attitudes without an accommodation of institutions. The attitude is inherent, the natural characteristic of institution accountable, if it is a joint stock company, to its shareholders; and, if it is a trade union, to its members. Neither is accountable to the unemployed nor, in a free society, to the Government. By the middle of the last century, trade unionism had already declared that 'scarcity of labour was one of the fundamental principles', that the way to make labour dearer was to restrict the supply of it.[23] All the more strange that the advocates of a return to Victorian values should chide trade unions for refusing to forgo or minimise pay rises in order to create more jobs or to contain inflation. As an implicated part of Capitalism, the trade unions must be expected to play by Capitalism's rules; and government by admonition is, as always, ineffectual.

Yet, despite the critical debility of the national economy, it is no less difficult to deny Mr Jay's further proposition: that though it would almost certainly serve the general interest to prohibit trade unions, in a free society such a prohibition would be unthinkable. He comments:

> The perception of social advantage in general abstention from collective bargaining is too remote from the circumstances of the individual worker for him ever to support through the ballot box a general prohibition on trade unions, let alone to abstain privately from their immediate protection in a world where there is no reason to expect other workers to confer a reciprocal advantage on him by similar abstention.[24]

So, the cure will not be found in tinkering with the present institutions. The need is to change them; to find for the means of production and provision another structure such as will of its nature avoid the dilemma with which the present dispensation ultimately confronts the country: either unacceptably high and chronic unemployment or unacceptable and uncontrollable inflation, each so operating as eventually to destabilise society to the point where the purposes of liberal democracy can no longer be entertained, let alone fulfilled. The macro-economic case for the widespread and general adoption of the industrial co-operative form is that it is just such another structure; that the structural change lies in making labour the employer of capital rather than, as at present capital the employer of labour; that such a change would fuse the interests of ownership and labour, interests which so long as they remain separate must also remain ultimately opposed; and that, because relations among co-operatives and between producers and providers on the one hand, and consumers and users on the other would be determined by the operation of a free competitive market, the workers in each co-operative will be exposed to its imperative discipline. In a properly managed co-operative, the workers will know that their business cannot prosper and support excessive wage claims. They will know, too, that the ultimate responsibility for the success or failure of the business is theirs. That knowledge, extended through manufacturing and service industry would ensure generally that the wages suit was cut according to the profitability cloth; and would remove from the operation of the national economy the inflationary propensity of the trade unions' monopoly of the supply of labour and, with it, a main cause of the United Kingdom's industrial debility.

It is all too easy to blame the unions, to argue that they must know perfectly well that the effect of excessive wage settlements is inflationary but that they nevertheless still seek and get them. But that is to miss the point that it is not the unions' business to manage the firms with which they negotiate the settlements, nor to manage the national economy. That is not what unions, under the present dispensation, are about; and that is why, after three years of wage restraint under the compulsion of economic crisis, there was in 1979 what the *Financial Times* properly called a return to normality, with all its faults. To those who remain unpersuaded, there is this to say: that, in response to that recent survey, three-quarters of the directors questioned did after all consider that the pay settlements they had conceded were not too high. Why then should the trade unions have settled for something less? What the critics, of the trade unions and managements alike, are really saying is this: that they do not like normality with all its faults. They would like normality, but without its faults. And that they cannot have. What they have not yet recognised is that, if that is normality, if those are the institutions the system requires and that their normal behaviour, then the system is wrong and another is needed, a new economic model which will mark an advance from the sterile confrontation between Capitalism and Socialism, thesis and antithesis, to the synthesis providing a long overdue advance in democratic practice and a means of treating the chronic and disabling debility of the national economy.

To conclude: we have found that the industrial co-operative, in a market economy, is a fully effective form of organisation for production or provision in the United Kingdom as in other liberal democracies; that there is no necessary reason to attach to it limitations of size or kind; and that the general adoption of the form would import into the national economy such a structural change as is urgently needed to resolve the problem, ominous and intractable, of securing near-full employment without inflation at other than an insignificant rate. So, to the moral case for the general adoption of the form we may now add the practical imperative. We need the third way, urgently.

Most certainly, it would pay us to do the right thing.

— 9 —

Parties and Prospects: Left and Right

'The question is,' said Alice, 'whether you *can* make words mean so many different things.'

'The question is,' said Humpty Dumpty, 'which is to be master – that's all.'

Lewis Carroll: *Through the Looking Glass*

What are the expectations of changing the composition of the national economy so that the use of the industrial co-operative form of organisation became general, rather than exceptional? The first need is to persuade political opinion of the case for change, the second to show by what the possibilities might be. If there is no political will, there will certainly be no way. Over the last decade and more a broad current of opinion for the Industrial Co-operation has strengthened. The Co-operative Development Agency Act, 1978, brought before Parliament by a Labour administration maintained in office by Liberal support, was passed as agreed legislation. Since 1979, Conservative administrations have twice extended the life of the Agency: in 1981, by asking Parliament to make available to it a second tranche of money earmarked for but not guaranteed to it by the 1978 Act; and again in 1984, when the Co-operative Development Agency and Industrial Development Act provided funds for the Agency for a further six years. Of both Acts it might be said that, when they were passed they represented the most that could have been done and the least that ought to have been done. Of the second, critics would insist that the supply of £200,000 a year for the Agency represented a good bit less than least that ought to have been done. The Working Group on a Co-operative Development

Agency had put the figure at £300,000 a year at 1977 prices. Still, successive governments have thought it right that the Agency, which has made the promotion of the industrial co-operative sector its first priority, should continue. That the Agency's grant for 1987-8 is to be £440,000 is certainly cause for some satisfaction.

Often enough the right things are done for the wrong reasons. And perhaps it is more true of political than of any other activity that the occasion for applauding an interested party's performance is also one for most considering its motive. So, while we may take comfort in the fact that the promotion of the industrial co-operative sector commands general political support, we would do well to recognise that, as the lowest common denominator of opinion among contending political parties, that support is the minimal prescription for the active promotion of the sector; and that, given the marked tendency of the present constitutional dispensation greatly to over-represent the dogmatic extremes of political conviction, any policy much beyond the minimum would in all probability imperil the present general political support and so fail to survive the Government introducing it. This is no more than to say that, like any other reforming policy requiring, in order to mature, a period of time extending over more than one and, probably, several Parliaments, the greatly extended use of the industrial co-operative form of organisation is more likely to proceed and succeed under a constitution changed so as more sensitively to reflect the variety of opinions, expectations and aspirations and hence to require that accommodation among them which is the firmest foundation for enduring structural policies: to proceed, because such a constitution would reduce the represen-tation and influence of dogmatists, at either extreme, who are likely to declare the promotion of the industrial co-operative form of organisation, or the form itself, to be bad doctrine; to succeed, because such a constitution would much reduce the risk of abrupt reversals of policy as governments of sharply differing persuasions succeed one another, and so permit the persisting pursuit of long-term objectives.

That broad consideration noted, we need next to inspect the reasons brought by each of the parties to the minimal consensus for Co-operation. For the reasons are likely to differ; and the differences to show contrasting, even conflicting, perceptions of the role it might play upon the national economic stage. Some may so far misunderstand its essential character as to cast it in an unsuitable part or to expect of it an impossible performance: of that, the story of the *Scottish Daily News*, KMS and Meriden is reminder enough.

First, then, the Labour Party: first because it is commonly thought of as providing the organisation through which the Co-operative Movement seeks political expression. Commonly, but mistakenly: for it is better understood as acting in alliance with the Movement and with its political arm, the Co-operative Party. The latter has retained its own separate existence since 1917 when a resolution of the Co-operative Congress declared the intention to secure direct representation in Parliament. Cole's account of the relations between the two parties shows that although from the outset they worked in alliance in Parliament, elsewhere relations were uneasy; and that the uneasiness arose from difference on both policy and organisation.[1] He comments that, after the emergence in 1918 of Labour as a national party, it was impossible for the Co-operative Party to establish itself as a working-class party, if the two stood for essentially the same policy.[2] The comment assumes, of course, that the necessary purpose of the Co-operative Movement in politics is to provide a working-class party; and again follows from that view of history which sees it as programmed to displace Capitalism by Socialism, in its ideological version, through the agency of a working class organised to that end. And the qualification 'if the two had stood for essentially the same policy' has to do a lot of work. For what comes through Cole's account of the relationship is the Co-operative Party's continuing reservations about the centre piece of Socialist policy: the public ownership and control, national or municipal, of a wide range of essential industries. Of the state of the relationship in 1918, he records: 'Co-operators, however, were not prepared to commit themselves to "Socialism" as an objective, even if the immediate Socialist programme was acceptable to most of them.'[3] Then again, of the programme drawn up by the Co-operative Party in 1922: that it was 'remarkable for its silence on the broader questions of ownership and control'. Remarkable only if Socialism and Co-operation are, as nearly as makes no essential difference, synonymous. Cole interprets that silence as avoiding 'the Socialist issue'. Of the Co-operative Party's programme as it developed in the aftermath of the defeat, in 1931, of the Labour Party by the National Coalition, he says: 'the question of Co-operative versus State ownership was still, to some extent, evaded; but there was a decisive approach to the advocacy of State ownership of vital industries which could not be transferred to Co-operative control.'⁴ However, he goes on to record the Co-operative Party conference of 1933 as declaring the Party's objective to be the collective ownership of the means of production, distribution and exchange, while the Labour Party's thinking pointed to the establishment of public corporations 'in which Trade Unions would be able to claim a share in the control'. Let us take note of that claim. Prolonged discussions between the two parties were, Cole tells us, inconclusive.⁵

So much for the differences of policy. On his appraisal, they were no more than differences of degree. If that is so, then it is surprising that discussion over several years failed to resolve them. The other view is that, in the end, the differences were fundamental; that though Co-operation, and Socialism in its ideological version, might very well have agreed in seeing much wrong with Capitalism, they differed then – and so may continue to differ now – on the remedy to be sought. The Co-operative Commonwealth is not an array of State or municipal businesses, the limbs of a corporate state articulated by an omnipotent central planning agency. Nor is state or municipal ownership properly seen as collective ownership in the sense in which it was declared in 1933 by the Co-operative Party Conference to be the Party's objective. The phrase is collective ownership and not, as in Clause IV of the Labour Party's Constitution, common ownership. One thing is clear: the Consumer Movement was founded on individual ownership, by members of shares in their retail societies, by societies of shares in the movement's wholesale and insurance undertakings.

Seen by Cole as primary and more significant than that about policy, the dispute between the two Parties about organisation arose from 'what can only be regarded as an attempt by the Labour Party Executive to force the Co-operative Party into a position which would have destroyed its independence and meant to all intents and purposes the acceptance of a subordinate position inside the Labour Party's electoral machine'.⁶ That is as if to say that, though each was reading from the same piece of music, the Co-operative Party was unwilling to play second fiddle to the Labour Party's first. Pride of place is a common enough human failing; but it strains belief to suppose that procedural difficulties would have prevailed over a co-incidence of objectives had it in reality been so nearly complete as to make Co-operation a socialist rose, but by another name. Writing in 1944, Cole concluded that there could not be room for two separate parties, Labour and Co-operative, representing largely the same views and very largely the same body of political thought. And then, prophetically: 'if a two-party, or even a three-party, system holds, Co-operators must in practice align themselves with the Labour Party so as to form a virtually single political force ... unless the Labour Party itself breaks apart, or gives place to some new comprehensive organisation of the political Left.'[7] He seeks to prove his point by observing that Co-operative Members of Parliament had from first to last found it easy to work inside the Parliamentary Labour Party and in unity with the Labour Party outside Parliament. In 1986, we have the benefit of hindsight comprehending the picture of the · Labour Party in a prolonged crisis of identity, a crisis which included the secession of a number of its Members of Parliament to establish in 1981 a new party of reform, the Social Democratic Party. Of that number, four were members of the Co-operative Party. For them, alignment with the Labour Party was not in practice compelling and had become intolerable. In that secession we may see further evidence, if evidence is needed, that the Webbs' prescription for Socialism is ultimately incompatible with Co-operation; and that, for all Aneurin Bevan's advocacy in 1952 of the mixed economy,[8] Socialism had not by the late 1970s and early 1980s so far dissociated itself from that prescription as to make compatibility possible.

But has it now? There are two main considerations. The first is what perception trade unionism as the Labour Party's *alter ego* and its paymaster, is to have of its own purpose in future; and whether that purpose would be consistent with the development, as a strategic objective, of Industrial Co-operation. The second is whether the Labour Party is willing and able, in a revised description of Socialism, to renounce the common ownership of the means of production and provision as an essential objective, and so to remove the historic impediment to the assimilation to itself of the positive objectives of Co-operation. In the past, the two considerations would not have been distinguished; and Clause IV of the Labour Party's Constitution would have been quoted as the authoritative comment on both. Thus Clause IV:

to secure for workers by hand and by brain the full fruits of

their industry and the most equitable distribution thereof that
may be possible upon a basis of the common ownership of the
means of production and exchange and the best obtainable
system of administration and control.

Ownership, in the particular form of common ownership, is
declared to be the basis upon which is to be founded a fair system
of distributing among the workers the wealth they have created.
For the trade unions this has meant, certainly until quite recently
and to quote Cole, the establishment of public corporations 'in
which Trade Unions would be able to claim a share in the control'.
For the Labour Party, certainly for its left wing, Clause IV is the
keystone of the socialist arch. No Clause IV, no Socialism.

So, since the case for the adoption of the industrial co-operative
form of organisation is primarily that it provides for industrial
democracy, the test of the trade union movement's intention is
this: does it continue to see it as something exclusively different, as
the participation by trade unions in the management and direction
of conventionally organised businesses whether privately or
publicly owned, the unions nevertheless retaining as their essential
function an unqualified right to engage in joint collective
bargaining with a view to selling their members' labour at the
highest price they can get for it? If so, then the trade unions will
expect a Labour Government to pursue policies the general effect
of which would be to make the market for labour more a seller's
and less a buyer's; and, more particularly, that it would put into
effect the recommendations of the Bullock Report, or something
like them. And they would have ruled out the development, as a
strategic objective, of the industrial co-operative sector. This is
simply to recognise that the industrial co-operative removes a large
part of their present *raison d'être*; and that unless the trade unions
are ready to take a new view of their purpose, to look beyond the
limitation of their present function as purveyors of labour to
capital and towards a reconciling synthesis of the different and
ultimately opposed objectives of the two sides of industry, their
response is bound to be conservative and reactionary. They will
remain as they have been described by Professor Eccles: 'a major
impediment to worker co-operatives in the British manufacturing
industry.' For, in their view, worker co-operatives would continue
to 'pose a major threat to the health of existing occupational trade
unions' so that 'far from being the natural institution to help

workers' self management in the enterprise [employing them], trade unions are operationally opposed to the development of worker co-operatives as a significant force in manufacturing industry'. In support of that judgment, Eccles quotes from *Worker Co-operatives*, a Labour Party publication, to show that both the Party and the trade union movement had tended to emphasise the concepts of public ownership and collective bargaining rather than Co-operation. For the trade unions' operational opposition to industrial co-operatives, he identifies two main reasons: first, that since the workers, as members of the co-operative, are themselves the ultimate custodians of its policies including those on pay and conditions of employment, there is no place for a union to represent them against themselves. No 'them and us', no union. The second is this: that the natural disposition for the members of an industrial co-operative will be to attach greater importance to their common and immediate interest in the success of the business, rather than to their demarcated, sectional interest in this or that union's general concern with this or that occupation: 'its office workers, electricians, lorry drivers, draughtsmen and production workers [have] far more common cause with each other than with, say, electricians working hundreds of miles away in another company in another industry.' In effect, Eccles argues, the industrial co-operative presents in a specially sharp form a threat to the 'basis of existence for multi-company, multi-industry general unions as well as a distinct challenge to the primacy of craft and specialist unions'.[9] Redundancy and irrelevance; if indeed that is, or is seen to be the implicit sentence passed on trade unions by Industrial Co-operation, then we cannot expect them to offer it unstinting support. On the contrary, the trade unions' attitude to Industrial Co-operation will, on such an appraisal, at best be ambiguous and at worst dismissive; and that attitude is likely to be reflected by the Labour Party.

The other possibility is that the trade unions will be ready to take a new view of society, and of their own place in it; to see their present selves as others increasingly see them – as impediments to socially beneficial change rather than as agents of it. Such an agency is available to them if they will take a new and better view of it, one which prefers Industrial Co-operation, as an authentic description of industrial democracy to the Bullock Report's misapprehension which, in seeking to fortify the unions' place in the *status quo*, would fortify the *status quo*. Such an agency would involve the trade unions generally as the active protagonists of the rapid development of the industrial co-operative sector. It would seek to make unions especially the advisers and consultants to industrial co-operatives, existing or prospective. It would become the unions' concern to ensure that proposals to establish co-operatives, whether as new starts or conversions from conventionally organised enterprises, were critically appraised; that the need for effective management was properly understood and provided for; that there is available to Industrial Co-operation a source of finance where existing sources are not. Such a concern would never invite men and women to invest their hopes, and expectations, and money into projects which could not be reasonably sure enough of commercial success soon enough. It would not delude them into supposing that Co-operation was Cockaigne, a guarantee that each and every job would be preserved. It would be hard-headed and realistic. All it could guarantee them would be an opportunity to make their working lives their own business, their own business part of their lives. That would be its ethic, its moral force: the restoration to each man and woman of his or her full rights in the disposal of his or her working life in a community of interest. In contradiction of the Webbs' prescription for trade unionism, it would make a reality of the change in their definition of a trade union from its first version to the second: from the maintenance or improvement of the wage-earners' conditions of employment, to the maintenance or improvement of their working lives.[10] But where the Webbs admitted the change as a concession to historical accuracy, remodelled trade unionism would understand it as a denial that the aggregation of the working lives of men and women into a thing, a commodity called labour, put at the disposal of this or that trade union, could by itself be anything like a sufficient cause for the movement. It would not be content to remain an implicated part of Capitalism.

But it would have had to recognise that the alternative was not Socialism so long as an essential part of its definition is comprehensive State ownership of the means of production. If that is what Clause IV of the Labour Party's Constitution means, then it remains a formidabe obstacle to the adoption by the movement of a new and progressive purpose.

Meanwhile, the signals from the trade union movement itself are confused and confusing. Its expressed sympathies for workers' co-operatives are helpful, but its behaviour is equivocal. There are some shining exceptions; and conspicuous among them is the initiative taken, at the prompting of Mr George Wright, by Wales TUC. A study it commissioned in 1980 concluded that:

> the trade union movement in Wales must back workers co-ops; that a resource centre to provide the necessary professional and managerial skills to would-be and new start co-ops should be established; and that an independent investment fund dedicated to the provision of risk capital for new co-ops be founded to operate in parallel with the resource centre.

And the annual conferences in 1982 and 1983 formally endorsed the establishment of a resource centre. Significantly, the study drew upon an examination of the banking and professional services provided by the Caja Laboral Popular in Mondragon and an assessment of the trade unions' involvement in the co-operative sector of the Italian economy.[11] More significantly, the fact that the initiative by Wales TUC implied a qualitative change in the trade unions' role was, at least, touched upon. To quote George Wright:

> We are seeing that workers can create their own jobs, that they do want to share decisions and ultimately that they are ready to take responsibility for their own workplaces. This may pose something of a challenge to traditional trade union thinking but it is not one we should avoid.[12]

A leaflet, *Wales Co-operative*, prepared for distribution at the annual conference in 1984 of Wales TUC, considered the challenge more particularly:

> Why do workers need a trade union if they have control and ownership? Theoretically, the worker co-op should remove the conflict between those who own capital – the employers – and those who sell labour – the employees.

Again:

> Why should trade unionists help to set up co-ops? Most trade unions constitutions express similar sentiments to that of the Labour Party which sets out to achieve common ownership of the means of production, distributions and exchange. Usually this has been interpreted to mean supporting nationalised industry and the public sector.

The answers given were, to the first, that trade union officials would be needed to resolve conflicts between members of an industrial co-operative and to ensure minimum standards of health and safety; and to the second, in effect, that state or municipal ownership on the one hand, and industrial co-operatives on the other, were alternative means to the same end. We may question whether the answers are sufficient. And we will not find them so if we accept the conclusion, reached earlier, that the differences between trade unionism's traditional objectives and those of the Co-operative Movement are fundamental.

What the leaflet might have argued is that trade unionism needs a new view of society and of the part that the unions should play in realising it; a part which, seen at the outset as complementary to its traditional but limited function, must be expected increasingly to displace it. The argument might have continued, and from what better place than Wales, by losing 'patience with those socialists, so-called, who in practice would socialise nothing, while in theory they threaten the whole of private property'.[13] It might have declared for authentic industrial democracy. It might have. But it did not; and given the *Realpolitik* of the trade union movement, it is hard to see how it could have done. Nevertheless, Wales TUC declared the promotion of the industrial co-operative sector a strategic objective, to be pursued for its own sake and not, as had almost invariably been the case since the advent after 1850 of the new model unions, a tactical incident to what had become their essential and ultimately exclusive traditional business.

For the *Realpolitik* and a definitive pronouncement of the TUC'S perception of its role in the future, we must turn to *A New Partnership, A New Britain*, published in August 1985 by the TUC and the Labour Party jointly. This document describes the framework of the economic, industrial and social policy to be pursued by a Labour Government. Those who look in it for a new view of society such as would comprehend the widespread and general development of the industrial co-operative sector as an urgently necessary change to the national economy will find it disappointing. Its recognition that the need is 'not just to reduce unemployment but also to improve British long-term industrial performance', its statement of broad intention to 'develop a high investment, high productivity, high wage economy' - presumably through the agency of a sufficiently profitable manufacturing base - all this is laudable as any self-evident good. Its declaration that the intention can be achieved 'if we work together and draw upon all our resources, especially the talent and enthusiasm of working people themselves' is unexceptionable as an appreciation of the obvious. There is, of course, still much virtue in 'if'. But, all the same, the statement acknowledges that the sustained commitment of the workforce is an essential ingredient, that considerations of morale are three-quarters of the game. It is when the means to achieving good intentions are propounded that the questions arise. The document declares:

> A key feature will be to provide workers with positive rights to information, consultation and representation in company decisions. The aim will be not to impose any particular model or method, but to widen the collective bargaining agenda beyond wages to crucial investment decisions. We see new rights for workers as a catalyst for the extension of democratic involvement and accountability not just within the enterprise but also beyond it in sector and national planning.

The document goes on to outline an industrial policy structured upon a framework of central planning. The business plans of public and private sector industries would be discussed and negotiated with Government and trade unions. Not just discussed: discussed and negotiated. But one possible feature of economic planning is forsworn: 'Statutory norms and government-imposed wage restraint offer no solution.'[14]

The general appraisal of *A New Partnership, A New Britain* focused on two points. The first was the assumption that it would be possible to reach at national level a meaningful agreement among Government, employers and trade unions on the allocation of resources to income, and on its distribution among the various classes of claimant: investors, savers, wage-earners and so on. That assumption, necessary if the two prime objectives, growth and the rapid reduction of unemployment were to be assured, was seen to be insecure. The second was extreme doubt whether, even if a meaningful agreement could be reached it would be made to stick. For the sole reason for adhering to it would be that, as all would know, the achievement of those prime objectives required adherence: that is as much as to say that fear of the shame and blame which should and perhaps would attach to any on the one side of industry who asked for more than was consistent with the agreement, or on the other who conceded or offered it, would be deterrent enough. It assumes a compelling sense of moral obligation: and it is bound to do so because neither side is an organic whole and so always and everywhere obedient to orders from headquarters. Obedience of that kind is available to the government of the authoritarian state where, because disobedience brings punishment, its orders are enforceable; or to the government of the deferential state where, because shame is unendurable, they are unquestionable. The United Kingdom of Great Britain and Northern Ireland is neither authoritarian nor deferential. And, more particularly, the conduct here of industrial relations is an unintegrated medley of negotiations between employers and trade unions. The only certainty in the TUC–Labour Party document is that free collective bargaining rules.

How does that appraisal bear upon the question whether the TUC, and hence, the Labour Party, would in the event so act as to promote the general adoption of the industrial co-operative form of organisation as to bring about structural change in the national economy? It offers no expectation that the political party which, since 1918, has stood for reform will do anything of the sort. For the insistence on the sanctity of free collective bargaining is, in effect, an insistence on the structural *status quo*. And its idea of industrial democracy remains the chimera pursued in the majority report of the Bullock Committee. The workers' further 'positive rights' would not be only and uncontentiously to information and consultation, but also and imprecisely to 'representation in company decisions'. Imprecisely: meant to mean either that employees who are members of trade unions are to have through them the right to make representations to management with a view to influencing prospective decisions, or that trade union members appointed in that capacity and as of right to the directing boards of privately owned companies would participate in those decisions. Of the two irreconcilable meanings we may, so far, choose whichever we like. But there is more. The intention is 'to widen the collective bargaining agenda beyond wages to crucial investment decisions'. Plain words, please: that blurred presentation can only mean that trade unions continue to claim a right, which a Labour Government would recognise, to make conditional upon the unions' agreement decisions as to how assets owned by others are to be used. And still more: where the Bullock Committee's terms of reference avoided the constitutional impropriety that the inclusion within their scope of nationalised or other publicly owned industries would have imported, *A New Partnership, A New Britain* is not so deterred: 'Public enterprise must be made more accountable to its workers and more responsible to the community it serves.' More accountable to the one, more responsible to the other: so even though the statement is properly read as meaning that those charged by whatever appropriate authority with the conduct of a publicly owned industry are to be made accountable to each of two differing constituencies, the workers in the industry and the population served by the industry, yet some distinction is presumably intended. We may infer that accountable to the workers means answerable to them as ultimate custodians, whether in whole or in part, of the affairs of the industry; but that responsible to the community means something less, means – in the looser usage of the word – showing a decent concern for the dependent community. The obligations to the workers would be mandatory; that to the community, moral. Yet perhaps the inference is premature. 'We intend', the document declares, 'to come back to this issue and come forward with proposals next year.' Even so, two related observations can be made at once. The first is that it is as true now as it was in the days of the Rochdale pioneers that the interests of producers and providers are opposed to those of consumers and users in this essential: that those who produce or provide will want to sell goods or services at the highest price, those who consume and use to buy them at the cheapest. If the industry is a monopoly, the effect of implicating the trade unions in the management of it must be to create a conspiracy against the consumers' or users' interests; that is to say, against the general interest. The second observation is that it is as true now as when the terms of reference of the Bullock Committee were devised that the right to decide whether and how assets shall be used inheres in the ownership of them; and that, unless the trade union movement is to be established as the co-equal of Parliament, accountability for the management of an industry owned by the State is to Parliament and only to Parliament.

In the end, *A New Britain, A New Partnership* is not new at all. It is old, at least as old as the report of the majority of the Bullock Committee, and as misconceived. It recognises the fundamental importance of the moral factor to the regeneration of industrial Britain, and the consequent need to restore to workpeople their alienated rights in the disposal of their working lives, but supposes that the representation of trade unions on the directing boards of privately or publicly owned businesses will satisfy that need. It continues to present the change as merely one of degree, as an 'extension of democratic involvement', when in fact it asserts a new and unsustainable principle: that trade unions have the right to determine how the property of others is to be used, to have title without ownership. If it is a new view of anything, it is a new view of Clause IV; for, in effect, it no longer sees common ownership of the means of production and exchange as the necessary basis upon which to secure for workers by hand and brain the full fruits of their industry and the most equitable distribution thereof that may be possible. Because trade unions are to assume in the cause of 'democratic involvement' a partial but presumably sufficient control of industry, it is no longer necessary to nationalise or municipalise it as a preliminary to controlling it.

To conclude: as the instrument of the trade unions' political aspirations, the Labour Party sees the development of the industrial co-operative sector neither as the primary, let alone the only, means to authentic industrial democracy, nor therefore as the principal means of engaging the aspirations of working men and women in a sustainable project for the regeneration of British industry. Those who consider that that regeneration requires the extension of the powers of unreformed trade unions so as to enable them to participate or intervene positively in the management of industry where now they may only influence or check it, will find *A New Partnership, A New Britain* a substantial pronouncement. They will do so either because they believe with those who signed the majority report of the Bullock Committee that such an extension implies industrial democracy as the inspirational and essential factor; or because, more simply, they believe that the implication of trade unions in management will make for industrial efficiency, whether or not it makes for industrial democracy. Those who do not equate industrial democracy to trade union authority and so, if only for that reason, would not confer upon unreformed trade unions additional power such as the document envisages, will see in it not the substance but only the shape of policy, an inflated simulacrum, a blown-up look-alike whose limp anatomy is found on inspection not to be of bone, sinew and muscle, but of hot, stale air.

The trade union movement is not, however, the only constituent of the Labour Party; and we need to consider what else it has had in recent years to say about the promotion of industrial co-operatives. Under the heading 'Jobs and Prosperity', its manifesto for the general election of 1979 stated that a Labour Government would 'develop the work and funding of the Co-operative Development Agency in expanding co-operative enterprise'. There are other incidental references: under the heading 'Rural Areas', the Party undertook to ensure that the Agency would 'play an active role in rural job creation'; and under 'Building and Our Future' to 'encourage the development of building workers' co-operatives'. Mr Callaghan's own perception of the merit of industrial co-operatives had focused upon its organic assimilation of the employer-employee antithesis. In an address to the Co-operative movement in October 1977 he referred particularly to an observation in the recently published Report of the Working Group on a Co-operative Development Agency, an observation to the effect that successfully organised and conducted industrial co-operatives might offer a solution to a problem seen by many as a major cause of the country's economic difficulties: the problem of engaging all those who work in an enterprise in the pursuit of ends which should be complementary but were too often opposed. And again, in April 1983, at the launch in Cardiff of the Wales Co-operative Centre, he observed that industrial co-operatives abolished the division between 'them and us'. For that reason he regarded them as one of the highest forms of work organisation.[15] That perception might be held to recognise a strategic need for Industrial Co-operation and to proceed from an inspection of factors contributing to an urgent and major practical problem, rather than from an ideological premise. It does not depend upon Clause IV, though it could on an unexacting reading of 'common ownership' be said to be consistent with it. But the manifesto[16] cannot be said to give a strategic place to the promotion of the industrial co-operative sector as a means of a synthesising structural change to the national economy. Instead, it founded its expectations on the central idea of the management of the economy by reference to an agreement among Government, employers and unions 'on how to expand output, incomes and living standards'. This it contrasts with a Conservative free-for-all in pay and prices. Elsewhere, the manifesto declared: 'Industrial Democracy – giving working men and women a voice in decisions which affect their jobs – is an idea whose time has come.' Here, industrial democracy is presumably defined in Bullock's version of it. In sum, the manifesto did not envisage structural change, but the implication of the trade unions in the management of the economy in the expectation that, the movement being so implicated, its constituent unions would not materially exploit their monopoly of labour against the general interest in sustainable industrial growth and stable prices; and that the admission of industrial democracy defined as a qualitative extension of the powers of the trade unions would guarantee their overriding concern for that interest. As we have seen, the electorate thought otherwise in 1979. And as we have also seen, *A New Partnership, A New Britain* returns to the same prospectus. So hope continues to triumph over experience.

Next among the pronouncements by the Labour Party on industrial co-operatives was a discussion document. Its contents were therefore provisional. Published in 1980, it is interesting not only for its content but also for the contention it aroused between the Party and the Co-operative Party. The main cause of contention was a proposal that workers should be given a conditional statutory right to take over the plant they work in, and run it as an industrial co-operative. In principle, the right would have attached to any plant whatsoever, not only to those threatened with closure; and could have been acted upon whether the owners of the plant agreed or not. Chaired by Mr Leslie Huckfield, the working party which prepared the discussion document numbered among its members Mr Peter Clarke, representing the Co-operative Party. He dissented. His memorandum of dissent was not published. The Co-operative Party was critical of the principle of a general right of conversion as being, in itself, highly controversial. It involved an open-ended commitment on public funds, invited commercial disaster, and was likely to bring the Co-operative Movement into disrepute. Successful co-operatives were started by co-operators: that is to say, by the uninduced volition of men and women who were ready to assume the responsibilities of membership along with the rights. In short, the proposals in the Huckfield working party's document were unrealistic and misunderstood the essential character of Co-operation.

For its part, the Co-operative Development Agency told the Labour Party that, because the principle of establishing a right of workers in an enterprise to convert it to a co-operative was bound to be a matter of great political controversy, as a public authority

148

the Agency would not express any views upon it, but would confine public statements to its view of the practical effect the conversion scheme would have on the development and growth of a viable industrial co-operative sector. The Agency's considered view was that it would be damaging. In an interesting comment on detail, the Agency challenged the document's dismissal, on the ground that it provided for individual rather than collective ownership, of the share capital invested, of the Mondragon model. Collective ownership in workers' co-operatives was, throughout the world, the exception rather than the rule: and if individual ownership were not allowed, the effect would be to limit severely the possibilities for extending the industrial co-operative sector in the United Kingdom; to disqualify well-established workers' co-operatives, some of many years' standing; and to add a restriction not required by the statement of co-operative principles agreed by the International Co-operative Alliance. At the Co-operative Party Conference held at Weston-super-Mare, Easter 1981, the executive recommended rejection of the central proposal, the right to convert. And reject it the Conference did.

In Parliament, the Party's dissent was registered by Mr Ted Graham; and the occasion for it was the debate in the House of Commons on the Order making available to the Co-operative Development Agency the second tranche of money, the date 22 July 1981. Mr Huckfield had led for the Opposition. He was, said Mr Graham, aware of the strong reservations the established Co-operative Movement and Co-operative Party had about the discussion document's proposals. He and the Co-operative Group of Members of Parliament would have a contribution to make which 'might not be different from that of the established Co-operative Movement in the past'.[17] The reference to the Movement as established distinguished it from the Industrial Common Ownership Movement. Incorporated in 1975 after operating for nearly twenty years on a voluntary basis, by contrast with the Co-operative Union representing primarily the Con-sumer Movement, ICOM is a relatively recent body. Though it recognises that common ownership is not a necessary but an optional characteristic of Industrial Co-operation, ICOM's concern is to promote only the common ownership form. This it associates with the advocacy by the Labour Movement of the common ownership of the means of production, but dissociates from the Fabian insistence on State ownership. While many among ICOM's members took a live-and-let-live view of co-operatives in which members held personal property rights, some did not. So, though it cannot be said of ICOM that its general preference would have been that the CDA, insistent for its own part that both options must be presented to prospective co-operators to choose from, should be dissolved, some among ICOM's members would have found it a matter for satisfaction if the Conservative Government had decided to dissolve the Agency. None of this is to detract from ICOM's considerable contribution to the revival of Industrial Co-operation. But it goes far to explain why relations between the established Movement and ICOM were not always co-operative.

If the established Co-operative Movement dissented from the proposals contained in the Labour Party's discussion document, the trade unions were unenthusiastic. Industrial co-operatives, of whatever kind, did not enter much if at all into the unions' scheme of things. A sub-committee of the TUC-Labour Party liaison committee had been established under the title *Planning and Industrial Democracy*. It was reported at the time that the most senior members of the TUC and the Party were meeting monthly: that their attention was concentrated on what was, in effect, the preparation of a new social contract between the TUC and a hypothetical Labour Government; and that co-operatives were not featuring in the sub-committee's deliberations. The report continued: 'As minutes of the committee's first meeting in January [1981] show, their work programme is heavily focused on the reform of "existing institutions and this does not fit in well with the long-term goal of establishing full workers' self-management."'[18] That repeats, in effect, that in the TUC's perception of it, industrial democracy remained the Bullock Committee's prescription, and was not the promotion of the industrial co-operative sector; and, in the repetition, it affirms indeed that the major impediment to worker co-operatives is the trade union movement. In short, while the Co-operative Movement objected to the proposals contained in the Labour Party's discussion document because they were not Co-operative, the TUC did not care for them because it supposed they were.

Published as a statement by the Labour Party's National Executive Committee to the 1981 Conference, *A Strategy for Workers' Co-operatives* reflects the ambivalent internal response to the discussion document from which it derived. As evidence of a major revival of interest in industrial co-operatives, it recalls the financial aid given by the last Labour Government to the *Scottish Daily News*, KME and Meriden. But it overlooks the fact that the three were regarded generally in the Co-operative Movement as misconceived and damaging. Admission of misconception and damage by one's own side is not of course the stuff of political parties' publications. Still, some recognition that at the least there were lessons to be learned would have helped to carry conviction that, next time, something better than disastrous good intentions would be on offer. More significantly the pamphlet asks whether workers' co-operatives are truly socialist; and, after accepting that some people would say not, concludes:

> We believe, however, that co-operatives offer a positive and socialist sway forward. In the first place, the practice of co-operation should give workers the invaluable opportunity of developing the skills necessary to run the enterprise in which they work. Second, the co-operatives we wish to encourage would be an integral part of the trade union and labour movement. Third, co-operation is generally agreed to be a desirable form of 'common ownership' as called for in Clause IV of the Labour Party Constitution, not as a substitute for traditional public ownership but as an additional socialist means to the same socialist end.[19]

Of these three attributes, the first does not relate only to Socialism; and we need not dwell on it. But the second and third pose awkward questions. The second seems to assert that there are different kinds of industrial co-operatives. There are those which are integrants of a larger whole: that is, of the trade union and labour movement; and there are those which are not. The first are to be preferred, the second not. And the first, as part of the larger organic whole, must be supposed to conform in the end to its will and intention. What this exposes is the continuing failure by the Labour Party and the trade unions, a failure identified though not satisfactorily explained by Cole, to understand – or if they understand, to accept – that a co-operative exists for its own reasons and not as an incidental expression of their policies; that co-operatives are of their own kind, and not to be categorised as either socialist and good, or non-socialist and bad. More specifically, if the essential case for industrial co-operatives is the realisation of industrial democracy, then so long as the trade unions persist in their version of it, the objectives of Industrial

Co-operation and that of the trade unions remain incompatible. The third attribute, common ownership, is no less awkward. Common ownership is generally understood to mean, of a co-operative, that its members do not own personal stakes in the business, and that the only title to the property is the corporate one. As in Robert Owen's America co-operative community, *New Harmony*, none owns anything, all own everything. But as in most co-operatives of all kinds, individual ownership is the rule, then unless for the purposes of Clause IV common ownership includes individual ownership, most co-operatives could not be regarded as 'an integral part of the ... labour movement', but as 'a substitute for traditional public ownership' and hence as unacceptable. This is, of course, an old tale. It retells Cole's perception of Socialism, one which cannot accommodate authentic Industrial, or as he has it, Producer Co-operation.[20] It might be Capitalism with a human face. 'Co-operative enterprise', declares the NEC's statement to the 1981 conference, 'plays a major role in many countries, though it is not always founded on socialist principles.' And though the Mondragon co-operatives are no longer dismissed out of hand, reservations about them remain: 'some features of these co-operatives have been criticised.' Yet the statement also admits, as one of the reasons why the progress in Britain of Industrial Co-operation has been limited, the fact that the backing of the Labour and trade union movements has been 'less than wholehearted'.

If anything is clear, it is this: that, on the central question whether individual ownership of shares in co-operatives is proper Socialism, the writers of the statement are unclear. What we can conclude is that, if on a proper understanding of Clause IV, individual ownership is not proper Socialism, then its positive objectives are materially different from those of Co-operation which admits it. One begins to see more clearly why, in the years of discussion before the war, the two parties were unable to resolve their differences.

The difficulty is very real. The Co-operative Development Agency found it necessary to pronounce upon the fact that some local co-operative development groups in effect defined Co-operation as exclusively common-ownership. Discussing its working relationship with local co-operative development groups, the CDA commented in 1984:

> Equally diverse are the political colour, the motivation and the composition of local CDAs. Inevitably, some disagree with our non-ideological stance or with our attitude, in principle, non-discriminatory, towards the alternatives of collective or individual ownerships in co-operatives. We see co-operation as a non-exclusive and broad church.[21]

And earlier, the Agency stated that its work did not bring it into ideological conflict with any co-operative or support body which accepted as the characterestics of a bona fide co-operative those set out in paragraph 6 of the Registrar of Friendly Societies' *Guide to the Law relating to Industrial and Provident Societies*.[22] Plainly, the ideological objection which, on an exact reading of the Labour Party's constitution, some find in individual ownership of the means of production and exchange, continues to prevent them from seeing Co-operation, which allows it, as Socialism. And if common-ownership means common-ownership, they are right. Still, they could understand the reference in *A Strategy for Workers' Co-operatives* as one to co-operatives of the kind the Party wished to encourage, those which would be 'an integral part of the ... labour movement', as meaning those which insisted on common ownership. Others could read in the document's recognition that the Labour Party had not, in the past, given Industrial Co-operation full support, the expectation that such support would in future be forthcoming; and that, in consequence, a more generous interpretation of Clause IV would allow individual ownership in industrial co-operatives. We may conclude that the Labour Party's philosophy on Industrial Co-operation remains uncertain and equivocal.

Nor, if we choose to ignore it and to ask instead what the Party proposes to do, will we find much comfort. For, in face of the objections voiced by the Co-operative Party and the CDA to the right to convert proposed in the discussion document, the NEC's statement, *A Strategy for Workers' Co-operatives*, retained the proposal with little change of substance, thus:

> if workers in a private firm wish to convert their enterprise into a workers' co-operative, they should have the legislative right, subject to the consent of government, to acquire the assets of the firm and, if necessary, to receive some financial assistance for the purchase.

The one significant concession it made to the Co-operative Party's criticism of the discussion document was to postulate expenditure of 'say, initially, £100 million a year for this purpose'. But it did not defer to the Party's view that the creation of a general and publicly subsidised right to convert privately owned enterprises into industrial co-operatives was impracticable, and misconceived the essential motivation of Co-operation.

To sum up, despite the alliance with the Co-operative Party, the Labour Party is unlikely in practice to contribute effectively to the development of the industrial co-operative sector; and for two reasons. The first is that it will not admit the essential case for that development: that it is necessary to authentic industrial democracy. It will not do so because the trade unions will not agree. They will not agree because the admission would deny their view of industrial democracy as an extension of their powers to include participation in the management of all industry, whether privately or publicly owned; and because Industrial Co-operation destroys the *raison d'être* of unreformed trade unionism. The second reason is that Co-operation admits individual property rights in industry and so is incompatible with Clause IV. Unresolved in the 1920s and 30s, the differences of policy between the Labour and Co-operative Parties remain unresolved to this day because they cannot be resolved: not, that is, so long as Clause IV remains part of the Labour Party's Constitution; or so long as Co-operation refuses to confine itself to what critics regard as the limiting, and ICOM the better, specification – that is, common ownership. The fact that the trade unions' perception of industrial democracy, control – or shared control – of industry without the preliminary step of obtaining ownership, is inconsistent with Clause IV, will not help the Co-operative cause. The determinant is that two elements of the Labour movement, unions and Clause IV purists, share misgivings about industrial co-operatives. That the misgivings are different and opposed does not matter. Nor will it help if Marxists observe of the trade unions' perception that, just as did Robert Owen's, it fails to face the problem of ownership and power, to see that the second depends on the first. Though the logic of the trade unions' prospectus stands on a false premise, it would enable the Labour Party, ignoring the falsity, to declare redundant the objective of common ownership as the means to control. But even if the Party were to beat a tacit retreat from the objective, its leadership would not make the declaration, nor fight and fight again for it. We may conclude, to put it mildly, that

Labour's backing for industrial co-operatives will continue to be less than wholehearted: to put it starkly, that the Labour Party will remain a major impediment to them.

The more the pity, this, since Consumer Co-operation – the established Movement – has moved from the traditional in indifference, or even objection, to Industrial (or Producer) Co-operation where the latter was not an incident to its own operation and under its control. In 1977, the Co-operative Congress resolved that the Co-operative Union and the Co-operative societies members of it should give all practicable help and assistance, within the limits of their resources, to support the formation of new co-operatives in all fields where these appeared to have merit. The Union itself responded by setting in train a study to establish how help might best be given, in collaboration with the Co-operative Development Agency; and did so in the knowledge that the Agency was to concentrate its attention on the industrial co-operative sector. But it is of course, to Consumer Co-operation's banking arm, the Co-operative Bank, that one would look for evidence of the Movement's new found commitment to the general promotion of that sector. Under two successive Chairmen, Sir Arthur Sugden and Mr Lewis Lee, the Bank has contributed much to its development over recent years. All this is a very far cry indeed from the dismissive view, attributed by Cole to the Consumer Movement, of Industrial Co-operation as embodying 'the rival doctrine of producers' control'.[23] How far Consumer's Co-operation will be able to help is another question. It has its own, pressing, problems.

For pressing they are. Chapter 1 observed that the present ills from which co-operative stores in general suffer are only too likely to prove terminal, that nothing less than an organic change would provide a cure. In support of the observation, it referred to the warning given in October 1984 by the Chairman of the Co-operative Wholesale Society at its half-yearly meeting that the fabric of the movement as a whole was at risk. In 1986, one possible organic change, the merger of Co-operative Retail Services with the CWS, was rejected. Operating in various areas throughout England and Wales, the CRS is the largest retail society. The prime function of the CWS remains the traditional one of supplying goods and services to independent retail societies.

At the annual Co-operative Congress, held in 1986 at Llandudno, the CWS was described by Mr W. Farrow, President of

Congress and Chairman of CRS, as 'to some extent a handicap'. He said that the old trading supply line from manufacturer or importer through a wholesaler had, for big retailers, been superseded by direct supply from source to retailer. Though the CWS had made adjustments, they had not been enough to diminish the handicap it placed on large retail societies in responding to competition. This comes close to saying that the larger retail societies, at least, would be better off without the CWS; and that for them, Consumer Co-operation's production arm, seen by the Webbs and by Cole as virtually the only admissible form of Producer Co-operation, had become redundant. As to the proposed merger, abandoned after protracted talks, the essential arguments were these. As the CWS management saw the matter, the merger would have made for more effective control and direction of the Co-operative retailing business and a more effective response to competition from the supermarket chains. As the CRS saw the matter, the merger would have spelt the demise of co-operative retailing, considered as a consumer controlled undertaking. For the merged CWS–CRS would inevitably have become the basis of a single national society. And it would not have been a true co-operative, answerable to its members. 'The health of this movement', said Mr Farrow, 'will be determined solely by the performance of our retail societies and I do not see, nor do I wish, that retail societies should be controlled by the federations (these include the CWS).'[24] Co-operative health, or commerical health?

A sympathetic observer would note that, since 1982, the policy of the Co-operative Congress has been to reduce the number of societies to 25, where in 1958 the number was 918; that about 80 per cent of trade is conducted by some 15 retail societies; that in Scotland, Northern Ireland and South London, the CWS is already – through the rescue of local retail societies – in control of retailing; and that the CRS's operation is dispersed over many and differing places. And he could reasonably infer that the Consumers' Movement had already become so far dissociated from locality as to lose its sense of 'belonging', of being an expression of local intentions and aspirations, that it had ceased to draw strength from the grass-roots, that it had lost the democratic impulse which is the dynamic of Co-operation, that it was no longer a thing of the people, by the people, for the people. And of the Movement's commercial health, he would understand Mr Farrow to mean that the prognosis was poor. The Co-ops' High Street performance was seen as 'bland mediocrity'. By the end of the century, the movement could have collapsed. Since 1960, its share of the retail market had declined from more than 11 to just over 5 per cent in 1984. Adjusted to present financial values, an overall profit in 1960 on £507 millions had been reduced to a current £20 million.[25]

The sympathetic observer might go on to suppose the obvious: that, its consumer arm having lost the democratic impulse and being faced with the commercial disaster, the imperative need for Co-operation was to restore the one and to avert the other. Mr Farrow, for the CRS and other retail societies, and the management of the CWS were both right: the one in seeing that a national consumer society would not be Co-operative, the other in declaring the commercial necessity of central control of a nationwide organisation. If both were right, then either Co-operative retailing was doomed or it must take some other form, a form suited to the environment in which in the last decades of the twentieth century it found itself. The amiable dinosaur would have to change. It would have to become some other kind of Co-operative animal. What kind? The observer would note that consumers were voting with their feet. They were shopping elsewhere because they found no advantage in Consumer Co-operation. If it were no longer needed, some other form of Co-operation was surely to be preferred to collapse by the end of the century. The Movement's concern must be about Co-operation first, and only secondarily about this or that form of it. A form which would reconcile the need to preserve democratic principle and restore the practice, and at the same time to realise the requirement of a nationally controlled organisation to compete in a market economy, was the industrial co-operative. A chain of retail stores, owned and ultimately controlled on the basis of one man, one vote, by the people working in them, would be Co-operative and need not lose their essential character for being organised and run nationally. He would see that such a change would be hard for many devoted to Consumer Co-operation to accept; but ask them: would it not be better by far than the worst possibility, the one they have been asked to face – collapse by the end of the century. It would be sad indeed if the Consumer's Movement in catastrophic decline, continued to cling to the shadow of Co-operation till it finally disappeared, rather than grasp at its substance, but in a different mode: the industrial co-operative.

In other words, the established Movement might well now ask

itself whether, if Industrial Co-operation is the wave of the future, the time had come to lay the distinguished but fading Fabian ghosts of the past, who in their prospectus saw a place only for Consumer Co-operation. And, if it concluded that that time had indeed come, then it might go on to ask itself what good reason could exist for the Movement's continuing its political association with a Labour Party still haunted by those ghosts whose influence, acting through Clause IV, operates now as it did between the wars to exclude Industrial Co-operation, comprehensively and properly described, from Socialism; which, so long as it identifies industrial democracy as unreformed trade unionism's model of it, is unlikely to promote Industrial Co-operation as the Party's preferred and exclusive alternative; and which, if it does take up the cause of Industrial Co-operation, is less likely to do so for its own sake and values, more likely in pursuit of a misdirected perception of it as an incidental means of satisfying a doctrine – to achieve the common ownership of the means of production. Finally, the Movement might ask how, given these considerations, it could rationally expect the Labour Party's support for the promotion of the industrial co-operative sector to be different in the future from what it has been in the past: in a mild judgment of it, less than whole-hearted.

The answer might be that attitudes within the Labour Party and the trade union movement are changing belatedly, but changing nevertheless. Besides the initiative taken by Wales TUC, there is now some evidence of a shift away from the established position of the trade union movement and the Labour Party. In April 1986, it was reported that Unity Trust, a financial institution established jointly by the Co-operative Bank and the movement, had set up a company to promote employee share-ownership plans – ESOPs – in the United Kingdom. The Trust is reported as envisaging an arrangement such that there would be acquired on behalf of all employees a block of shares in the firm employing them; and as favouring a holding of between ten and thirty per cent. ESOPs are distinguished from other forms of share-ownership by the fact that the shares are held in a trust. By giving corporate form to the employees' ownership of an interest in the company employing them, the structure ensures permanence. Trade unions were said generally to have welcomed the development; and the welcome itself was noted as unusual in its support for employee ownership.[26] A straw in the wind of change, perhaps? The idea has much in common with that of the Employee Participation Co-operative, devised in 1980–81 by the Co-operative Development Agency, and discussed in the next Chapter (see page 175). If trade unions generally were to decide to throw their full weight behind employee participation in the ownership of the firms employing them, that would indeed mark a fundamental change in their perception of their role. For they could then be said to be taking just such a new view of society as is, earlier in this Chapter, suggested for them; to be assuming just that agency that is available to them to promote it, to become agents of a beneficial change rather than protagonists of a *status quo* increasingly seen to be defective. If, if only, trade unions were so to decide. But that would be to raise expectation above judgment. If we are not to do so, then we have to conclude thus: that the traditional and restricted role will be reaffirmed. And we should hope profoundly that events would prove us wrong. Some may see just such a proof in the statement, contained in the Labour Manifesto, June 1987, of intention to encourage co-operatives of all forms. Others will continue to doubt whether good intention can prevail against the constitutional imperative of Clause IV, and trade unionism's traditional objections.

After the intricacies and confusions of the relationship between the Co-operative Movement and the Labour Party, the attitude of the Conservative Party has one shining merit: simplicity. True, the simplicity has, in the main, been that of indifference. Between the wars and after, as the party of consolidation, it had taken no initiatives to promote Industrial Co-operation as an alternative form of organisation for production and provision. Nor should it have been expected to since, until the late 1970s, neither did the established Co-operative Movement, nor its political ally and party of reform, the Labour Party. But when in 1979 the Conservative Party displaced Labour to form the Government under Mrs Thatcher's leadership, it had been stirred from its indifference by Mr Benn's misdirected enthusiasm for industrial co-operatives as the vehicles for rescuing failed privately owned businesses. And though, of the three cases, the *Scottish Daily News* was already four years and KME two months dead, Meriden was still alive and the memory fresh. To Conservatives and others, it seemed that if these were indeed industrial co-operatives, then Industrial Co-operation looked very like unprofitable businesses run at the tax-payers' expense by shop stewards in pursuit of an ideological goal.

So it came as no surprise when Sir Keith Joseph, the Secretary of State for Industry, refused to allow Meriden to defer interest payments on loans made to it by the Labour Government, a refusal seen at the time as likely to kill off the co-operative. In the event, Meriden lingered on until August 1983. Still, the Co-operative Movement itself had long since pronounced serious reservations about the rescues and questioned whether the rescued organisations could properly be called co-operatives. And if Co-operation's parliamentary affiliation to the Labour Party ranged it with the Opposition to Conservative Government, yet its maxim *Self-Help and Mutual Aid* had the authentic ring of Samuel Smiles, the appeal to Victorian values to which Mrs Thatcher's administration would have the nation return. When, later in 1979, Sir Keith met Lord Oram, the Chairman of the Co-operative Development Agency to discuss its future, he told him that he regarded industrial co-operatives as a desirable expression of private enterprise, but that they should not be subsidised out of public funds. They should be given the same consideration, no more and no less, as other forms of enterprise.[27] On 18 February, at a showing at the Houses of Parliament, of the BBC's television programme about the Mondragon co-operatives, he referred to the co-operative form as a product along with other forms of organisation for business, characteristic of the flair and inspiration of the mid-nineteenth century; and suggested that that characteristic was needed now. Here, then, we have a recent and authoritative declaration of the Conservative view of the industrial co-operative. It sees it, quite simply, as another and in itself perfectly valid form of doing business.

Seen thus, the industrial co-operative could be held to exemplify another objective of Conservative industrial policy: participation. The Conservative Trade Unionists' publication *Participation – The Next Industrial Revolution* is interesting on two counts: first, for its general discussion of the need for and meaning of participation; and second, for its particular references to the industrial co-operative form. Containing a foreword by Mr James Prior, the booklet is declared to be a statement of the author's personal view and not an official pronouncement by the Party. In his preface, the author – Mr Ken Daly – quotes from the 1980 Granada TV Lecture given by Mr Len Murray as General Secretary of the TUC, on the need to involve people, as workers, in the responsible exercise of power, so as to strengthen democracy in our society; and from Mr James

Prior, as Secretary of State for Employment, in a statement also made in 1980, on the need to recognise the importance of fully involving employees in the conduct and fortunes of the business. We might infer from these contemporaneous observations a coincidence, or near coincidence, of view from the political Left and Right. But we should remark that, where Mr Murray spoke of involving workers in the responsible exercise of power and of democracy, Mr Prior spoke of involvement in conduct and fortunes; and that the first kind of involvement might be understood to involve a good bit more than the second. For himself, Mr Daly settles for this: 'Participation, if it means anything, means seeking ways and mechanisms of improving the industrial dialogue so that individuals can be more involved.'[28]

For involvement, the case is that the interests of employer and employee are interdependent; and that 'the philosophy of "two sides of industry" and "us and them" has done much harm'. That there are two sides is, of course, a fact rather than a philosophy. It is one thing to say that the interests of the two parties, Capital and Labour, are like those of any other two trading one with the other, complementary. It is quite another to ignore the fact that there are two parties to the transaction. The marriage is of convenience, not love; and, therefore, only contractual. Except perhaps by implication in the chapter 'Financial Participation' the booklet does not examine that consideration. As share-ownership or profit-sharing by employees, participation might be said to admit it: for, in seeking to give the employee an owner's interest, it invites him to balance a concern to maximise profits available for distribution as dividends to shareholders or as bonuses to profit-sharers, against a concern to maximise wages payable to employees. Whether the invitation would persuade employees to forgo or reduce wage increases is debatable. However, like purse Socialism, the idea of employee share-ownership or of profit-sharing does at least face the fact that ownership is the governing factor; but where Socialist purity cries Clause IV and common-ownership of the means of production and exchange, Conservative conviction proclaims individual property rights in a property-owning democracy. 'We are all', it might say, 'Capitalists now.'

Not that the booklet's chapter 'Shareholders' Rights' discusses, as we might expect it to, ownership as solely entitled to determine the use of the property owned. It contents itself with the declaration that shareholders, both individual and institutional, must bear some responsibility for the social consequences of their actions; and that, given participation as the booklet sees it, there would not be the same compulsion for shareholders and workers to insist on their respective rights. This is, in effect, to say that our forms of industrial organisation may continue to be worse than they should be, in the expectation that people will be better than they are known to be. The only statement in the booklet which may be said to touch, and then only by tenuous inference, on ownership as the sole entitlement to determine use of the assets owned, appears in the extracts from the Industrial Participation Association's guidelines for voluntary codes of practice on participation. Printed as Appendix A, the extracts state: 'Eventually there could be the possibility of employee representatives on boards of directors – whether unitary board, or policy board in a two-tier structure.' That is so different in degree from the trade unions' claim, whether as presented in *A New Partnership, A New Britain* or as in the Bullock Committee's formulation $2x + y$, as to be absolutely different.

The chapter 'Is There a Role for Co-operatives?' passes lightly over what it calls some recent co-operative experiment in Britain', observing only that they may have failed 'because they were attempts at "rescuing" virtually impossible situations'. It goes on to cite the Mondragon examples as evidence of the successful use of the industrial co-operative form. 'Workers', it says, 'in the Mondragon co-operatives all share in the profits; there is a considerable degree of participation and a tremendous air of commitment.' Unsurprisingly, the example of commercially successful Industrial Co-operation uncongenial to the Labour Party's sticklers for Clause IV purity, appeals to Conservatism. Finally, the chapter finds that there may be value in co-operatives as a means of helping to revive depressed areas. In sum, *Participation – The Next Industrial Revolution* sees Industrial Co-operation only as a possible but inconspicuous feature of participation.[29]

More recent pronouncements by the Government itself suggest that the Conservative Party has warmed somewhat towards industrial co-operatives. In 1984, Mr Norman Tebbit, then Secretary of State for Trade and Industry, sent a statement to a conference organised by the *Royal Institute of Public Affairs* emphasising the Government's support for worker co-operatives and wider share ownership. And when, in 1983, Mr David Trippier announced the Government's decision to fund the Co-operative Development Agency for a further six years, he drew attention to the contribution that industrial co-operatives make to employment and job-ownership. It is too much to see in this, as did one commentator, an 'ideological U-turn' by an administration which 'has a traditional scepticism of anything tainted with grass roots socialism'.[30] At the most, the association of Industrial Co-operation with job-ownership seen as an objective of Conservative policy, shifts the Party's attitude from passive indifference to one of modest but none-the-less positive support. What it does not do, and what none of the Party's pronouncements have done, is expressly to make the point that the case for Industrial Co-operation is that it is an extension of democracy to include authentic industrial democracy; that it acts upon the principle that all men and women are equal in esteem; that it restores to working men and women their alienated right to make their working lives their own. The point may be inferable; but again the inference is tenuous. The better view is that, for Conservatism, Industrial Co-operation is valid not for its own sake, but as an expression of private enterprise tempered by participation. That indifferent attitude has its value. It allows, indeed expects, the growth of the industrial co-operative sector to proceed from the volition of prospective co-operators. The support it offers is minimal; but it is not conditioned by a distorting ideological objective. It does not require of Co-operation, as does a Labour Party pre-occupied with Clause IV, an achievement which it cannot deliver, and remain Co-operation. But, left to its own devices, what the Conservative Party will not do is advocate the general adoption of Industrial Co-operation on grounds of democratic principle, or as a structural change necessary to the regeneration of industry.

It remains for us to consider the third way.

— 10 —
Parties and Prospects: The Third Way

Last season's fruit is eaten
And the fullfed beast shall kick the empty pail,
For last year's words belong to last year's language
And next year's words await another voice.

T.S. Eliot: *Little Gidding*

On the general ground that it would much reduce the excessive influence of the extremes of Left and Right, the advent on the parliamentary scene of the SDP-Liberal Alliance in sufficient strength should of itself improve the prospect of introducing and maintaining a policy of positively promoting the industrial co-operative sector. For, in such circumstances, moderate opinion could insist that politics is the art of the possible rather than the assertion of doctrine. Moderate Labour opinion could be content to promote Industrial Co-operation without requiring that it should be a means of securing the objectives of Clause IV. Nor need it defer to that trade union view, demonstrably unacceptable to general opinion, of industrial democracy as an extension of the power of unreformed trade unionism. Moderate Conservative opinion could recognise in Industrial Co-operation not merely one among various forms of private enterprise equally meritorious because they are private but one which, because it distributes wealth by distributing ownership, works to the special advantage of the national social and economic interest and on that account deserves special support. So, the political Third Force could, by the sole fact of its existence in enough strength, actuate a latent consensus for the special promotion of the industrial co-operative sector. It could: but would it? To appraise the prospect for Industrial Co-operation in the political scenario that the Alliance

164

would write, to see whether as parties of progressive reform, the SDP and Liberals would provide for it the effective and continuing political advocacy it needs, we need to look at their statements of policy and the reasons for them.

The SDP addresses the subject in the Party's *Policy Document No 4 on Industrial Relations*. The document is sub-titled *Industrial Democracy* and so sets the development of the industrial co-operative sector firmly in the right context. In the introduction, the document states: 'Britain has long been a political democracy. Yet in industry and commerce, which create the wealth on which our society depends, there is too little democracy and too little participation.' It goes on to a general description:

> By industrial democracy, then, we mean the development of a structure and climate at work which enables all employees to share in the process of decision-making, and gets away from the 'them' and 'us' confrontation which has bedevilled too much of industry in the past and for which management and unions share blame. Under our concept of industrial democracy, the right to participate belongs to people as individuals, not only as members of trade unions which may or may not reflect their individual aspirations. When human dignity and efficiency point in the same direction, the cause must be worth-while.

The case for industrial democracy is seen as a moral one and as necessary to the regeneration of the national economy's industrial base. So far, so good those who are persuaded that the case for Industrial Co-operation is that it realises industrial democracy, itself a moral and practical necessity, will approve the approach. They may, however, reserve judgment on a formulation which seems to equate industrial democracy with participation, until they know what participation implies and, in particular, how the document deals with the problems of ownership as a pre-condition of authority.[1]

Three kinds of participation are identified: direct participation; representative participation; and participation through ownership. Direct participation would involve 'those at work in the form and content of their own jobs'. It makes no fundamental change in the relationship between employer and employee, or manager and managed. It adopts the practice of consultation and consideration characteristic of good personnel management. That is not to deny its value but to recognise that it is a palliative, and minimal at that. It is not a cure.

Representative participation offers much more. The document describes it as:

> a way of giving employees, through a hierarchy of councils, a share in the running of their organisation. Such shared responsibility may extend all the way from the mere giving of information to joint control. The purpose of a formal structure is to enable employees to be consulted before decisions are taken. Full consultation means that suggestions and initiatives from employees may be integrated into the decision process. Employees may be given more authority than this if management adopts consensus participation whereby a decision is reached with which all participants are comfortable. The decision may go further and the decision be delegated to the representatives.
>
> Finally, management may share its ultimate authority and agree that the consent of all parties is to be required for some decisions. Any or all levels of participation may be present in an agreed structure. Representative participation, which may culminate in the election of employee directors means sharing of control and responsibility between managers and other employees and the development of a true industrial partnership.[2]

On a first reading, the description is of a progression: consultation, full consultation, consensus participation, shared ultimate authority; and each stage is at the discretion of management. The governing proposition is this: that employees are to be given a share in the running of their organisation. That proposition is not, of course, to be read as suggesting that employees would in effect have the same rights in an organisation as do those who own its assets. The organisation is 'theirs' – the employees' – only in the sense that they work in it. And a 'share' may be so little as to be virtually nothing, the mere giving of information; or so much as to be, at face value, very great indeed, no less than joint control. Yet both extremes of the range of possibilities are seen as shared responsibility. Responsibility to whom and for what? Management is primarily responsible to owners, by whom it may be replaced, for the use of the assets owned. Employees' representatives would presumably be responsible to the employees they represent for something or other: as the mere recipients of information, for nothing more than conveying it to them. Under conditions of full consultation they would be responsible to employees for the advocacy of their suggestions and initiatives to management, for seeking explanations from management, for offering criticism. Under conditions of consensus participation, employees' representatives would have, in addition, something very like a power of veto. Management would decide not to adopt the course of action it had intended if, after the employees' representatives had been consulted, they declared that they were not 'comfortable' with it; and the representatives would presumably have to account to their constituents for using, or not using, the power. It is difficult to see why management should voluntarily limit its power to act in the best interest of owners and unlikely, therefore, that consensus participation would be adopted in matters liable to affect that interest materially. Indeed, that seems to be recognised: the fourth and final stage of representative participation, itself something more than consensus participation, envisages that the consent of all parties is to be required for some – but not all – decisions. But for those decisions for which the consent of all parties would be required the employees' representatives, who might have been elected in that capacity by the employees to the board, would have to account to their constituents. If, on a literal reading, decisions by the board are conditional upon the consent of the worker directors, then they would have an absolute power of veto and, again, would have to account to their constituents for the exercise or not of the power. If, on a less exacting reading, the decisions of the board are corporate and subsume the various views and opinions of the individual board members, the employee directors would have no such power and so could not rationally be held accountable to employees. Like any member of any corporate authority, implicated in its decisions and finding any one of them intolerable, an employee director might resign. No doubt the threat of resignation would serve to check unjustifiable corporate intentions of the board with respect to the employees' interest. What it could not do would be to relieve the board of its obligations to the owners. Of the two readings, the second is therefore to be preferred; and the preference is borne out elsewhere in the document. Under the general heading, *Options for Top Level Participation*, it discusses as one of them the election of representatives to serve on executive boards. They should, the document recommends, form a substantial minority of a board; and company law would be amended by an enabling clause 'expressly stating the right to confer on employees a power to elect directors'.[3] A permissive right would be conferred upon management, not a mandatory duty imposed. And though the worker-directors would be able to inform and advise the board about the employees' opinions and likely reaction, as a minority they would not be able to secure that the board decided in the interest of the employees against those of the owners. The board would have available to it advice delivered to it at first hand and with an authority perhaps otherwise lacking; and, having it, might sometimes conclude that the owners' interests would be better served by deferring to the employees' interests. But authority would still derive from ownership; and the board, including the employee directors, to which its exercise had been delegated, would still be corporately answerable to the owners. The test question is; who is to pay the worker-directors' fees? The document does not say; and we have therefore to infer that, like those of the other directors, the worker-directors' fees would be paid by the firm, not by the employees as would have to be the case if they sent their elected representatives to the board as delegates to a negotiating committee. So, the duty of the worker-directors to the employees would be to inform and explain. If the electorate found the information or explanation unacceptable, the worker-directors could either resign, and forgo the fees payable to them by the firm; or they could await dismissal by the electorate at the expiration of their term of office. The alternative, to constitute the board as a negotiating committee and to appoint to it worker-directors elected and paid by the employees to serve as their delegates to it, would be a nonsense. Operational command simply is not a matter for negotiation. If a board were so constituted, then any effective control would be exercised elsewhere.

Does representative participation then, in the final form as described in the document, amount to industrial democracy? The difficulty lies in the various meanings of the word 'representative'. Political philosophy sometimes distinguishes between representative and responsible government, thus: that representative government provides for a freely elected assembly with which an executive appointed by and answerable to a benign superior authority is meant to work in harmony, while responsible government provides that the executive must command the general support of the freely elected assembly, is answerable to it and may be dismissed by it. The first may be described as the co-option by the government of the governed into the practice of government. The second asserts the principle that power derives from the governed. With that distinction in mind, let us look again at representative participation. Its final form provides for the direct election by all employees of their representatives to the board: that is, to the executive. The assembly, that is, 'the parliament', is the whole membership of the workforce. But, as we have seen, the elected representatives are not in any meaningful way accountable to, nor open to effective censure by, the employees. So, representative participation may be said to resemble representative government. The owners are the benign superior authority. The board is the executive. The employees are the assembly with which the executive is expected to work in harmony. To justify that expectation, some members of the assembly are, with the agreement of the benign authority, elected to the board – the choice being solely that of the assembly. Evidently, representative participation cannot be said to proceed from the principle that power derives from the governed: or, more precisely, from the 'managed', from those whose working lives are managed as part of the process of managing the business in which they are employed. And on that appraisal, it cannot be said to constitute industrial democracy. Nor, in order to do so, does it need only to be modified; for where, for the purposes of political democracy, the proposition that power derives from the governed is perceived on grounds of natural justice or of practical necessity as axiomatic, the proposition that for the purposes of industrial democracy power is derived from the managed is not. It derives, as Robert Owen failed to recognise in 1833 but as Marx, the new model unions of the eighteen-fifties, the Fabian authors of Clause IV of the Labour Party's constitution, and everyone since has recognised perfectly well – it derives from ownership. Everyone, that is, until in the 1970s trade unions supposed that, in the cause of industrial democracy, they could be legislated into control without first getting ownership. So, unless representative participation is restructured to comprehend ownership by employees, it cannot do more than formalise and maximise consultation by, or on behalf of, those who own the assets of industry with those whom they employ to use them to produce and provide. This brings the humanising, the palliative virtue and value of consultation to its conclusion.

There is virtue, too, in its use of the form of democracy, of the election of representatives. It insists, thus far, on the primacy of the individual; and, if only for that reason, is to be preferred to that essentially reactionary view which would make 'industrial democracy' solely a function of trade unionism, and which owes more therefore to the idea of government as a concert of the interests of the major estates in the body politic. But whatever its conciliatory merits and values, representative participation is not by itself industrial democracy, nor can it lead to it. The view of it as a progression to what the SDP's policy document calls 'shared control' is illusory. It civilises but does not remove the ultimate confrontation between 'them and us'.

That ownership is the governing factor is, in effect, conceded by the document's description of the third kind of participation it identifies: partnership through ownership which 'entails full or partial ownership of the organisation by its employees. The rights and duties of shareholders and employees are merged. As owners, employees will be concerned about and have power to help decide the business the firm is to be in, its commercial policy, its investment plans and its future.'[4] Expressly, it is in their capacity as owners that employees have power: power as of right, not influence allowed by authority. One might pause on the pronouncement that the power is 'to help' decide. Those who own a controlling interest are in ultimate control. The pronouncement might mask the absolute difference between representative participation and participation through ownership, a difference which challenges their common classification. Or it might imply that the employee-owners would be open to influence, whether by the owners of a minority interest or by management – 'the executive' – considered as their principal advisers. Whatever the explanation, there can be no doubt that it is as the owners in whole or in sufficient part of an enterprise that employees ultimately control it. And it is, of course, because an industrial co-operative is wholly or largely owned by the men and women working in it that it is properly said to be ultimately controlled by them.

Ultimately controlled by them: but on the basis one man, one vote. It is that assertion of equality of esteem that vindicates the claim that industrial democracy is inherent in Industrial Co-operation. Under the heading 'Proposals for the Promotion of Employee Ownership', the document puts support for co-operatives first. 'These enterprises', it observes, 'which employees own and control normally on the basis one member, one vote, are clearly democratic.' It goes on to refer to the support provided, by way of services, in other European countries for the development of the industrial co-operative sector; and singles out for special attention the services provided by the Caja Laboral Popular as a support organisation for the Mondragon group of co-operatives. Because it argues, a wider distribution of ownership and, more particularly, the development of an employee-owned sector as another option beside those of the publicly and privately owned sectors would be socially beneficial, positive support should be provided by Government to promote Industrial Co-operation as a means of realising the benefit. The support would include tax and other incentives and a service to provide business consultancy and managerial advice, as well as financial support. The service would be provided by a publicly funded agency. But when the sector had grown large enough to do so, it would establish its own banking and advisory services, on the Mondragon model. This, the document observes, would take some years: and the agency would need in the meantime to have the full support of the government.[5] In summary, the SDP's case for the development of the Industrial Co-operative Sector is founded on the moral necessity for authentic industrial democracy; and on the practical necessity of securing through it the commitment of employees to the regeneration of British industry. Where the Labour Party, out of deference to the trade unions' conception of industrial democracy, is inhibited from giving whole-hearted support for the best reason for it, the SDP bear no such burden of inhibition. Where, from a need to justify Industrial Co-operation by reference to Clause IV of its constitution, the Labour Party has hitherto failed to provide it with unremitting and effective support, the SDP is constrained by no such ideological strait-jacket. And though the Labour Party, largely in response to the challenge of the SDP, is seeking to throw off its ideological inhibitions and remove that challenge, there can be no guarantee that the Labour Party will not resume them: not so long as Clause IV remains the key-stone to the arch of the Party's intentions; not, that is, so long as it remains socialist and will not become social democratic.

Elsewhere, the SDP's Policy Document does consider ownership by employees as a possible feature of participation generally. It sees it, though, as an optional extra: desirable, but not necessary. The need is to recognise that it is necessary, not merely desirable; that, in the end, it is that structural change that is required, nothing less. Better lubrication and maintenance will not do. The failure of recognition provides a reason for the mistaken assertion of a condition which partnerships and co-operatives would have to satisfy before they could be 'automatically acceptable models of participation'. They would only pass scrutiny 'if the employee owners had decision making responsibilities at all levels as well as formal ownership and control'.[6] Just a moment, though; the employees own the business, not as a mere matter of form, but actually. As owners, they will be able to exercise control to the extent and in such detail as they choose. If they are well advised, they will delegate authority to management made accountable in due form and at due intervals to them. The act of delegation might prescribe that, as employees, the owners should be fully consulted. A paper tiger is no bad thing as a reminder that there is behind it a real tiger, alive and waiting; and the real tiger, the effective discipline on management would be its constant awareness that, as owners, the employees would be calling it to account for the exercise of the powers delegated by them to it, including its practice of personnel management. So it would be liable to explain to the satisfaction of the owners why it had adopted this practice, that policy; and if it could not do so, either change them or, if it would not, expect to be replaced. No need, then, for this off-stage parade of scrutineers ready to march heavy-footed onto the industrial co-operative scene and tell co-operators how to participate. Co-operators are, of their own unqualified right, participants; and it is wholly and solely up to them to exercise their right. Industrial Co-operation is democracy, in action. Where there are grounds for criticism, democracy can bring it most directly and immediately to bear upon authority in charge of an organisation; and for this reason provides a better regimen for the health of the organisation than others which delay or mask the exposure of incompetence. It is harder on management. But that, too, is no bad thing. The industrial co-operative form is to be preferred to others which, because they are less immediately exposed, are less sensitive to change and challenge, more liable to complacency. Only the need to ensure so far as possible that, against their natural dispositions, organisations conduct themselves properly can justify the imposition of supervisory apparatus. That need is not there where authentic industrial democracy, such as the industrial co-operative form of organisation of itself provides, operates. That it is necessary where, there being no sufficient ownership by employees, participation is not a structural feature, is understandable. Indeed, the creation of an Industrial Democracy Agency, such as Policy Document No. 4 envisages, with the task among others of validating participation agreements between employers and employees, may be held to demonstrate again the flaw in the case for representative participation. By admitting the need for a body to supervise a treaty-like arrangement between two sides, the SDP's document acknowledges that participation so described cannot assimilate 'them and us', capital and labour, in a progression from Capitalism, but leaves them fixed as implicated and contending parts of it.

Of the SDP's *Policy Document No. 4 on Industrial Relations*, we may conclude: first, that its identification of participation with industrial democracy is mistaken and that, in the absence of a means of securing for employees sufficient ownership of the assets of the firm employing them it cannot be said to be capable of developing into industrial democracy; secondly, that though the immediate palliative value of representative participation should bring some remission to British industry from its debility, it is not a cure; and thirdly, that though in order to become a cure representative participation needs to include as a necessary objective ownership by employees, there is no reason in principle why it should not do so. The failure in the Document's exposition of representative participation to recognise the central importance of ownership contrasts sharply with the clarity and emphasis with which the point is presented in the description of participation through ownership. Subject to one reservation, Policy Document No 4 provides a generally satisfactory basis for the support by government for the development of the industrial co-operative sector. The reservation is that it is wholly unnecessary to encumber self-regulatory Industrial Co-operation with external regulation – and that merely because the Policy Document has associated it with participation which, in general, may well need supervision.

Equality and the Ownership Question, a paper published by the Tawney Society as a contribution to debate within the Society and the SDP, demonstrates the essential difference between industrial participation and employee ownership. The paper opens with a statement of Social Democratic belief in the gradual and democratic transformation of Capitalism into an economic order in which power is more equitably distributed among all adult citizens. Until other forms of industrial organisation are known to be as effective as those developed by Capitalism in producing goods and providing services, the Party's first concern would remain to make the present system fairer and more efficient.

> In the long run, however, Social Democracy is not merely about making Capitalism of the traditional sort work more efficiently; or blurring the distinction between capital and labour; or applying Japanese techniques of personnel massage in British conditions. Nor is it simply about encouraging the development of a small co-operative sector alongside the private and public sectors: if the commitment of the SDP to co-operative enterprise is a matter of principle, it surely follows that we seek to apply that principle as broadly as possible. Our aim has to be the creation of a genuine common interest, not the illusion of one.[7]

More specifically, in the chapter 'Industry and Ownership' the authors state under the sub-heading 'Industrial Democracy' that their main concern is 'the transfer of the ownership of public [i.e. private] limited companies into the hands of the workforce to a degree which is compatible with the measures of social ownership we consider later'. In contrast to the Party's *Policy Document No. 4 on Industrial Relations*, they identify 'genuine forms of profit sharing' leading to the ownership by employees of a 'significant stake in their company' as a necessary ingredient of meaningful industrial participation. Declaring that Social Democracy should regard some form of co-ownership as the minimum acceptable reform, the paper argues that legislation should be introduced to begin a gradual conversion of conventionally owned businesses into co-ownership; and, to this general end, supports the proposal that the Co-operative Development Agency should be given 'a financing capacity in addition to its present advisory and promotional responsibilities'. To the objection, that, as a form of organisation for production and provision, enterprises owned by employees were most likely to succeed if they wished of their own uninduced volition to own them and to accept the concomitant obligations, the authors reply that, perfectly true though that may be, it is not a reason for refraining from 'campaigning on the issue of popular ownership'. Indeed not: it is a reason, though, for ensuring that employees are fully aware of the obligations; and, being aware, are willing and made ready to accept them. Because the method of conversion envisaged is gradualist, it would provide time and opportunity to satisfy that requirement. It envisages the accumulation from a sum set aside from gross profits, and administered by the workforce, of 'a collective workers' stake of about 5 per cent after 5 years'; and looks towards a ceiling of 20 per cent.[8]

Some years ago, the Co-operative Development Agency devised a Co-operative model *The Employee Participation Co-operative*, for the management of such a stake. In its *Annual Report and Accounts* for the year ended 31 March 1981, the Agency stated that the Registrar of Friendly Societies had approved a set of rules providing that a Co-operative might hold a minority interest in a Company; and that the value of the Co-operative's shares might be allowed to appreciate. The merits seen in the model by the Agency were that, by involving employees in the corporate oversight of their holding in the firm employing them, it provided opportunity and time for the workforce to prepare itself to take on the responsibility at a later stage of running the whole enterprise as an industrial co-operative.[9] It could, in short, be envisaged as an educative half-way house towards the eventual goal of conversion to the co-operative form. The idea canvassed in *Equality and the Ownership Question* and the Co-operative model – which that idea might adopt – proposed by the Agency, contrasts sharply with the Labour Party's proposal published in 1980. This, as we have seen, advocated that there should be a general right of conversion, exerciseable on the initiative of its workforce in the expectation that the exercise would be state-funded. And the essence of the contrast is this. The first would provide conditions such that the progression, in a conventionally organised business, towards the industrial co-operative form was matched by a corresponding and trained progression towards full responsibility for the oversight of its affairs. A workforce would come to the ultimate goal knowing what it was about; and, in that knowledge, would have decided to attain it because it wanted to. The second offers no such opportunity. It invites the probability that the workforce would come neither fully aware of nor fully prepared to assume new responsibilities; and unsure whether it would have wanted to assume them. The contrast at the other extreme with the Conservative Party's advocacy of industrial participation with wider share-ownership and profit-sharing as the intended motivator is this: that it neither offers a sure way of involving employees corporately in the ultimate control of the organisation employing them, nor admits the principle of equality of esteem. It cannot therefore be, or become, industrial democracy.

Like that of its SDP partners in the Alliance, the Liberal Party's approach takes as its starting point the premise that a restoration of morale is necessary to the restoration of the country's industrial performance; and that industrial democracy is the precondition. Its manifesto for the 1979 General Election declared:

> We see a revolution in attitudes amongst all at work through the introduction of *Democracy in Industry* as the key to reversing Britain's economic decline. This means employees sharing control and profits with shareholders. We would achieve this by giving all employees (irrespective of trade union membership) legal rights as individual members of their Company; a direct vote in electing the board of directors jointly with shareholders; rights to information about its plans and prospects; to participate in decisions through elected works councils; and to share in the profits. Liberals would encourage producer co-operatives by establishing a Co-operative Development Bank'.[10]

That declaration chimes in with the proposals elaborated in the SDP's policy document; and is open to much the same appraisal. Notoriously, manifestos present general and contingent intentions, rather than reasoned explanations. Nevertheless, an explanation is required; and again it is how, without sharing enough of the ownership of the firm employing them, employees are in reality to share in the control of it; how directors elected by employees, but presumably corporately answerable with the other directors to the owners, could meaningfully account to their electorate; how, if employee-directors are not like the other directors answerable to the owners, the board could be anything but a negotiating committee; and how, in that case, it could manage except by out-voting the employee-directors whenever it wished or needed to. But it would be tedious to rehearse over again the argument that, for all its virtues, if it lacks a mechanism for securing ownership by employees, participation is neither in itself nor can lead to industrial democracy. We may note the Party's affirmation of its support for the promotion of the industrial co-operative sector. We cannot however be persuaded that participation, as so far described, would bring about the revolution in attitudes the Manifesto recognised as essential to the reversal of the Country's economic decline.

As so far described: but more recent pronouncements have had more to say. Published in July 1982, *The Liberal Programme* is stated in its foreword to be a statement of Liberal priorities for government. As part of its general industrial strategy, the Party 'would introduce a series of measures designed to provide positive discrimination for people starting up and developing small businesses, with particular emphasis on co-operative and community enterprise.' This is of course only to regard co-operatives as a kind of small business, though one deserving special attention. A much more significant reference follows under the sub-heading 'Partnership at Work – a Positive Role for Trade Unions'. Confrontation between the two sides of industry is, the programme observes, partly the cause of Britain's resistance to change and innovation. It continues:

> Liberals believe that the introduction of genuine industrial democracy will progressively transform attitudes and enable people at work to participate fully in decisions that affect their working life and to share more fully in the wealth they help to create. Our proposals are two-fold:
> 1   Employee Participation in Decisions – through democra-tically elected Works Councils with rights to key information and upper, supervisory, boards elected equally by employees and shareholders.
> 2   Employer Participation in Ownership – by an expansion of employee share ownership schemes.
>
> Decentralisation of decision-taking, particularly in large enterprises, is essential. Liberals would discriminate in favour of community enterprises, producer and service co-operatives, and other forms of co-ownership as good examples of industrial democracy in practice, attracting to business life many young people wholly alienated by hierarchical and bureaucratic companies.

The passage goes on to describe the role it envisages for trade unions.[11]

Again, the case is founded upon the necessity for industrial democracy as a pre-condition of industrial revival. Again, the co-operative form is identified as exemplary. More importantly, however, the passage brings together participation and ownership; and so may be understood as seeing both as essential components of genuine industrial democracy. Yet, this niggle remains; the statement does not expressly admit that meaningful participation by employees in the ultimate control of the firm employing them is a function of the ownership by them of a sufficient corporate share in it. Nevertheless, it registers a material advance on that earlier view of the SDP's which seemed to regard ownership as an optional extra rather than a necessary characteristic.

Finally, the SDP's and the Liberal Party's thinking are brought together in the consultative paper *Partnership for Progress*, published in July 1986 by the Alliance. The section 'Partnership and Opportunity' affirms in brief but does not materially add to, the proposals already published by each of the Parties on employee participation and employee ownership. It is enough to observe that the two, participation and ownership, are described as complementary; and that, in the two cases – those of the National Freight Corporation and the John Lewis Partnership – cited in support of those proposals, participation by employees is a function of ownership.[12]

So, to turn back to the question posed at the beginning of this Chapter: are the statements of the policy proposed by the Alliance and the reason for them such that we can confidently expect it to provide for Industrial Co-operation the effective and continuing advocacy that it needs? That the two Parties intend to promote the industrial co-operative sector there can be no doubt. But the first test of intention is the reason for it. For both the SDP and the Liberal Party, the reason is that the introduction and rapid attainment of industrial democracy as a normal condition in British Industry is a moral and economic imperative. It would pay us to do the right thing, to enlighten self-interest. Those who are persuaded by the case argued in this book will agree, therefore, that the Alliance passes the first test of intention. They may however see the Parties' identification of industrial participation with industrial democracy as a distraction, damaging if it were to lend credence to the idea that there was a soft option, an easy way to establish industrial democracy, one which dodged the central problem of ownership. That major reservation is largely satisfied, though, by the view to which the Alliance has come: that is, that employee participation and employee ownership are comple-

178

mentary characteristics of industrial democracy; for it marks a decisive advance from that innocent supposition that consultation, carried to the limits of goodwill, of employees by employers would be enough. There remains the minor reservation that the Alliance does not explicitly recognise that the right to employee participation is a function of employee ownership. It is minor because, whether the Alliance recognises it or not, the fact of sufficient and corporate employee ownership will result in the function; and it could well adopt the model, *The Employee Participation Co-operative*, proposed in 1980–1 by the Co-operative Development Agency. Because the right to participation is a function of ownership it is open to question how far there would remain a general and continuing need for an external supervisory body, an Industrial Democracy Agency, to ensure that owners could participate. That question lies outside the scope of this book. But it does stand repeating that, exemplifying authentic industrial democracy as they do, industrial co-operatives should be exempted from any such general supervision or regulation. One does not validate the ideal.

To conclude: it is to the third force in British politics that we may most confidently look for the effective promotion of Industrial Co-operation, the third way. Next year's words are finding another voice.

— 11 —

A New View of Society: After Recessional

Surely, every medicine is an innovation; and he that will not apply new remedies must expect new evils: for time is the greatest innovator; and if time of course alter things to the worse, and wisdom and counsel shall not alter them to the better, what shall be the end?

Francis Bacon: *Of Innovation*

Ah, but a man's reach should exceed his grasp, Or what's a heaven for?

Robert Browning: *Andrea del Sarto*

The purpose of this book has been to review the history of Co-operation and to try to assess, in the light of that review, its relevance to the social and economic condition of the United Kingdom today. It is time now to summarise and conclude. Essentially, the proposition is this: that Co-operation is another way of getting things done and one for which there exist legal forms suiting it to the corporate conduct of business today; and that the application of the principles of Co-operation should, and could with much advantage, be applied to the organisation and management of industry generally. By industry, I mean manufacturing and service industry; and by Co-operation, therefore, Industrial – or Producers' or Workers' – Co-operation, distinguished from Consumer's Co-operation which, for all its past achievements, is a failing cause.

For the general adoption of the industrial co-operative form of organisation, the case is both moral and economic. It offers a new view of society. Not absolutely new, of course: all societies are, in their nature and in some measure, co-operative; but new in the kind and degree of co-operation now proposed. And new as an alternative to either Capitalism or Socialism, considered as mutually exclusive alternatives between which society must choose; new as a reconciling synthesis of their opposed intentions.

A new view of society becomes necessary when the circumstances in which society finds itself prompt the generality of the men and women who compose it to a new view of the possibilities it provides for their fulfilling themselves. For it is at such times that the structures, that is to say, the forms of institution and organisation, which had seemed sufficient to that end are now seen to have become insufficient, whether because old possibilities have died and the structures which subserved them have lost relevance, or because new possibilities require new structures. A new view of society perceives the need to create new, or adapt existing institutions to the design most likely to provide the means by which people may, if they choose, take advantage of the opportunities, the life-chances, now apparent to them. A political democracy will act upon that perception; for democracy, properly described, declares of the civilised society that its institutions shall so provide that the individual may best realise his or her potential for thought, feeling and volition, the qualities of mind; and so grow in spirit. This is not to ignore the material basis of life; nor to suppose that its constituents do not contribute, whether directly or in sublimation, to that growth. We need cakes and ale as well as virtue. And often we need them first. It is only to recall that there is for mankind more to living than getting and begetting; that each human life should be a discovery of meaning and value; and that the essential purpose of a society's institutions is to offer freely-choosing men and women the best possible prospect of giving their lives that quality. One has only to look at the alternative: that is, that men and women should find contentment in the condition of sensual robots, physically satisfied and obedient, to know that the thought is unbearable.

Robert Owen lived in a time when a new view of society had become necessary, when institutions and forms of organisation had to change in order to accommodate both the development of the industrial revolution through its second and potent phase, the age of coal and iron, steam and railways; and the possibilities provided by that development. His new view came late to its finest idea, that of industrial democracy: not until 1833 when he proposed through the instrument of trade unionism to reconstitute society as an industrial co-operative commonwealth. We know now that the idea was premature, conceptually flawed and impracticable. It was premature because, in the logic of history, the prior need was to establish a sure foundation for political democracy; and because, to support the accelerating progress of the industrial revolution as the means to an unprecedented mastery of natural circumstance, an exponential growth of wealth and the completion of a world-wide economic system, Capitalism had first to triumph. It was conceptually flawed because, for moral justification, it relied upon an ideal view of perfectible human nature and upon the labour theory of value. It was impracticable because it failed to recognise that control of the means of production and provision derives from ownership of the material resources used to produce and provide; and because it supposed that a peaceable challenge by labour would prompt owners to relinquish control. These are serious criticisms. But they are, largely, criticisms of previous innocence by subsequent experience. And they leave untouched the central idea: the ultimate necessity for industrial democracy. Though at the wrong time, for the wrong reasons and in the wrong way, Robert Owen was right in one essential: that there should be restored to men and women their rights as individuals in the management, the application, of their working lives in the business of production and provision; of their rights in the disposal of that part of their existence which, because hitherto the interests of system have – whether in fact or belief – been seen to require it, has been alienated from them.

Here is the root cause of the 'them and us' confrontation in British industry. However, what the system offered increasingly from the mid century, was a share in the growing prosperity it provided; and, in the British century, a pride in being British that ranged from popular jingoism to a vision of the Parliament of man, the Federation of the World. So Tennyson saw it; on the British model and under British guidance, no doubt. In an age that seemed to prove the special quality of the model and to justify the guidance, the possibilities offered by economic and colonial dominion were by and large enough.

Enough, given the successive changes society made in adjusting to the absolutely new conditions of the industrial revolution, very different though those changes were from the revolutionary change Owen had seen as the necessary response to it.

Constitutional change, starting with the Great Reform Bill, accommodated the growth of political democracy; liberal economic philosophy, the triumphant progress of Capitalism. In the process, trade unionism and Co-operation, momentarily fused together by Owen as the means to his illusory new order, became each a separate part of developing Capitalism: trade unionism, as the purveyor to capital of labour, and so disposed to seek control of the supply; Co-operation, eventually defining itself as the Consumers' Movement, coming to deploy large resources of capital and standing in exactly the same contractual relationship to labour as did any other capitalist. This is not to say that social ideals were wholly lost. Certainly, Co-operation continued for decades to examine its social conscience. Conspicuously, what neither trade unionism nor Co-operation did was to respond to Marx's great shout of indignation, if indeed either of them heard it all all. Members of trade unions, members of Co-operative societies may or may not have seen themselves as shackled in his metaphoric chains; but, if they did, they must be supposed to have judged that they did have something to lose besides them; and might well do so if they obeyed his imperious summons to the class war.

So, in their formative stage when purposes and objectives were moulded and hardened, neither trade unionism nor Co-operation were moved to shape them by reference to this new view of society, a proletariat engaged in inevitable battle, which it would as inevitably win, against a bourgeoisie. Just as well: because, for all Marx's influence on modern thought, his vision of a society has proved as millenarian and as mistaken as was Owen's. But where Owen's view came to assert the principle of industrial democracy, the application of Marx's thinking has denied it. And more: where nations have acted upon his thinking, the result has been destructive of liberty of thought and action.

It was left for Socialism much later to proclaim itself the necessary and exclusive successor to Capitalism; and to found its proclamation on the thesis derived from Marx, that ownership of the means of production and provision was a pre-condition of the full control of the creation and distribution of wealth. In the United Kingdom, it was not until the Labour Party emerged towards the end of the First World War that the replacement of Capitalism by Socialism was formally declared to be a political objective. Clause IV of the Labour Party's constitution was, and remains the essence of the declaration. Incongruously, trade unionism as an implicated part of Capitalism, is, in its political manifestation as the Labour Party, committed to the abolition of Capitalism. For there is no role, except as the Party's claque, under Socialism defined in denial of the propriety of competition as the organisation of society on the basis that the state or municipality owns the means of production and provision and employs labour. Those who are unpersuaded have only to look at eastern European countries where Marxism, in its Russian model, is practised. They might ask themselves why it is that Solidarity, which sought to assert the rights of Polish working men and women against the State, has been crushed. Solidarity: Trade Unionism's evocative call to the moral duty of the brotherhood of man is the face of oppression, raised now against Socialism. There would be no room, either, for Industrial Co-operation in its own right: for, although for differing reasons, neither the trade unions nor the Clause IV Socialists have a meaningful place for it in their prospectus.

Socialism's view of society is, then, not new but old, a derivative from Victorian circumstances and thought, a response to the loss in the late nineteenth century of confidence in the ability of liberal economic practice to assure indefinite progress. Between the wars, Keynes came to provide such an assurance and so to deny both the Marxist prognosis for Capitalism and the necessity for the Marxist solution. That denial may be said to have provided the basis for the post-Second World War politics of consensus in the United Kingdom. Socialism could mean the mixed economy, Conservatism the managed economy. Both insisted on full employment and the welfare state: and assisted in the dissolution of Empire. For a time, a new view of society founded on that consensus and the large measure of shared moral concern it subsumed seemed possible. It was common ground that the physical and cultural well-being of the individual in society was a matter for public care and concern by society.

But the centre did not hold. In both the Conservative and Labour Parties, opposed politics of conviction were increasingly proclaimed. The final cause of the break was the demonstration in the winter of 1978–9 by the trade union movement that for it, normality was full freedom to exploit against capital, and in characteristic capitalist practice, its monopoly of the supply of labour; and to do so even though the result must be inflationary and seriously to harm the general interest in the maintenance of stable prices and an internationally competitive manufacturing

184

industry: in sum, to put at risk the means of supporting the moral concern of the civilised society to care for all its members. As if that were not enough, the movement continued to assert a right to share in the management of capital owned by others; that is, a right to the representation of trade unions on the boards of companies employing their members. Explicitly, the exercise of that right was not to reduce the unions' full freedom to engage in collective bargaining. In effect, the movement was to have a voice in buying the labour which it exists to sell.

Represented as the realisation of industrial democracy, an idea whose time had come, it purported to be a structural change necessary to the regeneration of British industry and hence necessary in the general interest. On that representation, it could perhaps be said to offer a new view of society. But the representation was, and remains, spurious. It has nothing to do with authentic industrial democracy. It fails to face the problem of ownership. And such a failure by the movement whose political expression, the Labour Party, asserts the necessity of common ownership as a condition of the just society, cannot be ascribed to innocence. Again, not a new view of society: for it boils down to an attempt to reinforce the power of trade unionism within the existing order. A new view of society could have proceeded only from a recognition by trade unionism that it would have to accommodate itself and its attitudes to the new circumstances created by a commitment to maintain, by Keynsian policies, full or near-full employment; and to act upon that recognition. Instead, the movement preferred the old view: 'a return', as one of its leaders was reported to have put it, 'to the philosophy of the pig-trough'.[1]

More than anything else the trade union movement's failure opened the way for, and, some would say, justified reactionary Conservatism. This is not the place to dwell upon the consequences of its insistence upon a particular economic prescription. We may, however, take note of the criticism by traditional Conservatism of the present Conservative per-formance: that though the prescription is increasingly seen to be wrong and the national economic condition in consequence still more debilitated, a Government which nevertheless knows that there is no alternative, is bound either to deny the gathering evidence of failure, or to attribute it to wilful obstruction, or even to sabotage. So it comes to see all opposition as mischievous or factious, criticism as tendentious or even as sinister conspiracy, objective but inconvenient advice from officials as demonstrating the case for a politicised Civil Service; to mistrust other publicly accountable authorities which, observing that the effect of the prescription is to preclude the proper discharge of their functions, may be disposed to resist it. Thus, the traditional Conservative criticism goes, present Conservatism has become authoritarian, centralist and intolerant; and hence the instrument of an attack on national institutions where formerly their maintenance and preservation stood first among the Party's purposes. Severer critics should add that present Conservatism confuses propaganda with presentation, regards the deployment of what is euphemistically called 'disinformation' as acceptable practice, and is impelled to meet by growing repression the growing discontents its policies have exacerbated if not created. We are, they would infer, witnessing the erosion of political democracy, the invariable outcome of the politics of conviction, whether of the left or right. For, once reached, convictions are not open to amendment by rational argument, to the proposition that to almost any question worth asking there are at least two sides. Convictions are either asserted, or suppressed. So, they would conclude, Socialists or not, we should all recognise for the zealotry it is Mrs Thatcher's reported intention to destroy Socialism and likely, therefore, to smell it in virtually any kind of social care, or concern, or interest publicly funded; and more, that in common prudence we should insist upon a specific account of the items of 'Socialism' due for destruction and of those that are not. Having inspected the account, and read the political small print, we shall be able to judge how far Conservatism now regards as Socialism in action what once it would have seen as a necessary publicly-funded commitment to the elevation of the material and cultural condition of the people it formerly sought to comprise within one nation.

For the purposes of this book, however, it is enough to observe that the economic policies of present Conservatism are not mere inertia, the continued use from habit of institutions and the observance of attitudes which, formed in response to Victorian circumstances, now stand in urgent need of adaptation. They are a conscious attempt to revive and apply mid-Victorian liberal economic theory. It is not innovative but atavistic; and so strengthens the expectation that time, the greatest innovator, left to itself will alter things to the worse. No more than Socialism does present Conservatism, for all its claim to be radical, present a new view of Society; but one that is old. It looks back to the triumphant age of British capital. But, lacking the material and moral basis on which Britain in the British century could present itself to itself, and to the world, it is uninspired and uninspiring. Certainly, that presentation was too often idealised, all too often ignored grievous sins of commission and omission. Nevertheless, a nation's ideals are part of what a nation is. They represent its best self, the condition towards which it continues to reach even though it fails to grasp. It is as irrelevant now to complain of the Victorian faults as it is to point backwards to their achievements. That day is done. We have lived through the Recessional; and there is no future in the past.

We would do better to look forward, and for wisdom and counsel to alter things to the better. It is high time to take a new view of society, to recognise that present structures are no longer well enough suited to its purposes as these are now understood in the western democracies. Changes are needed, as they were in Robert Owen's day, in the governance of the country and in the organisation of the means of production and provision.

The first would proceed from a recognition that, since the politics of conviction have been preferred to those of consensus, a constitutional design which so greatly inflates the representation of a minority opinion against others exceeding it in total can no longer be justified. For, in the proper practice of democracy, forbearance is a condition of the exercise of power by those who, whether as a majority or a dominant minority, hold it against those who do not. Now that the British Constitution, unwritten, may no longer rely upon a sense of moral obligation as an impulse to forbearance, now that the checks against government impelled by conviction towards intolerance of opinions, interests, concerns and aspirations other than those held by the party are seen to be insufficient, we need another and an assured guarantee. And the need is the more urgent because, when conviction is taken to be the measure of fitness and ability, it is towards the extreme of conviction within a political party that authority will gravitate. The guarantee must be inherent in the structure, the function of the constitutional machinery at work in Parliament. Emphatically, it must not be litigable prescription for ultimate interpretation by the courts, a determination not by public opinion but by arbitrators and, therefore, arbitrary. Such a guarantee would be provided by

187

reform of method of electing Members of Parliament; and the reform would be election by proportional representation in place of election by simple majority. That reform, and the structural change it would generate, is as necessary now as was the progressive development of political democracy from 1832 onwards. If it is a requirement of political democracy that it will, as fairly and sensitively as possible, express the variety of opinions, interests, concerns, and aspirations, then the adoption of proportional representation may well be seen as completing that development. In its time, each step in the progress was needed to secure a political basis for general consent of the governed to government. For the same reason, we need the next step now. It has the support of some Conservative and of some Labour Members of Parliament. But only the SDP and Liberal Party advocate it as their policy. It is to them that·we must look for the impulse to that structural change.

The second change needed, change in the organisation of manufacture and services, would proceed from the general recognition that the commitment of working men and women is necessary to the regeneration of British industry. And the dominant theme of this book is that the creation of the attitude of mind, the high morale indispensable to that commitment, can be secured only through the general adoption of the industrial co-operative form of organisation as the third way, as a reconciling progression from the either-or contention of Capitalism and Socialism. Nor need the start of the change in the organisation of industry wait upon constitutional change, much though the prospects for the first would be improved by the adoption of the second: by the consequent restoration of consensus, the rejection of uncompromising extremes and the inconsistencies of pendulum politics. Here again, it is only to the parties of the Alliance, uninhibited by ideological fixations, that we can look for declared and unequivocal support for Industrial Co-operation operating in a market economy, for support given for the right reason. And that is the promotion of authentic industrial democracy as the means to the re-assertion of the right of men and women, working in a community of equals in esteem, to the ultimate control of their lives at work; and the recognition that, to this end they must first become wholly or largely the owners of the enterprises they work in.

So, the case for Industrial Co-operation is primarily moral. But it is also, in the best sense of the word, expedient: that is to say, like all morality, practically necessary to the realisation of the general purposes of society as they are now perceived. Demonstrably, the industrial co-operative is a fully effective form of organisation for production and provision in a market economy. More than that, the general adoption of the form would make just that structural change in the economy that is required to resolve the problem that threatens eventually to destroy the economic basis of consent to government: the problem of securing, in a free society and through the application of Keynesian policies, near-full employment without generating inflation at an intolerable rate and as a chronic condition. The general adoption of the form: it is not a matter for instant and universal change, but one for declared intention, sustained application through the duration of several Parliaments, and a steady but accelerating progression as experience accumulates. It would probably use the sort of educative half-way house, the Employee Participation Co-operative, devised by the Co-operative Development Agency, to that end.[2] The expectation might reasonably be that the industrial co-operative sector would by the end of the century have become a major feature of the economic landscape of the United Kingdom; and that during the twenty-first century it would have become the common form of industrial organisation. We would have established the Industrial Co-operative Commonwealth.

Our society needs a new and better view of itself, a new and better perception of the ideal purpose it should pursue, the ideal condition it should reach towards. It needs a view to put in place of that which, in the age of the maturing industrial revolution and of the constitutional and organisational changes it required, had come to be its vocation: the cause of British economic and colonial domination justified as the instrument of progress and enlightenment, liberty and justice; and as the means of asserting the values of a democratic civilisation as they were commonly understood in western Europe; a view which, having reached its Victorian highnoon, survived with declining force until after the Second World War and may be said to have died at Suez in 1956. In support of its moral justification we may recall that British power was deployed twice, in the greatest wars mankind has known, in the defence of those values; and was essential to it. On the second occasion, Churchill's great rallying call to the nation declared that what the British Empire had stood for was 'the urge and impulse of the ages, that mankind would move towards its goal'. Manifestly just, the cause 'would not be suffered to fail among men'.[3] It was one which outweighed the faults, grievous though some were, of British dominion and so finally justified it. It brought together the English-speaking world to lead a moral mission: the defence of the values which in the ultimate crisis, it saw as giving meaning to history.

It was a Frenchman – Léon Blum – who, on the day in May 1945 which marked victory in Europe, said: 'Who would not be English today?'[4] Just for that one day, of course. A Frenchman will be pardoned by them for assimilating Scots, Welsh and Irish into the English; and one at least of Léon Blum's great compatriots would never have wished on VE or any other day to have been anything but French. But the comment stands recording: first because, since he spoke as one of a nation which more than most might see reason to dissent from the British justification of British history, for its generosity; and second, because as a French view it adds persuasively to that justification.

This much is certain. After VE Day, both the power and the justification were gone. After the tumult and the shouting, there came the Recessional.

Yet the urge and impulse of the ages, that mankind should move towards its goal, is unchanged; the goal proclaimed by the democratic imperative to be that society should strive to create conditions such as will open to the men and women who constitute it the best possible opportunity of making, through their own free choices, actualities of the hopes and expectations life is now seen to hold out. The Industrial Co-operative Commonwealth provides the means by which society living in the developed industrial state may best respond to that imperative; and, in the task of achieving it, a great purpose for it to pursue. It offers reasons for commitment: a more complete, and so better, description of democracy as a practice; a better realisation of the idea of liberty of thought and action, of equality of esteem, of fraternity in operation. It is a better appeal to the humanity in humankind.

Among those of us who are old enough to remember school-time celebrations of Empire Day as an affirmation of the special place and quality of the British in the world, who sang 'Recessional' with little if any awareness of its disillusioning message, and whose reflexes are still conditioned to twitch a bit when we recall past grandeur and glory, many will find no compensating inspiration in the idea of the Industrial Co-operative Commonwealth as an instrument for the achievement of new possibilities to replace the old. But that would be to miss Kipling's point. It would be to mistake the grandeur and glory of dominion for the justification for dominion, and to forget that the affirmation of human values is the only timeless cause.

For those who are young enough to see in the twitch of an older generation's conditioned reflex evidence at best of a ludicrous if not senile nostalgia, at worst of an ineffectual but still damaging chauvinism, the Co-operatve ideal may however offer a cause to which they could dedicate themselves, a vocation worth the expenditure of a life-time's potential. They may see it as spelling an end to old, irrelevant confrontations; as an urgently needed extension of democracy, a distribution of authority and responsibility; as insisting that we are members one of another. They, who embody humanity's capacity for getting on, may see the Industrial Co-operative Commonwealth as offering a relevant and necessary new view of society.

I hope so.

Notes

I The Third Way

1 During its half-yearly meeting held in October 1984, the Co-operative Wholesale Society reported that its half-yearly profits were down 15.4 per cent at £6.6 m on a turnover of £958 m. The Chairman warned the meeting that it could not allow large co-operatives to continue to make large losses and thereby weaken the fabric of the co-operative movement as a whole. The meeting discussed the possibility of reducing the number of retail societies, of the already greatly reduced, from the present 100 to about 25.
2 Industrial and Provident Society Act, 1965: Section 1(3).
3 See Chapter 5 of the Registrar's *Guide to the Law relating to Industrial and Provident Societies* (HMSO, 1978) for a full account of the matters for which the rules must or might provide.
4 Industrial and Provident Society Act 1961: Section 18(1)(a).
5 L. Stettner, *Establishing Criteria for the Economic and Social Performance of Producer Controlled Enterprises* (A Social Science Research Council Project), unpublished, 1980, Chapter 4.

2 A New View of Robert Owen: The Vision and the Visionary

1 G.D.H. Cole, *A Century of Co-operation*, Co-operative Union Ltd, 1946, Chapter II.
2 Robert Owen, *A New View of Society*, Everyman edn, Dent, 1975, first essay.
3 *Ibid.*
4 *Ibid.*
5 *Ibid.*
6 E.P. Thompson, *The Making of the English Working Class*, Pelican, 1968, pages 862 ff.
7 George Woodcock, Introduction to William Cobbett, *Rural Rides* Penguin, 1967, page 23.
8 E.J. Hobsbawm, *The Age of Revolution*, Weidenfeld & Nicolson, 1962, page 215.

192

9 William Cobbett, *Rural Rides* (1830), Penguin edn, 1967, page 168.
10 H.L. Beales, *The Early English Socialists*, Hamish Hamilton, 1933, page 67.
11 Robert Owen, *A New View of Society*, Everyman edn, Dent, 1975, Report to the County of Lanark.

3 A New View of Robert Owen: Owenites and Owenism

1 G.D.H. Cole, *A Century of Co-operation*, Co-operative Union Ltd, 1946, page 20.
2 Ralf Dahrendorf, *The New Liberty*, Routledge & Kegan Paul, 1975, page 14.
3 G.D.H. Cole, *A Century of Co-operation*, Co-operative Union Ltd, 1946, pages 34–6.
4 *Ibid.*
5 Sidney and Beatrice Webb, *History of Trade Unionism*, Longmans Green, 1926, page 120.
6 E.P. Thompson, *The Making of the English Working Class*, Pelican, 1968, pages 875–76.
7 G.D.H. Cole, *A Century of Co-operation*, Co-operative Union Ltd, 1946, page 28.

4 A New View of Robert Owen: Reform or Revolution

1 A.A.W. Ramsey, *Sir Robert Peel*, Constable, 1972, pages 124 ff.
2 *Ibid.*, page 160.
3 E.P. Thompson, *The Making of the English Working Class*, Pelican, 1968, pages 892–96.
4 Bertrand Russell, *History of Western Philosophy*, Allen & Unwin, 1946, page 809.
5 Sidney and Beatrice Webb, *History of Trade Unionism*, Longmans Green, 1926, pages 155–6.
6 Manhood Suffrage; Vote by Ballot; Equal Electoral Districts; Payments of MPs; Annual Parliaments; Abolition of Property Qualifications for Candidates.
7 G.D.H. Cole, *A Century of Co-operation*, Co-operative Union Ltd, 1946, page 26.
8 Robert Owen, *A New View of Society*, Everyman, edn, Dent, 1975, page 159.
9 *Ibid.*, page 206.
10 Robert Owen, Speech to the Congress of Owenite Societies, London, 1833.
11 It is not so often recalled, however, that it was on the initiative of a member of the Government (Lord John Russell) that the Tolpuddle Martyrs were pardoned. Melbourne, at the Home Office, had refused to receive a deputation presented on their behalf by a grand demonstration led by a clergyman. Lord John wrote to Melbourne

advocating their release. Melbourne demurred; but when Lord John, seeing the matter as one of principle, persisted, Melbourne gave way.

12 Sidney and Beatrice Webb, *History of Trade Unionism*, Longmans Green, 1926, page 1.

13 Herbert Heaton, *New Cambridge Modern History, vol. X, chapter II*, 1960, revised edn 1971, pages 45, 46.

5 Producers and Consumers

1 G.D.H. Cole, *A Century of Co-operation*, Co-operative Union Ltd, 1946, page 76.

2 *Ibid.*, pages 89–90.

3 *Ibid.*, Chapter XXII, especially pages 394 to 401.

4 *Ibid.*, page 97.

5 *Ibid.*, page 131.

6 *Ibid.*, pages 168, 169.

7 *Ibid.*, page 170.

8 On the ground that it tempted Government to extravagance and tax payers to evasion.

9 G.D.H. Cole, *A Century of Co-operation*, Co-operative Union Ltd, 1946, page 170.

10 E.J. Hobsbawm, *The Age of Capital*, Abacus, 1975, Introduction, especially pages 14–16.

11 For a development in domestic trade and centred on Lancashire, it is especially relevant that where between 1820 and 1850 the export of cotton piece goods had grown by about 1,100 million yards, between 1850 and 1860 it grew by more than 1,300 yards. The number of cotton operatives had grown by about 100,000 between 1819–21 and 1844–46, but at double that rate in the 1850s. See Hobsbawm, *The Age of Capital*, page 44.

12 G.D.H. Cole, *A Century of Co-operation*, Co-operative Union Ltd, page 125.

13 *Ibid.*, page 196.

14 *Ibid.*, page 210.

15 The Co-operative Development Agency's *Directory and Resource Guide*, September 1984, lists three on page 57.

16 G.D.H. Cole, *A Century of Co-operation*, Co-operative Union Ltd, 1946, page 291.

17 *Ibid.*, pages 209, 210.

6 Dogma and Diffidence

1 E.P. Thompson, *The Making of the English Working Class*, Pelican, 1968, page 865.

2 *Ibid.*, page 912.

3 *Ibid.*, page 883.

4 Karl Marx, *Selected Writings in Sociology and Social Philosophy*, eds T.B. Bottomore and N. Rubel, Pelican, 1956, page 68.
5 Roger Boyes, *Spectrum, The Times*, 17 October, 1984.
6 Bertrand Russell, *A History of Western Philosophy*, Allen & Unwin, 1946, page 767.
7 C.D. Darlington, FRS, *The Evolution of Man and Society*, Allen & Unwin, 1969, pages 540 to 549.
8 E.P. Thompson, *The Making of the English Working Class*, Pelican, 1968, page 915.
9 L.C.B. Seaman, *Victorian England*, Methuen, 1973, page 42.
10 Karl Marx, *Selected Writings in Sociology and Social Philosophy*, eds T.B. Bottomore and N. Rubel, Pelican, 1956, pages 177–8.
11 Isaiah Berlin, *Karl Marx*, 4th edn, Oxford University Press, 1983, pages 95–6.
12 *Ibid.*
13 Chapter I, pages 12–15.
14 M. Voslersky, *Nomenklatura*, Bodley Head, 1984.
15 L.C.B. Seaman, *Victorian England*, Methuen, 1973, page 315.
16 George Lichtheim, *A Short History of Socialism*, Flamingo, edn, 1983, page 212.
17 Sidney and Beatrice Webb, *History of Trade Unionism*, Longmans, Green, 1926.
18 George Lichtheim, *A Short History of Socialism*, Flamingo, edn, 1983, page 212.
19 Sidney and Beatrice Webb, *History of Trade Unionism*, Longmans, Green, 1926.
20 *Ibid.*, pages 159 to 164.
21 Douglas Jay, *Socialism in the New Society*, Longmans, pages 319–24.

7 The False Start

1 Lord Bullock (Chairman), *Report of the Committee of Inquiry on Industrial Democracy*, HMSO, 1977, page v.
2 *Ibid.*, page 169.
3 *Ibid.*, page 20.
4 *Ibid.*, page 20.
5 *Ibid.*, pages 20–5.
6 *Ibid.*, page 41.
7 The Town and Country Planning Act of 1947 provides an interesting parallel. Under it, the State was to acquire the development values in land. The owners were to be paid due compensation and to retain only the value of land for its existing use. Rather than dispose of land at a price reflecting its existing use value, and not its enhanced value for development, they did not dispose of it at all. The system could only have been made to work if land for development were first acquired, at its existing use price, by or on behalf of the State – and then resold to developers at that price. In short, whatever the statute

contemplated, owners would not forgo the exercise of their rights – even though they were to be compensated.

8 Lord Bullock (Chairman), *Report of the Committee of Inquiry on Industrial Democracy*, page 59.
9 *Ibid.*, pages 92–8.
10 *Ibid.*, page 54.
11 See Chapter 6, page 71.
12 Lord Bullock (Chairman), *Report of the Committee of Inquiry on Industrial Democracy*, page 112.

8 The Awkward Corner

1 Bertrand Russell, *History of Western Philosophy*, Allen & Unwin, 1946, page 756.
2 Chapter 1, p. 13, 14.
3 Keith Bradley and Alan Gelb, 'Motivation and Control in the Mandragon Experiment', *British Journal of Industrial Relations*, Vol. XIX, No. 2, July 1981.
4 Alistair Campbell, *Mondragon 1980*, Industrial Common Ownership Movement, Pamphlet No. 9, pages 5, 16, 17.
5 Henk Thomas and Chris Logan, *Mondragon, An Economic Analysis*, Allen & Unwin, 1982, page 101.
6 Keith Bradley and Alan Gelb, *The Replication and Sustainability of the Mondragon Experiment*, British Journal of Industrial Relations, Vol. XX, No. 1, April 1982.
7 L. Stettner, *Establishing Criteria for the Economic and Social Performance of Producer Controlled Enterprises*, Social Science Research Council Project, 1980 unpublished, Chapter 4.
8 David Spreckley, Foreword to *The Co-operative Way*, ICOM Co. Publications, Pamphlet No. 8, 1979, page 3.
9 Rupert Cornwell, *Financial Times*, 28 March 1970.
10 Dennis Lawrence (Chairman), *Report of the Working Group on a Co-operative Development Agency*, HMSO , Cmnd 6972, 1977, page 5.
11 Co-operative Development Agency, *Annual Report and Accounts for the year ended 31 March 1979*, HMSO, 1979, pages 16, 17, 23.
12 Co-operative Development Agency, *Annual Report and Accounts for the year ended 31 March 1981*, HMSO, 1981 page 9.
13 P.A. Management Consultants Ltd and Co-operative Bank plc, *Workers Co-operatives, Past, Present and Future*, PA Management Consultants Ltd, 1985, pages 30–5, 39, 43–44, 48–56.
14 Co-operative Development Agency *Annual Report and Accounts for the year ended 31 March 1979*, HMSO, 1979, page 17.
15 Co-operative Development Agency, *Annual Report and Accounts for the year ended 31 March 1985*, CDA, 1985, pages 5,6.
16 Co-operative Development Agency, *Annual Report and Accounts for the year ended 31 March 1981*, HMSO, 1981, page 4.
17 J.E. Bolton (Chairman), *Report of the Committee of Enquiry on Small Firms*,

HMSO, Cmnd 4811, 1971, pages 1–4.

18 P.A. Management Consultants Ltd and Co-operative Bank plc, *Workers Co-operatives, Past, Present and Future*, P.A. Management Consultants Ltd, 1985, page 130.
19 Joan Robinson, *Economics: An Awkward Corner*, Allen & Unwin, 1966 page 19.
20 *Winning the Battle Against Inflation*, HMSO, Cmnd 7293, 1978, page 3.
21 Peter Jay, *A General Hypothesis of Employment, Inflation and Politics*, Institute of Economic Affairs, 1975.
22 *The Times*, 20 December 1985.
23 Chapter 4, pages 48–9.
24 Peter Jay, *The Workers Co-operative Economy*, Manchester Statistical Society, 1977, page 16.

9 Parties and Prospects: Left and Right

1 G.D.H. Cole, *A Century of Co-operation*, Co-operative Union Ltd, 1946, pages 316–34.
2 *Ibid.*, pages 317, 318.
3 *Ibid.*, page 319.
4 *Ibid.*, pages 326, 327.
5 *Ibid.*, page 328.
6 *Ibid.*, pages 327, 328.
7 *Ibid.*, pages 333, 334.
8 See Chapter 6, page 90.
9 Professor A.J. Eccles, *Trade Union Behaviour towards Workers' Co-operatives*, Plunkett Foundation, Sixth Co-operative Seminar, April 1981.
10 See Chapter 4, pages 47–8.
11 Wales Co-operative Centre, *Annual Report 1983–4*, page 5.
12 *Wales Co-op Centre News*, Wales TUC Special Edition 1984.
13 Aneurin Bevan: see Chapter 6, page 90.
14 The TUC and Labour Party, *A New Partnership, A New Britain*, August 1985.
15 Wales Co-operative Centre, *Annual Report 1983–4*, page 7.
16 The Labour Party: *The Labour Party Manifesto 1979*, pages 10, 21, 22; page 4.
17 Hansard, House of Commons, 22 July 1981, cols 448–9.
18 *New Statesman*, 17 April 1981, 'Labour in Co-op Plan Row'.
19 The Labour Party, *A Strategy for Workers' Co-operatives*, 1981.
20 See Chapter 5, pages 68, 69.
21 Co-operative Development Agency, *Annual Report and Accounts for the Year ended March 31, 1984*, CDA, 1984, page 6.
22 See Chapter 1, pages 6, 7.
23 See Chapter 5, page 68.
24 *The Times*, 20 May 1986.
25 *Ibid.*
26 *Co-operative News*, 15 April 1986; *Financial Times*, 8 April 1986.

27 Co-operative Development Agency, *Annual Report and Accounts for the year ended 31 March 1980*, HMSO, 1980 page 4.

28 Ken Daly, *Participation – The Next Industrial Revolution*, Conservative Trade Unionists Publication, 1981, pages 2, 5.

29 *Ibid.*, pages 20, 21.

30 *Financial Times*, 12 June 1984, '*A Resurgence of Interest*' (article on Co-operatives by David Churchill).

10 Parties and Prospects: The Third Way

1 The SDP, *Policy Document No. 4 on Industrial Relations 1. Industrial Democracy*, 1982, pages 1, 2.

2 *Ibid.*, page 7.

3 *Ibid.*, page 19.

4 *Ibid.*, page 8.

5 *Ibid.*, pages 27–31.

6 *Ibid.*, pages 21, 22.

7 Richard Gravil (ed.), *Equality and the Ownership Question*, The Tawney Society, 1986, page 1.

8 *Ibid.*, pages 9–14.

9 Co-operative Development Agency, *Annual Report and Accounts for the year ended 31 March 1981*, HMSO, 1981, pages 7, 8.

10 The Liberal Party, *The Real Fight for Britain*, Liberal Publication Department, 1979, page 10.

11 The Liberal Party, *The Liberal Programme*, Liberal Party Headquarters, 1982, page 9.

12 SDP-Liberal Alliance, *Partnership for Progress*, SDP, 1986, pages 24, 25.

11 A New View of Society: After Recessional

1 See page 125.

2 See page 175.

3 Churchill: House of Commons, 13 May 1940.

4 The author relies on his memory for this attribution. The quotation may not be exact.

Index

criticism of, 82–88; social utility of rational education, 19–23; Villages of Co-operation, 25–8, 31, 152
Owenism, Owenites, 31–37, 40, 44, 45, 46, 63, 71

Peel, Robert, 40, 42
Pickering, 40
Place, Francis, 42
Planning Agreements, 100, 101
Political Democracy, 38, 39, 44, 51, 102, 111, 165, 181, 182, 186, 188
Prague Spring, 81
Prandini, Ornelli, 115–17
Prior, James, 127, 161

Ralahine, Ireland, 32
Ramsey, A.A.N., 41
Reform Bill, 36, 38–46, 111, 183
Registrar of Friendly Societies, 3, 6–8
Ricardo, 24, 25, 35, 36
Robinson, Joan, 125, 128, 129
Rochdale Co-operative Manufacturing Society, 54–7
Rochdale Pioneers, 53–7, 145
Rotunda, 45
Rousseau, 22, 27
Russell, Bertrand, 44, 112
Russell, Lord John, 40, 42, 44

Scargill, Arthur, 125
Schiller, 31
SCOP, *see* French Confederation of Producer Co-operatives, 114
Scott Bader, 123
Scottish Daily News, 115–18, 135, 151, 159
Seaman, L.C.B., 82
Socialism, 70–2, 80, 82–92, 115, 119, 140, 151, 183, 184, 188
Solidarity, 184

State ownership, 68, 85–90, 95–6, 145
Stettner, L, 113
Sudgen, Sir Arthur, 155

Tawney Society, 173
Tebbit, Norman, 162
Tennyson, 51, 77, 182
Thatcher, Mrs, 127, 159, 186
Thompson, E.P., 22, 43, 71–2
Times, The, 42, 75–6, 129
Tolpuddle Martyrs, 47
Trade Unions, Unionism, assimilation into Capitalism, 48–50; and Co-operation, 33–6, 51–2, 183; and employee ownership, 158–9; and industrial democracy, 92, 93, 101, 138–44, 185; and the Labour Party, 137–9; the new model unions, 48; the winter of discontent, 125–7, 184
Trippier, David, 162
TUC, 101, 142
Turner, 51

United Employees' Association, 59
United States, 30, 32

Villages of Co-operation, 27–8, 50
Voslensky, 81

Wales Co-operative, 141
Wales TUC, 141–2, 158
Watt, 24
Webb, Sydney and Beatrice, 44, 48, 97, 140, 156; criticism of Robert Owen, 82–91
Wellington, 41
White Paper on Pay Policy, 1978, 103
William IV, 41
Woodcock, George, 28
Working Party on a Co-operative Development Agency, 116, 147
Wright, George, 141